六十年之追求

忠恕堂

孟治

Chinese American Understanding

A Sixty-Year Search by Chih Meng

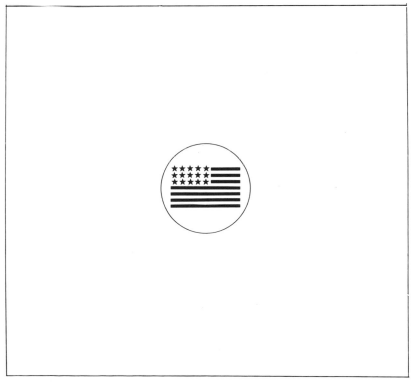

China Institute in America, New York, NY (1981)

Photographs on pages 55, 80 (bottom), and 98 (top) are from the Sidney D. Gamble Photograph Albums and reprinted by the courtesy of the Princeton University Library.

Photograph on page 240 (left) by LeNang.

Spellings of names of Chinese persons and places:

In English, spellings of names of Chinese persons and places have been changing in recent years. To insure identification and to avoid confusion, the spellings of Chinese names in this book are those in use and widely known during their respective historical times.

For example: Confucius instead of Kung Fu-tze

Peking instead of Beijing

V. K. Wellington Koo instead of Ku Wei-chün

Chou En-lai instead of Zhou Enlai.

Designed by Albert Squillace

AFFECTIONATELY DEDICATED
TO MY WIFE
HUAN SHOU KWOH

AND TO MY CHILDREN
PAUL NI-NI, ELIZABETH MEI-MEI, VIRGINIA WA-WA,
JAMES DI-DI, AND GLORIA YU-JU
WHOM PROVIDENCE HAS PLACED IN THE SAME BOAT OF LIFE WITH ME

Contents

Preface

This is the story of a young Chinese brought up in a courtyard within a series of courtyards, where his parents and his grandparents concerned themselves with his education in the classical Confucian tradition of *chia chiao,* or home education. One of his first memories is of his mother taking him by the hand to bow in filial piety before the ancestral tablets; one of his ancestors was Mencius.

From the *Chung Shu* of Mencius he learned that human nature is essentially good, and that he should not do unto others what he would not wish others to do to him. Only through *jen,* or humane behavior, and not through *pa,* force, could peace be achieved. From Confucius he learned that human relations are harmonized by good manners, and that there is no such thing as a righteous war.

His father considered him such a promising scholar that he was sent to Nankai, a famous school in Tientsin, and later he was admitted to Tsing Hua in Peking. There he was caught up in the student revolution known as the pivotal May Fourth Movement of 1919. The revolution was against the old ways, but it was also against foreign ways—particularly foreign encroachments on China's territorial integrity—and the young student was determined to exorcise both kinds of demons.

It is all the more remarkable that this same young man, befriended by Americans in Peking, and fortunate enough to win one of the prized Tsing Hua scholarships for study in America, devoted his whole life to interpreting Chinese civilization to Americans, and American ideals of freedom to the Chinese.

One of his heroes, and lifelong friends, was Hu Shih, one of the Chinese students in the United States most enamored of the American dream. Determined to find ways to communicate it to the great mass of the Chinese people, Hu Shih abandoned the elitist classical style of speaking and writing Chinese and undertook to popularize the language. His peers repaid him with vituperation, but history now remembers him as father of the Chinese Renaissance.

Chih Meng is known to a host of friends as Paul, the name suggested by my father, Henry W. Luce, an American missionary who recognized in his young Chinese friend a man with a message. Paul Meng's way of delivering that message is highlighted in this book.

His chief channel of communication was China Institute in America. When he took on the job as director of the Institute in 1930, it was an infant organization, with prestigious sponsors, vast potential—and a bank balance of one hundred and seventy-six dollars and seventy-three cents. When he retired in 1967, its resources had grown more than a thousandfold and its finances were sound. The Institute had its own headquarters, known as China House, with a small but choice art gallery, classrooms, library, music room, offices, and a Chinese garden. These facilities were crowded with a kaleidoscope of activities. The Institute's School of China Studies was teaching yearly more than one thousand adult students in Chinese painting, language, calligraphy, and philosophy. Other thousands of students, from China, had been served in a variety of ways, from scholarships to counseling to weekly parties featuring Chinese opera and American jazz, as well as an annual Labor Day weekend conference bringing Chinese students from all over the country. The wider community enjoyed exhibitions of Chinese art, lectures on a broad range of subjects, and social occasions with a Chinese flair.

Paul Meng collected around him a devoted staff and a Board of Trustees that caught his enthusiasm for the steadfast purpose of promoting deeper appreciation between Chinese and Americans, and encouraging genuine collaboration between the two peoples. Their stated purpose was to disseminate information concerning Chinese and American education; to promote closer relationships between Chinese and American institutions through the exchange of professors and students; to assist Chinese students in America in their educational pursuits and help American teachers and students interested in the study of things Chinese; and to stimulate general American interest in the study of Chinese culture. All this kept Paul Meng busy day and night for many years.

After World War II and the abrupt descent of the bamboo curtain, dividing not only Chinese but Americans, Paul Meng and his board rose above the thorny problem of political affiliations by clinging to the long view that Chinese culture was an enduring subject to be explored, and that the friendship between the two peoples was indestructible.

His wisdom in all of this derives from his intimate knowledge of Chinese history—its philosophers and its folklore.

11

His optimism reflects his Christian faith and his belief in the ideals of his adopted country. This book mirrors his conviction that the combination of the two is the surest touchstone for the long future.

Paul Meng and I share many interests, but our greatest bond is that Shantung is our home province, as it was for both Mencius and Confucius. Shantung is rich in wheat and millet and sorghum, but for centuries it has been regularly flooded by the Yellow River of Sorrows. In the Ming dynasty one of Paul Meng's ancestors established emergency granaries, a system which came to the attention, three hundred years later, of Emperor Chien Lung. In his own calligraphy the emperor caused to be inscribed on the Meng family tablet warm words of commendation.

Years hence Chih Meng's name will be inscribed on the family tablet in both Chinese and English to symbolize his lifelong dedication to strengthening the bonds between his two countries. His unwavering belief has been that "Under Heaven All Men Are Brothers."

12   New York, 1981

Acknowledgments

This book began as a history of China Institute in America, a project I was urged to undertake by members of the C. T. Loo Chinese Educational Fund, Inc., and especially by Elisabeth Luce Moore and Mousheng Lin. The first draft, although it covered only the first forty-one years of the Institute's existence, had become voluminous by the time I retired, in 1967. We then agreed that a more generalized effort should be attempted. It was hoped that a wider audience would perhaps be interested to read how an anti-foreign Chinese became an Americanophile and devoted his life to the search for Chinese-American understanding. This memoir is the result.

I wish to thank many friends for encouragement and support:

C. T. Shen, for his thoughtful reading of the manuscript and for many valuable suggestions; C. Martin Wilbur, for his cogent analysis of the original manuscript, K. Y. Ai, for corroborating my memory of our more than thirty years together in the service of the Institute; Dudley B. Tenney, for sympathetic counsel at all stages of the journey; Adolph Suehsdorf, for thorough and creative editing, and Bettyjean Tighe, whose efficient and cheerful work brightened the preparation of the first draft.

I am grateful to Beth Moore for writing the preface. In her own person and through the accomplishments of a lifetime, she has contributed greatly to the Search, and to a most reliable and mutually enriching way to achieve international understanding.

To these friends and to many others who have helped me in the Search, my profound thanks. Any errors which may survive in the text are my own.

Chih Meng   13

Part 1

Roots in Peking

Around the Moon Year

Foreign Devils and Generation Gaps

Around the Moon Year

My sojourn on this earth began at Chung Shu T'ang, the Meng family manor in the southern part of the metropolitan district of Peking. It was truly my world. I roamed it freely and discovered its wonders. Day by day, new and interesting things happened which initiated me to the concepts of Heaven, Earth, and Man.

Our home was in the classic Chinese design. It consisted of three main quadrangles, each surrounding a courtyard, along one axis, and one separate minor quadrangle and courtyard. A high wall enclosed the whole, perhaps six acres in all. The front faced South Main Street and had a main entrance and a carriage entrance. The main entrance was built on a terrace five steps high and opened onto the reception quadrangle, where visitors were ushered into waiting rooms. A decorative doorway led to the guest quadrangle with a much larger courtyard which displayed the family's best plants. The center of the guest quadrangle was the main hall, which was erected on a terrace of three steps, so that it topped all other structures. Here major banquets were held, and family and clan conclaves convened. Directly behind the main hall was the living quadrangle which, in my childhood years, housed three generations. In back of the living quarters was a spacious compound that contained the clan school quadrangle, the servants' rooms, the stables, the carriage house, and, to the rear, an entrance which faced West Street. Across the street was our farm tenants' town house, with our private well, barns, and a threshing floor.

For me, as a young child, it was great fun to go from quadrangle to quadrangle, exploring the various sheds and shops between them and the enclosing wall. There were sheds for storing wood, coal, and grain, for smoked meats, cured soya-bean sauce, and vegetables, and above all the storeroom for long-discarded and forgotten articles such as spears, broadswords, crossbows, and arrows. Equally exciting were the shops for grinding grain and for ginning, spinning, weaving, and dyeing cotton, and for making clothes.

Since my generation, most people have been born in hospitals, which seems to me cold, impersonal, and devoid of historical interest and sentiment. Fortunately for me, my advent was a privileged natural birth in my mother's bed. At birth I was given the "milk" name—an affectionate diminutive used only by adult family members—Pao Chu (Precious Pig), partly because I was born during the Year of the Pig, the twelfth and last of the animals of the earth, and partly because a pig usually has the best chance to survive.

From birth to six is a child's Golden Age. It enjoys freedoms and privileges, and immunity from punishment. I could ask for and get food and drink at any hour, day and night. I was allowed to wander into any room to see anyone. When I got into trouble or had a temper tantrum, all members of my family were expected to help. How wonderful it was to be the youngest of four children and the only son of my parents.

The dominant philosophy urged that bringing up children was of paramount importance, not only to the parents in this life, but also because it helped perpetuate the good family name, here and now, and in history. Primary responsibility was placed on the mother, the father, and the grandparents, in that order. *Chia chiao* (family or home education) had been worked out carefully and consistently for more than twenty-two centuries, so much so that filial piety was an absolute in Chinese folkways until the 1917 cultural revolution.

Mine was a most loving and wise mother. She knew well how to lead me step by step, pleasurably and yet firmly. There were many resources for her to make use of. Like all families, we maintained three altars at home: one for Old Heavenly Grandfather (the Creator), one for the ancestors, and one for the Kitchen God. Altars could be large or small, simple or elaborate, but each had to have an incense urn and two candlesticks. Ceremonial respects were paid to the Creator on supreme occasions, including the New Year, funerals, and weddings. The Kitchen God resided in the kitchen, where, as the local agent of the Creator, he got frequent kudos from all participants in cooking. Our particular family tradition was to offer incense every evening to the ancestors. Our ancestors' altar had been placed in the entrance hall

Author (left), four years old
and still addressed by the "milk name" of Pao
Chu—Precious Pig—is photographed
with Third Sister, Pao Shen, in a
courtyard of Chung Shu T'ang, the classic Chinese
home of the well-to-do Mengs in
Peking. The fearsome dowager empress Tzu
Hsi, last of the Manchus, rules from
the Imperial City, but a republican
revolution is in the offing.

of my parents' living quarters since my mother's appointment as definitive housekeeper by my grandmother.* As soon as I was able to walk she took me with her to perform this ritual. Sometimes she would let me hold an incense stick while she lighted it and called my attention to its fragrance. My mother explained that incense fragrance symbolized family fragrance and that she and I should pray that the Meng family fragrance would flow on by my becoming a good adult, marrying a good wife, and begetting good offspring.

My perceptions of this childhood world were formed through living among a family of three generations. The family tie had long, deep roots and was multiphased in that it was at once physical, psychological, and religious. Day after day I could not help but notice how my parents treated their parents. My grandparents' physical needs and comforts, and the satisfaction of their desires, and even of their whims, were a major concern and constant endeavor of my father and mother.

We thought of our God as Old Heavenly Grandfather, who created us all; but He delegated our own parents to bring us into this world. In this way He provided every family with the opportunity and freedom of choice as to how well and how differently it would develop. Individual efforts and achievements would count but in the eyes of God and society they would be credited to parents and ancestors.

Our family altar centered on five rows of wooden tablets representing five immediate generations of ancestors. As a new generation was added, the tablets of the sixth were retired and packed away. Each ancestor had a tablet on which was inscribed his or her vital statistics. Since the altar occupied a honored place in the living quarters, grownups and children passed it frequently. My three sisters and I liked to play in front of the altar on the rug, which was very thick and large. Hence, there were many occasions for us to ask questions about the tablets and whom they represented. My grandfather was our chief source of interesting anecdotes. I remember his relating the devotion of an ancestor whose father was paralyzed and remained an invalid, confined to bed, for eleven years. Even after the son had

* Grandmother, like all grandmothers, had authority over internal household affairs of the family. When she became enfeebled by age, she delegated Mother to act in her stead; she retained veto power, but never exercised it, to my knowledge.

become a governor and affluent enough to have servants, he waited on his father personally, feeding him, turning him in bed, and reading to him whenever he was home. Frequently, Grandfather would remind us of our long family history, which had a continuous record dating back to Meng Tzu (372–289 B.C.), the philosopher-sage known in the West as Mencius. Our nation ranks him with Confucius (551–479 B.C.) in greatness. We, the descendants, must try to be worthy of him. Hanging on a wall in our main hall was an imposing black tablet bearing a reminder of this in characters of gold: *Chung Shu T'ang Meng*. *Chung Shu* was the *T'ang*, or "hall," name of the Mengs, our family designation. It comes from the last of the *Four Books* in which Mencius expounded the teachings of Confucius, and which are the basic literature of China's traditional academic examinations. In one passage, students ask, "How can the Master's teachings be summarized in one sentence?" The reply: "*Chung shu* embodies all. *Chung* is faith in the goodness of human nature and loyalty to all mankind. *Shu* means not doing to others what you would not wish them to do to you."

Another great tablet that graced the top of our main entrance also was the subject of frequent inquiry by us children. "Why is it composed of blue background and gold characters? What are the inscriptions alongside the Chinese characters, and whose seal is it in the left corner?" Grandfather always smiled and then turned serious. His face lighted up with pride and his voice sounded deeper than usual whenever he explained this tablet. "It was awarded to our family," he said, "by the Emperor Chien Lung of the Ch'ing dynasty, who reigned from 1735 to 1795. Its inscriptions are bilingual: four Chinese characters and their equivalents in Manchu:

任 = Practice   可 = Set

郑 = Compassion   風 = Atmosphere or example

At the left in smaller characters are

乾 = Chien   御 = Personally

隆 = Lung   筆 = Penned

Imprinted underneath is the square imperial seal of vermilion and the date, Keng Wu year, First Moon, Second Day (March
9, 1750)."

The achievement this tablet celebrated antedated it by more
than three hundred years. The third emperor of the Ming dynasty,
Yung-lo (reigned 1403–1424), who is best remembered for planning
the Imperial City and the Temple of Heaven, also drafted one hundred
thousand scholarly and affluent families from several provinces to populate the newly established metropolitan district of Peking. As a result,
in our town there were originally four main clans from widely separated
parts of the empire: we Mengs from Shantung, the Chu clan from
Chekiang, Li from Anhwei, and Chung from Kiangsu. Some families
from these clans prospered and built mansions inside the city wall.

Nearly all families owning farmlands were located between
the wall and the great dike beyond, our barrier between the city and
our river, Yung Ting Ho, meaning Eternal Peace. Colloquially it was
called Hun Ho, the Confused or Muddled River, because every summer
it changed course, broke the dike, and caused floods. It was made
known to the West by Marco Polo, who traveled and worked in China
as an official of the Yuan dynasty and was a favorite of Kublai Khan
(reigned 1275–1292). On his way to the capital, Cambuluc, later the
site of Peking, he crossed the river on Lu Kuo Chiao (Reed Channel
Bridge), a beautiful marble structure ten miles west of the capital. Since
that time westerners have called it the Marco Polo Bridge.

Hun River is even more mischievous than the Yellow. It
causes minor floods annually and major floods biennially. For three
seasons of the year it is a narrow stream meandering gently through
marshlands overgrown with weeds. But each summer, suddenly melted

snow from the barren mountainside converts it into a roaring, mad, swollen torrent that breaks its dikes and inundates farms. Our ancestor, Meng Ch'uan-hsien, founder of Chung Shu T'ang, built an emergency granary and persuaded other families to do the same. These Meng-inspired granaries saved thousands of lives in times of flood and famine throughout the Ming and Ch'ing dynasties.

Three hundred years later, the Emperor Chien Lung, personally studying the flood problems of his capital, heard of our ancestor's precautionary system, which had been working effectively ever since. The emperor was moved to confer on us the great honor of inscribing the tablet with his own calligraphy.

Because the Chinese system of writing is so difficult and takes so many years to learn, the Chinese people have developed ways of transmitting songs, music, and literature orally, from person to person, from generation to generation.

"Mother Meng Moved Thrice" is a folk tale which has had universal circulation among all mothers for many centuries and also has been adapted in a large number of novels and dramas. It impressed me deeply when I first heard it as a small boy, because of our family descent from Mother Meng's son, Mencius. The story has become a time-honored legend, extolling a wise mother and an exemplary youth, repeated over and over as a source of inspiration for generations of mothers and sons:

"Mencius' father died when he was a young child and Mother Meng had to support the family by weaving cloth which she bartered for food and other necessities. Reverence for learning was the family tradition and she wanted her son to be a scholar. She was troubled when the boy got interested in imitating a butcher whose shop was nearby. So she moved their home to another location. It happened that a funeral parlor opened in the neighborhood, and her son talked about embalming as his desired career. The third home she moved to she made sure was near the school.

"One beautiful spring day the boy came home from school

and declared to his mother that he was tired of studying and had decided to drop out. Mother Meng led her son to her loom, where a piece of cloth was almost finished and, without comment, cut it to pieces with a pair of scissors. Amazed, the boy exclaimed, 'Mother, we need the cloth to barter for food!' 'Cloth destroyed can be replaced by another piece,' Mother said, 'but a boy who does not learn will not be a useful man.'

"Eventually, that boy became the great scholar who championed and expounded the teachings of Confucius and helped to make Confucianism China's dominant way of life."

On my mother's knees, at bedtime, or while I was recuperating from measles—indeed, whenever we were together—my mother would amuse me with stories, memories, and precepts which she treasured and which she thought would prepare me to grow into manhood. One virtue highly valued by the family was *chin chien* (industry, frugality). To cultivate this double-edged quality, she taught us not to waste food at the table. She made it fun by teaching us to recite a poem and to sing a folk song of the hoe:

"The Hoe" (song)

Take the hoe and cut out the weeds;
Gone the wild weeds, the crops grow.
Yi-yah-hey, yah-hoo-hey.
Wind blows, rain drenches, sun scorches;
Self-sow, self-reap, hence self may eat.
Yi-yah-hey, yah-hoo-hey.

For five thousand years the nation needs the
    hoe.
With the hoe the farmers secure their
    freedom.
Yi-hah-hey, yah-hoo-hey.
Wind blows, rain drenches, sun scorches;
Self-sow, self-reap, hence self may eat.
Yi-hah-hey, yah-hoo-hey.

"Hoeing" (poem)

Hoeing under the hot noon sun.
Sweat drops on the soil.
Food on the dinner plate
Is made of grains of bitter toil.

Every spring and autumn my grandfather took me to watch the volunteers repair the dike. It was much taller and thicker than the city wall. But the wall was a square structure of gray bricks built originally for defense, with battlements and gates and bell towers. The dike was made of clay, reinforced by thick grass and shrub cover on the sides and with trees planted on top. Both wall and dike were encircled by their own moats and required regular strengthening or dredging. Every family supplied manpower or refreshments. This was an occasion for do-it-yourself and see-it-for-yourself by the whole community. We children watched how some worked hard, some gave directions, many kibitzed, and all enjoyed socializing.

Indeed, the first six years of my life seemed to be all play, fun, and finding out about new things. Everybody wanted to make me happy and tried to do whatever I asked. My second and third sisters, being five and three years older, set examples for me to follow in my daily behavior. My eldest sister was twelve years older; she was my deputy mother and sometimes interceded for me when I was naughty and got into difficulties.

My life, while free, was also fully orchestrated by time-honored customs and by the clearly demonstrated division of authority and labor among the grownups. By tradition, Grandfather was the head of the family, but Grandmother nevertheless exercised unquestioned prerogatives in domestic matters of food, clothing, and the welfare of the women and children. How we greeted one another, our table manners, and the hours for retiring at night and for rising in the morning were strictly observed. Celebrations of festivals and anniversaries were noted on the calendar and details of their preparation were made and explained in advance.

On the anniversary of my birth, because I was the youngest,

I received gifts from all others. But early in the morning of that day I had to kowtow to all, one by one, and formally thank them for taking care of me. On the Second Day of the Second Moon we celebrated the return of spring and a new cycle of life. At dinner we ate the symbolic food of spring roll, which is cooked bean sprouts rolled in thick sheets of pancake, like crêpes. The Dragon Boat Festival came on the Fifth Day of the Fifth Moon and was celebrated with real or symbolic boat races and with *tsung*, a rice pudding with various fillings which is placed in bamboo leaves and tied into little pyramids. This festival commemorates the heroic death of a great poet and statesman, Chu Yuan, who drowned himself in Tung-ting Lake, in Hunan, in 296 B.C. As a minister of state, he had encountered overwhelming opposition by corrupt politicians who not only blocked his policies, but also succeeded in bringing about his dismissal from office and banishment. Chu Yuan thought of a way to make known his philosophy of life. He composed an epic autobiographical poem which he called *Li Sao*, (Parting Regrets), and left copies of it with his friends. He pinned a copy on himself, rowed out to the center of that famous lake, and committed suicide. He chose the Fifth Day of the Fifth Moon because it was the occasion for multitudes to come from far and near to pay homage to the zenith sun of midsummer and to indulge in water sports. His heroic deed set a historical precedent for frustrated idealists to publicize their causes by committing suicide.

The Mid-Autumn Festival was our Thanksgiving and took place on the Fifteenth Day of the Eighth Moon. By that time of the year we had finished harvesting. The family assembled on the threshing floor to give thanks to the harvest moon and the immortals who lived therein. At the center of the long table facing the full moon was a bushel of beans in which was planted a framed portrait of the White Rabbit, pharmacist-in-chief to the mythological mother who lives in a palace on the feminine Moon and oversees the affairs of womankind on behalf of Old Heavenly Grandfather. In our portrait the White Rabbit stood with dignity on its hind legs, pounding ingredients in a mortar in his never-ending search for an elixir conferring eternal youth and beauty on women. Flanking the incense urn and candlesticks was the choicest produce of our farms—apples, pears, grapes, and pumpkins. Next to the long table were two round tables set for dinner for the family. After we paid our respects to the Rabbit, who had restrained his earthly followers from destroying our crops, we sat down to enjoy our feast, climaxed by the Moon Cake.

The moon-year calendar was devised in antiquity and calculated on four seasons of three hundred and sixty days. The full moon is the fifteenth day of each of the twelve moons, or months. The year has some months of twenty-nine and some of thirty days; once every five years it employs a leap month to adjust inequalities and make the full cycle run true. Until the founding of the republic in 1911 the national astronomical bureau published the moon calendar as an official document of the empire. It not only contained schedules and guidelines for the seasons, suitable times for farming and dates for festivals, but also traditional advisory notes on auspicious dates for traveling, weddings, funerals, and other undertakings.

The most important annual community event was the New Year Festival. Lasting twenty-three days, it was the longest holiday and the only one that included everybody, even housewives and farmers.

Getting ready for the Kitchen God party, we children helped to make candies and cookies out of various materials, such as barley, sesame seeds, and molasses. By the evening of the Twenty-third Day of the Twelfth Moon, the start of the festival, we had picked out the best batches of candies and cookies in all kinds of fancy shapes and flavors, and brought them to the altar of the Kitchen God. Children were allowed to stick pieces of candy in his mouth. All offered incense and prayers that this resident agent of Old Heavenly Grandfather would render a good report when he returned to Heaven for his vacation.

The last seven days of the old year were full of exciting activities for all members of the family. The womenfolk's chief concern was to prepare new clothes to be worn on the first sixteen days of the New Year, and to cook all kinds of wonderful dishes and pastries for the spirit altars, and for the family and expected guests. My grandfather directed the men in giving a fresh new look to the outer walls, and especially the three entrances, in redecorating the front quadrangle and the great hall, in hanging new paintings and planting additional posts for all kinds of lanterns. Other families took similar action. The streets of our town were colorfully and brightly lighted. I was permitted to go out after sunset and set off my private hoard of firecrackers, and to explore other parts of the town with my playmates. New Year's Eve was the occasion for each family to out-firecracker its neighbors outside its front gate. The noisy contest shook the earth and lighted the air until midnight.

The first day of the New Year was dedicated to the spirits. We put on our best new clothes in the morning and assembled behind our grandparents, who led us to the altars of Old Heavenly Grandfather and the Ancestors, where we expressed our supreme thanks and hopes by kowtowing—thrice kneeling and nine times prostrating—and by lighting incense and candles. After we had paid our respects to the heavenly beings, our grandparents sat down beside the family altar to receive felicitations from their offspring, and then my parents from theirs. As the youngest, I bowed to everyone. However, the older ones had to give appropriate gifts, each in accordance with his or her rank. It always delighted me that New Year was a windfall of wonderful things from my loved ones. To further impress us children with the importance of starting the New Year right, we ate only vegetable dishes that first day and were warned that what we thought and said during the first sixteen days would determine the pattern of our lives for the rest of the year. This made it essential to refrain from cursing or even mentioning such words as death, sickness, or hate.

From the second day of the New Year through the sixteenth was a time for assuring a good start and for merrymaking. For grown-ups it was a matter of common decency and self-respect to pay all debts. Other family members divided up to pay New Year's calls on relatives, neighbors, and friends. With some we left red cards of best wishes. On others we dropped in to offer greetings in person. With some we stayed for lunch or dinner or for a game of mah jongg, dominoes, or cards.

Grandfather saw to it that we all made amends with people; he praised and rewarded me when I apologized to my mother for any past disobedience. He also insisted that I make up with any boys I had fought. We wore our best clothes, ate the best foods, and played to our heart's content.

We children especially enjoyed celebrating with grownups. Grandfather was very skilled in kitemaking. Though kites could be bought in the marketplace, we took special pride in flying our own. I learned how to attach bows of silk ribbon to produce humming music on kites, but Grandfather alone was able to make kite-lanterns and messenger-kites. It required patient and delicate balancing to suspend and to shield the little wick from the wind, and to send the tiny kite up the string to the big kite high in the air.

The First Full Moon Festival, lasting three days—the fourteenth, fifteenth, and sixteenth of the first month—was also known as the Feast of Lanterns. Families showed off their best lanterns, inside and outside their houses. Some lanterns were innovations, some were heirlooms. They presented a myriad of shapes, materials, colors, art symbols, and auspicious sayings and pictures of great and happy things to come. Grandfather always tried to cut ice-lanterns. He had a special way of freezing clear blocks of ice, which he cut into brilliant crystal rabbit- or turtle-shaped lanterns.

The climax of the First Moon Festival came on the evening of the fifteenth. The town treated the whole community to a gala display of fireworks in the public square. We were all amazed by the huge rockets which only the town could afford. But what stayed in our memory longest was the mandatory climactic scene sketched in multi-colored fireworks shot high in the air and finally exploded into ten thousand stars. In that scene was the Celestial Commissioner bestowing on the people of the earth—a symbolic group of male and female, old, middle-aged, and young—the four major blessings: peace, prosperity, honor, and long life.

After we returned home and before we retired, Grandfather

27

had us children gather around a kite. He asked us to think about all
the bad things we would wish to banish (such as colds and measles)
and to request the kite to take them away. We then flew the kite, laden
with our wishes, and let the wind carry it away, up, up into the night
sky, until it disappeared.

A farmer's life in old China was hard, especially in the North, where
rainfall was uncertain and floods occurred every year. Plowing, planting, and harvesting, emergencies and repairs, struggles with both human and societal foibles and the wicked incursions of ghosts and evil
spirits—his work was never done. He learned to lighten his burdens
by singing at work, by organizing festivals, orchestras, and processions,
and by staging theatricals. All these he managed to accomplish through
volunteerism and a do-it-yourself life style.

    In the storerooms of the municipal temple in our town, all
kinds of costumes, musical instruments, and other properties were
available for year-around festivals and processions. Now and then fresh
materials or efforts were contributed. In the long evenings, experienced
men trained and rehearsed young people in the temple courtyard,
preparing them to perform in dances, concerts, and processions for our
town and for others nearby. The standard repertoire consisted of the
dances "Flower Drum" and "Celestial Maidens Scattering Blossoms,"
the instrumental pieces "Flowing Stream" and "Three-Six-Four Together," and the "Wheelbarrow" and "Dragon" processions. Many were
trained; the best were chosen to perform.

    In contrast with western folkways, we Chinese have con-
sciously refrained from promoting boy-girl and man-woman get-
togethers for more than a thousand years. From the beginning of our
civilization to the T'ang era (618–906), social life between the sexes
was not much different from that of ancient Greece or Rome. They
danced, flirted, and courted together; they married and divorced easily;
there were women rulers, scholars, warriors, and beauties who caused
the downfall of cities and nations. There followed a long period of
reaction comparable to western Puritanism, when women and music

28

were repressed.

Emperor Hsüan Tsung of the T'ang dynasty (reigned 713–756) was a talented musician and actor. The empire enjoyed prosperity, so ample and so widespread that no doors were locked at night and things left in public were never taken. Emperor Hsüan had time to pursue his pleasures. He erected a concert hall and a theater in the pear-tree orchard of this palace and personally took part in the rehearsals. It so happened that His Majesty met and fell in love with a most beautiful dancer, Yang Yu-huan, whom he elected to *kwei fei* (high or honored concubine). In time she came to be blamed for his neglect of affairs of state, and for nepotism and corruption that aroused discontent among the people. After a powerful and successful revolt, the emperor was confronted with a choice between the throne and his mistress. He forsook Yang Kwei-fei and saved the dynasty. This episode is well known in Chinese history and literature as *The Eternal Regret*. Beyond the human tragedy, however, the popular reaction gave rise to a ban on music as an instrument of education and to the ousting of women from public affairs and the stage.

One festival survived to remind the Chinese people of their enduring affinity for feminine beauty and virtue, and the mystery of romantic love. Because they were forbidden to choose their loved ones to marry, they could pray to certain immortal spirits to help them realize their fond hopes. In the night sky, as one can see when it is clear, there is the River of Heaven (the Milky Way) and to one side of it a bright star (Aquila) flanked by two small stars; on the other side there is an equally bright star (Lyra) which holds a shuttlecock. For Chinese, the two bright stars represent immortal spirits who descended to earth and lived the lives of a Cowherd and a Weaving Maiden, exemplifying romance among peasants in spite of hardships. The two met under the new moon of the Seventh Eve of the Seventh Moon. The sincere love of the two stars so moved Old Heavenly Grandfather that He commnaded the *hsi chueh* (joyous birds; magpies) to form a bridge across the River of Heaven to enable the two lovers to reunite every year on that date.

What modern education offers as literature in classrooms and books, I received in oral doses in much more intimate and comfortable circumstances at my grandmother's knee, sweetened by frequent intake of nuts and candies. Western people know some of our classics well, such as *Monkey, The Romance of the Three Kingdoms, All Men Are Brothers,* and *Dream of the Red Chamber,* all of which have been translated into Occidental languages. But for Grandmother and me, they had simply been told, generation to generation, as grandmothers' tales. Grandmothers usually had more leisure to amuse their grandchildren, and our concepts of Heaven, Earth, and Man were absorbed gradually and pleasurably from them.

Folklore and folk tales were also basic components of traditional drama and fiction. Next in importance to grandmothers were storytellers and country theaters. There were several kinds of professional storytellers. The earliest were perhaps the puppet and shadow players, who popularized the miracle drama and later extended their repertoire to secular tragedies and comedies. By far the largest and most available groups were the blind men and women who traveled in pairs around the year, and who could be engaged to perform by the hour, the day, or the month. They usually sang their stories accompanied by a *san hsüan* (three-stringed banjo) or *ssu hu* (four-stringed cello), a hand drum, and wood or iron clappers (castanets). Most towns gave one or two free public theatricals a year. The town took up a collection of voluntary contributions, chose one or two likely periods of four days each, and booked a desirable company to perform four afternoon and four evening sessions. We had a permanent theater building at the southern end of our town square, facing the municipal temple in the distance at the northern end of the square. The theater consisted only of dressing rooms and the stage, which, by custom, had a space for the orchestra at the extreme left, with the entrance next, and the exit at the right. All were welcome, free of charge, to stand in front of the stage. Those who wanted to sit had to place their chairs or benches on the fringes. Overlooking the audience were the elevated boxes of wealthy patrons.

Grandmothers, storytellers, and theatrical performers, however varied their styles, dramatized for us the central themes of the Chinese way of life. Old Heavenly Grandfather loved us, they said, and tried his best to help us always, but we had to try our best to understand good and evil in all their forms and circumstances, so we could achieve happiness on earth and eternal bliss in heaven. Two particular classic sources, I think, were most illuminating for me.

First, and most widely known and loved, was the *Western Travel Journal*, better known as *Monkey* among foreigners familiar only with Arthur Waley's English translation. It is about an animated marble monkey who learned seventy-two magic tricks and was bent on attaining immortality. Buddha taught him to be patient. A monk, who also wanted eternal life, adopted him as his attendant, together with a magic pig and a white horse. The four set out on a journey to India to search for the scriptures and secrets of Buddhism in the land of its origin. They encountered all kinds of difficulties: demons which threatened to eat them, evil spirits which cleverly diverted them from their goal, and a most beautiful queen who tried her best to seduce them when they passed through her realm. Young people most enjoy the lurid and horrible episodes and the "Superman" stunts of the monkey, while adults appreciate the religious or philosophical overtones. But the story impresses all with the interaction of good and evil. *The Romance of the Three Kingdoms* (220–280) deals with heroes, battles, and intrigues following the decline and fall of the Han dynasty (208 B.C.–A.D. 220). Three particular stories made a deep and lasting impression on me. I later found that almost all the people I knew remembered them and that these three stories had exerted a profound influence on Chinese people generally. They were "Peach Orchard Three Righteous Ones," "Three Visits to the Reed Hut," and "The Empty City Ruse."

Tao Yüan San Chieh Yi (Peach Orchard Three Righteous Ones)

The decline and fall of the Han dynasty brought on a period of chaos and civil war out of which emerged three contending kingdoms—Wei, Shu, and Wu, all revolutionary groups. A shoemaker and farmer, Liu Pei, claimed that he was a scion of the imperial family and therefore a legitimate leader to save the dynasty and the people from other rebels. Among his devoted followers were Kuan Yü, a bean-curd peddler, and Chang Fei, a butcher and blacksmith. The three of them decided to organize a brotherhood, comrades-in-arms who would give their lives for one another and for the cause. Ordinarily, such comrades would take the vow of blood-brotherhood at the altar of Old Heavenly Grandfather and mingle blood obtained by biting their little fingers. But these three were starting a secret underground revolution. Therefore, under the cover of darkness, they went out to a peach orchard to observe the rite. Instead of burning incense, they used sprays of peach blossoms. For the next forty years, the three Righteous Brothers fought side by side through thick and thin, established the Shu kingdom, and sacrificed their lives as they had sworn to do.

Tao Yüan San Chieh Yi has become an example of the highest devotion to friendship and of dedication to a noble cause.

San Ku Mao Lu (Three Visits [to the] Reed Hut)

When the three Righteous Brothers succeeded in founding the Shu kingdom, they realized that they needed a statesman to help them to administer affairs of government. Inquiries disclosed that, in a grass hut in Sleeping Dragon mountain range, there lived a hermit who was really a statesman and strategist in retirement. Thereupon, King Liu Pei went with his entourage in search of the hermit. They found the rustic hideout, but the hermit was not home and his page boy would not tell them where the Master was or when he would be back: "My Master goes off frequently to look for rare species of herbs. It is not possible to guess how long he will be absent." The king left a written message with the boy, stating that he would return in ten days and would ask the Master to be his prime minister. Ten days passed. The king visited the grass hut a second time. The boy presented a reply from the hermit which said in part, "Please forgive my inability to accept your appointment because I have completely forgotten how to head a government and armed forces, and do not deserve the position and honor."

Chang Fei, no longer a butcher or blacksmith, but a general in the king's entourage, was enraged. "Doesn't this old fellow know his manners? He is rude not to be here to give his reply in person to his king. Let us comb the range to arrest and punish him."

"Third Brother," King Liu said, "perhaps I myself have not shown the respect due to a great scholar according to our tradition."

He left another message with the page stating that he would come again in ten days, but would be coming to seek advice and not to make an appointment.

On his third visit King Liu arrived at the hut dressed as a commoner and accompanied by one page. It was early in the morning. The gate was opened by the boy who whispered that the Master had returned very late the previous night, that he was too tired to write a reply, and that he still wanted to suggest to the king that there must be others who could better qualify for the position. Realizing that he was being tested further, King Liu asked the boy not to disturb the Master; he would wait outside the gate for a meeting until the Master woke up. King and hermit finally met. They conferred for three days and nights. Eventually, the hermit, Chu-ko Liang, accepted the king's offer, and as Shu prime minister (207–225), distinguished himself as a brilliant strategist and a dedicated official who served two kings, Liu Pei and his son, loyally. "Three Visits to the Reed Hut" emphasized for all people the dignity and importance of a scholar, which even a king must heed.

Kung Cheng Chi (Empty City Ruse)

Wei was much the largest of the Three Kingdoms and had a most powerful army. Wei was bent on conquering Shu, but Chu-ko Liang, the hermit prime minister, usually managed to win the battles. He was so successful that Ssu-ma Yi, the commander-in-chief of Wei, developed great respect for, and even fear of, Chu-ko's sagacity and tactics.

33

Once, in a serious engagement, the Shu field commander disobeyed the prime minister's directives, and as a result the Wei forces were able to threaten West City, where the prime minister was trapped with only a few bodyguards. On learning this bad news, Chu-ko ordered his guards to change into civilian clothes, while all others should continue with their normal daily work and all city gates should remain wide open, as in peaceful times. The prime minister put on a Taoist robe and hood, and took his seven-stringed *chin* to the tower over the eastern city gate. Wei's cavalry scouts soon arrived at the city wall, expecting the Shu forces to be demoralized by panic and to capture the city with ease. They could not believe what they saw: a man playing a *chin* atop an open gate, and the population pursuing its daily rounds in peace. Fearing a trick, they dared not enter and attack, but rushed back in confusion to Ssu-ma Yi. Ssu-ma himself then approached close enough to hear the music. The musician, his old adversary, politely invited the Wei general and his forces to come in. He would be delighted to have them as guests and would treat them with entertainment and refreshments. Chu-ko's music and spoken words evinced perfect calmness and confidence. Ssu-ma believed it must be a ruse. He held up the advance until he could be certain that the prime minister was not setting a trap for the Wei army. That delay allowed Chu-ko to slip away safely.

Such stories as these were the delight of my childhood, not only for their intrinsic interest, but for starting me on the path of Chinese cultural tradition. Like millions of others of the Chinese family, past and present, I learned through these stories an aspect of the moral values we shared. One sees this more clearly, of course, and appreciates it more fully, as one grows older.

I was groomed and ready for a school at six years of age. School was open to all, but only a small number of children actually was selected and admitted. All schools were funded privately by the clans, the labor guilds, and academies. Virtually all of them were preparatory schools for taking the academic and civil-service examinations conducted exclusively by the Government. Clan schools, such as ours, took care of the offspring and relatives of the family. Labor guilds, the largest of which were the carpenters and the masons, educated members' children. And academies usually were established by very wealthy, highly intellectual families to provide a setting for a particular scholar, or a public platform for his social or political point of view. Farm families depended so heavily on the labor of their children that only those deemed bright enough to attain a degree were sent to school. There was no compulsory universal schooling.

Third Sister and I were enrolled in the Meng clan school located in the rear quadrangle of our home. The other five pupils were cousins. Our tutor was an old scholar who had a *chü jen* (master's degree) and preferred scholarly pursuits and teaching to governmental service. According to custom, school commenced soon after sunrise and adjourned shortly before sunset. Morning and afternoon sessions were divided by period at the pleasure of the tutor. There were no weekends off. Our only holidays were the major festivals and the New Year.

The morning session was devoted to memorizing the text of the required books. The class followed the tutor in reading aloud, sentence by sentence, and each had his turn at the tutor's desk to undergo drilling in the sentences. In the afternoon we were taught how to make ink and use the brush, preparatory to learning calligraphy. Then followed a lecture on manners and discipline. The tutor pointedly showed us the regulation paddle, about two feet long, three inches wide, and one inch thick, which he would use to punish negligence in studying, and the rattan stick, about three feet long, which he would use to punish misbehavior.

Our prescribed reading list was *Three-Word-Line Classic, Filial Piety Anecdotes, Four Books, Five Classics.* The first reader was easily learned and committed to memory. Each line had three words. The Chinese language being monosyllabic, each line had three syllables and all lines more or less rhymed. The reader expressed in simple

35

terms a philosophy of life, an everyday manual of behavior and a history of the nation. For instance: "Man's beginning/Nature originally good/ By nature all men are similar/By habit they become different/Children misbehave/Parents' fault/They failed to study/Teacher's negligence."

It was not necessary to commit to memory the *Filial Piety Anecdotes*. But in leading us through the twenty-four historical examples, the tutor found ample and convincing proof of how much children owed to their parents, how the children should reciprocate by taking care of their parents, and how in this way the individual, the family, and the nation would insure their collective continuity and destiny.

The *Four Books* are the basic literature embodying the teachings of Confucius and Mencius. They are: *Great Learning, Middle Mean, Discussions and Sayings,* and *Mencius.* We were drilled daily until we were able to recite from memory whatever our tutor chose to question us on. After he was sure that all of us had committed to memory every part of the *Four Books,* he expounded their meanings, sentence by sentence, mainly according to the orthodox commentaries of the great scholar Chu Hsi (1130–1200). Much of the tutor's lecturing was over our heads, but he wisely moved from simple explanations to the more subtle and complicated, and emphasized the fundamentals so that they would stand out.

Ta Hsüeh (Great Learning) centers on the ability to recognize self-evident truths, to improve oneself, and to aim at ultimate goodness. Aim determines direction; direction brings peace; peace enables thinking; thinking makes creativity possible.

Chung Yung (Middle Mean) teaches moderation, a middle-of-the-road approach, and the avoidance of extremism in matters which are susceptible to differences of opinion or interpretation.

Lun Yu (Discussions and Sayings) concerns the Master's fundamental themes of self-cultivation, family building, sound national administration, and world peace. This sequential process grows with proper and desirable relations between parents and children, siblings and siblings, husbands and wives, rulers and the ruled, and between friend and friend.

Meng Tzu (Mencius) is a collection of the sayings of this teacher and philosopher, who was a student of the grandson of Confucius. The first three of the *Four Books* contain the teachings of the Master as they were recalled and recorded long after his death. Throughout his life, Mencius attempted to expound the teachings of Confucius and to have them understood and adopted by the rulers and the elite. He added his own ideas on human nature and on the affairs of state. Modern scholars, eastern and western, think highly of his philosphy of *T'ien Ming* (Mandate of Heaven), which posits the original goodness of human nature, and state control and the conservation of natural resources.

The Five Classics are pre-Confucian, but were edited by the Master. They were much more voluminous than the *Four Books* and we were not required to commit the texts to memory. However, we had to acquire a substantial mastery of their contents and to learn how to use them as references.

Shih Ching (Poetry Classic) is an anthology of about three hundred songs and poems selected by Confucius. He admired expressions of friendship, and reactions to fate and adverse circumstances. As for love, Confucius preferred restraint and propriety rather than an outpouring of intense romantic emotion.

Shu Ching (Book of Record Classic) comprises a collection of edicts, addresses, and proceedings of the government and rulers of ancient China. It shows how early Chinese society managed its affairs, from popular nomination of its rulers to the founding of dynasties, and the evolution of the emperor's dictatorship into the doctrine of the right to revolt by the people, and the concept of *kung ho* (all-together) people's rule. This ancient Chinese term was applied to the new republican form of government in 1911, and has been used continuously. In Chinese, the People's Republic is *Jin Min Kung Ho Kuo* (People's All-together Nation).

I Ching (Change Classic). *I* (pronounced *yi*) means "change." It deals with the ponderables and imponderables in nature and prescribes means and techniques of divination, including the calculation of chances by trigrams, which are stylized designs of the I Ching sticks, the calendar, and the choice of auspicious times for weddings and other undertakings. It has been used as a manual of divination by the masses. For scholars, including such modern western scholars as Carl Jung, *I Ching* also contains philosophical and psychological wisdom.

Li Chi (Rites Record) is a compilation or source book of rituals, etiquette, and manners. The detailed codification is more or less out of date, but the underlying meanings are still relevant and worth pondering. It teaches that good manners and politeness harmonize human relations and lubricate social friction, and that rituals and music moderate emotions and help us to travel the journey of life.

Ch'un Ch'iu (Annals of Spring and Autumn) is a chronicle of events during the middle of the Chou dynasty (722–479 B.C.). It is called the *Annals of Spring and Autumn* because those two seasons seemed to be the times for war and earthquakes and other unusual human and natural happenings. Among his rather terse observations on these events, Confucius makes it clear that woman is or should be the equal of man, and that no war is a righteous war.

In our town we had a Buddhist temple and a Taoist temple. From the outside the two temples were identical in their architecture. They both occupied scenic spots, each had a *pai lou* or ceremonial arch, quadrangles, goldfish and lotus ponds, green-tiled curved roofs, multicolored eaves, and so forth. Inside, the statues were different: Buddhist figures were Hindu in style, while Taoist gods were entirely Chinese in appearance. The Buddhist monks, who resided at their temple, shaved their heads and wore the orange robes common to Buddhist monks all over the world. Taoist monks let their hair grow long and wore their robes decorated with Chinese trigrams.

The *ch'eng huang miao* (municipal temple) closely resembled the other two temples in appearance, but was regarded as a local spiritual counterpart of the magistrate's establishment, the temporal seat of power. It probably resulted from our people's habit of eclecticism and Sinofying imported foreign things and cultures. With adult encouragement, we children frequently visited the Hall of Thirty-three Heavens and Hall of Eighteen Underground Prisons (or Hells) of the municipal temple. On the walls and ceilings of these two huge halls were painted dramatic scenes detailing life in each environment. Even a young child could understand the wonders of each heaven, each of which outshone the next up to the thirty-third and highest heaven, where the soul might enjoy eternal bliss in the company of Old Heavenly Grandfather. Prisons, on the other hand, showed what punishment fitted which offense, with those who committed the worst offenses, such as murder, cast into the eighteenth and lowest one to suffer torture forever. The Chinese believe that the soul is indestructible and will be treated by the spiritual establishment in ways similar to those in which human beings were treated by the governmental bureaucracy on earth. Rewards were graded and a soul was promoted upward for its good works. The penal system for souls allowed opportunities for redemption seventeen times.

The immortals in heaven were free to roam the earth, and many of them, on their own volition or by direction of the celestial authorities, offered helpful advice to confused human beings struggling with earthly problems. As frequently as needed, Old Heavenly Grandfather would send down specialists from heaven to be conceived and born by human mothers, so that their lives could serve as guidelines or inspirations. Among the best understood examples were the Cowherd and the Weaving Maiden, and the Eight Immortals who had lived on earth as scholar, warrior, physician, musician, alchemist, beggar, virtuous woman, and nonconformist woman. We all were comforted that even a beggar or nonconformist could become an immortal.

We also had a Confucian temple. Although architecturally the same, it had a color scheme of gray and white, and there were no statues or paintings inside, only memorial tablets and plaques. The main hall contained the tablets of Confucius and his seventy-two disciples, the east hall those of good men and the west hall those of good women, nominated by our community.

All temples were open to the public day and night. At the

Buddhist and Taoist temples the monks held daily worship with gala services on the first and fifteenth days and on special anniversaries. They also might be invited to officiate at funerals. The monks preached no sermons; there was no provision for the public to participate in their worship, no conversion, no membership. Support for the temples and monks came from their land and from voluntary contributions. The municipal temple was built and maintained by the town. Its staff also took care of the town square, the place for annual theatricals and fairs. The national Government built and maintained the Confucian temple and appointed a commissioner of education and a staff which cared for the buildings, gave examinations for the first academic degree, *hsiu tsai* (budding talent), and conducted two anniversary memorial meetings each year, celebrating the birth and death of the Master. In the modern western sense, Confucianism could hardly be called a religion, and the Confucian temple was not exactly a temple, because the teachings of Confucius had little to do with the supernatural, and people did not go to his temple to pray for blessings and forgiveness. Confucianism was really a philosophy of life, and the temple a shrine, like the Lincoln Memorial.

Confucius and succeeding generations of followers developed over a long period of years a philosophy which tolerated all religions and philosophies that were compatible with it. In the judgment of most people in China, especially scholars, the right attitude was to keep an open mind on supernatural matters and to avoid dogmatic conclusions on unprovable beliefs. Members of my family visited all three temples and treated our Old Heavenly Grandfather and our ancestors affectionately and naturally as an integral part of daily living. These practices and attitudes explain why China produces no theologians and why most western theologians consider Chinese faith in the supernatural primitive and anthropomorphic. Some even assert that Chinese are not religious, because we have not logically pursued religious or theological studies. It is true that, compared with the development of western thought, we have applied to religion less logic and more poetic license. To us the nature of God, revelation, ultimate beginning, and ultimate end are open-ended matters. We have not crystallized our religious beliefs into rival sects and denominations. We have had no wars or inquisitions caused by theological disputes.

Gradually and naturally, it dawned on me that Old Heavenly Grandfather had quite a hard time creating the universe. He started with the Yin and Yang forces. Yin led to the formation of the moon, water, and females, Yang to the formation of the sun, fire, and males. He needed and created assistants, and as His creation escalated the number of His assistants increased. Soon it was necessary for Him to establish a celestial government composed of a cabinet, numerous bureaus and independent agencies, and special agents and commissioners. After He had created Heaven and Earth, He created on earth human beings after His image. At first the Yin force dominated and there was too much water. He appointed Nü Wo, a female commissioner who could live in water and on land, as well as in the air. She made a survey and recommended that the Yin and Yang forces should be so controlled that they would work in harmony and be productive, rather than in conflict and destructive. A hydraulic commissioner dug nine rivers and drained the water into four seas. He then created females and males to inhabit the earth according to Yin and Yang principles and also to test their interaction. Soon violence broke out. Old Heavenly Grandfather, as emperor-on-high, had to spend considerable time and thought with his cabinet on how to deal with the quarreling and fighting females and males below.

The Minister of War, commander of the celestial soldiers, proposed, "Your Majesty made them. You have the right to destroy them. Let us wipe them out and then Your Majesty can create better beings for the Earth."

"Permit me to disagree," argued the Angel of Longevity, "because the women and men are the creatures of the emperor, they should be preserved and allowed to live the way they choose."

The Goddess of Mercy recommended that Old Heavenly Grandfather reveal Himself and proclaim exact rules of conduct for human beings to follow. There were prolonged discussions in heaven

41

and finally Old Heavenly Grandfather decided on a wise and benevolent policy which included the following:

Each human being shall be given a soul which is indestructible.

She or he shall be rewarded or punished according to her or his good or evil deeds.

Thirty-three heavens and eighteen prisons shall be established to encourage good and to penalize evil.

A bureau shall record the deeds of all beings and supervise and make assignments with regard to rewards, punishments, and reincarnations of each individual soul.

It seemed that all especially good, wise, and talented people were reincarnations of immortal spirits from heaven. According to our folklore, the souls or spirits of Lao Tzu (recognized originator of Taoism), Sakyamuni (originator of Buddhism), Confucius, and other great personalities are in the thirty-third heaven with Old Heavenly Grandfather. The Jews and Judaism were well received and well treated in China because the Ten Commandments coincide with the ethical concepts of Confucius. In 1624, when a flood destroyed the synagogue in Kaifeng, the people of that city contributed funds not only for its restoration, but also for a collection of Jewish scriptures to be translated into Chinese.

Foreign Devils and Generation Gaps

We had two "foreign devils" in our town. They resided in strange-looking buildings near the south city gate. One of the buildings had a pointed white steeple with a bell in it which rang every day. The two men were from beyond the west ocean. They were tall, had red hair and green eyes, and walked with long straight legs—the very personification of devils. We talked about them in hushed tones because we had heard so much that frightened us.

Long ago these two English missionaries had come to our town to persuade the people to change. They talked loudly on the streets and in the town square, and induced women and children to go inside their buildings. By and by, it was rumored that they wanted us to stop believing in our gods and ancestors, and to believe in theirs. They performed magic on the sick. All in all, they clearly were plotting to make our country their colony and our people their subjects. About 1900 the so-called Boxers rose up and attempted to rid China of all missionaries. They came to our town and massacred our two missionaries and some fifteen others. The foreign governments sent their soldiers to punish us. They shot all men on sight, violated women, and destroyed the temples. Forewarned, my grandmother, my mother, and the girls and I escaped to the corn fields, where I almost died from exposure and insect bites. Father was away in Peking. Grandfather was shot twice, feigned death, and lived to tell us about the barbaric deeds of these foreign devils.

Father was absent from home most of the time. He was a political activist, working first to establish a constitutional monarchy and, when that failed, the republican government of Sun Yat-sen. Visits to Peking and Tientsin brought him into contact with forward-looking and adventurous men of his age from all parts of the country. Like them, he had concluded that we must modernize through learning from the West. Consequently, he joined the revolutionary reform movement which later became Sun Yat-sen's Tung Meng Hui ("together-vow") resigned his position with the Imperial Government and went abroad to study. My happy and well-ordered childhood years were highlighted by his infrequent visits. He always brought home new and curious presents. I remember the first clock in my grandparents' room, which was admired by all, and the bottles of Doan's tonic for Grandfather. (A traditionalist, he would have nothing to do with them.) We children liked the modern toys, imported soaps, toothbrushes and powder, and a potted tomato plant.

Father also brought home foreign books and periodicals. He displayed them in the library, where they presented quite an assortment of covers, colors, sizes, and styles of printing. Some were intended for children. They contained colored pictures of such unheard-of things as electric lights, motor cars and telephones, and stories of western people, including Indians and George Washington. I looked at the many volumes, bound differently from our Chinese books. Most of them were incomprehensible, even their titles and the names of their authors. But I could and did read Lin Shu's translation of Shakespeare's *Hamlet* and Wu Kuang-chien's of *The Three Musketeers*, which, I thought, were not quite so good as our *Romance of the Three Kingdoms* and *Dream of the Red Chamber*. *The Adventures of Sherlock Holmes*, however, I thought superb.

Grandfather was more interested in heavy volumes of the works of Adam Smith, Thomas Huxley, John Stuart Mill, and Herbert Spencer, translated into Chinese. He and Father had lengthy discussions about them which they tried to explain and summarize for me. I heard but could not comprehend terms like economics, politics, or "constitutional monarchy," but I did understand "rapid-firing guns" and "modern schools." I could hardly wait to try both.

Grandfather conceded that some changes were necessary to improve things, certainly the weapons and the armed forces. He was undecided about political and social reforms. As for education, perhaps we should learn how to make better guns and battleships, and improve our science and engineering. As to our way of life, he never lost faith in our traditional family context, the extension of family relations to other relations, and humanism rather than the dogmatic theology preached by western missionaries.

As he passed the age of seventy, Grandfather began to prepare for his departure from this earth. He selected his coffin, supervised its carving and decoration, and placed it in the family vault. During his final two years he devoted more and more attention to me, reminding me repeatedly of my responsibilities as the sole heir of the long-rooted Meng family traditions. What has remained in my memory and stood by me all the years are his admonitions on "virtue rather than force," "learning rather than wealth," and "industry and thrift rather than idleness and licentiousness." He officiated at his own final farewell, attempting to persuade all assembled not to grieve or weep. He was actually holding my right hand and was saying that his presence would remain with us, as his tablet would be on the family altar, when he peacefully closed his eyes and breathed his last.

During all the years I lived with Grandfather, I never heard him raise his voice, never saw him walk other than deliberately. He was always courteous to Grandmother and refrained from taking off his jacket in her presence even in very hot weather. After his retirement from government office, his daily life was exactly regulated. He rose before the sun and retired only after making sure that all others had turned in. In addition to his duties as head of the family and clan, he enjoyed gardening, including evolving new species of chrysanthemums and tree peonies. The affection and respect between him and my father, his only son, were real and mutual, but remained unspoken. He missed the presence of his son during Father's long trips, but he told me and Grandmother often that he had wisely chosen a virtuous daughter-in-law who more than fulfilled the expected filial services. Grandfather's opinions on important matters differed from Father's only as to the degrees and the aspects of our country's modernization. Of course, Grandfather's traumatic experiences with European soldiers tended to make him somewhat antiforeign and anti-Christian, and this attitude influenced me consciously and emotionally. Father, on the other hand, understood better the West and westerners, and as an enthusiastic reformer was inclined to be more partial to innovation.

My second sister was the most outgoing of the children and a favorite of the family. One year, when she was twelve, she became very ill. When my maternal uncle, who was a doctor trained in the Chinese tradition, and other physicians proved to be ineffective, and her condition was desperate, Father sought the help of a modern physician, a German-trained M.D., a friend of his. The doctor arrived from Peking in the uniform of an army surgeon, with a sword and high leather boots. He changed into an all-white coat, examined the patient, and ordered me and my other sisters to be sent away to other parts

45

of our house. He prescribed cold baths and gave her foreign pills. Two days later my sister died. Father had a terrible time justifying his action. He did succeed in mollifying us somewhat by explaining that his doctor was called in after it was too late. But the family and the clan could not forgive the M.D. for wearing a white coat, because he should have known that this was the color for mourning the dead.

After Grandfather died, Father decided to start a modern school. He enlisted the help of an English missionary in our town and added arithmetic, English, and general science to our instruction. Our old tutor continued to drill us in the classics and calligraphy.

Those were the last years of the empire. The Ch'ing emperor, Kuang Hsü, seemed to be losing the Mandate of Heaven, his link with divinity and the authority by which he ruled on earth. In human terms he was a weak and ineffectual young man, not even in the direct line of succession, but the choice of his aunt, the ignorant, shrewd, unscrupulous dowager empress, Tzu Hsi, who expected him to be her puppet.

In 1898, aged twenty-six, he undertook a well-intentioned but doomed effort to accelerate China's advance into the contemporary world. With the encouragement of modern-minded tutors, he issued a series of edicts seeking to reorganize and strengthen the Chinese Government, so it could better absorb the West's ideas, while resisting its domination. The effort was short-lived. Kuang Hsü's so-called Hundred Days of Reform were thwarted by Tzu Hsi. She deposed the emperor, resumed the throne as regent, and had several of his entourage executed. Kuang Hsü spent the rest of his short life in a palatial island prison. And China plunged onward into the Boxer uprising and eventual revolution. From Father I heard many fascinating details of this heartbreaking story.

Among the major changes the reformers hoped to accomplish was transformation of China's absolutist rule into a constitutional monarchy, like Japan's. This dispersal of power, of course, threatened the vested interests of the Manchu bureaucracy and military, whose oppressive hand had controlled China for more than two centuries.

Since the reformers wanted, in fact, to reform the Government, not overthrow it, their forlorn hope was to persuade Tzu Hsi to agree to the change for the good of the country. Secretly, they got one of the few Chinese regimental commanders in the Imperial army to aid their cause. This was Yuan Shih-kai, more than a decade away from becoming president of the Republic of China.

Yuan was to head the escort guarding Tzu Hsi on her return from the Summer Palace to Peking in September. During the journey he was to approach her and request her agreement to a constitutional monarchy. If she acceded, the march would proceed. But if she refused, Yuan was to divert the convoy to another palace, where Kuang Hsü and his advisers waited to resolve the matter with her, face to face. It would be a virtual kidnaping of the dowager empress and extremely dangerous for the perpetrators.

The Manchu commander-in-chief of the army, Yung Lu, who, according to gossip, was Tzu Hsi's lover, learned of the plan from informers. A subtle strategist, he decided to confront Yuan. He had confidence in the young officer; Yuan was one of the first Chinese he had entrusted with command. But he was less sure of Yuan's loyalty to anyone but himself. Dressed in simple clothes, without military rank or insignia, Yung Lu appeared at Yuan's home one midnight. He was cool, unthreatening, ingratiating. Tell me the facts, he urged. What are you up to? Who are the traitors?

No treachery attaches to me, Yuan protested. As soon as I learned the details of the plan I was coming to tell you.

Good, said the general. Meanwhile, I will be watching your performance as escort closely.

Cornered, Yuan promised to tell Tzu Hsi everything.

The reformers also had their spies, who told them that Yuan was about to expose the plan. They held a series of secret meetings, searching for a way out of the agonizing dilemma: Should they take action before Yuan betrayed them, or should they yield? And what could be done to protect the advisers from the empress's wrath? After much discussion, it was decided their plan was doomed, and that the two principal mentors should escape, Kang Yu-wei to England, Liang Chi-chao to Japan, so that not all the voices for reform should be silenced. The rest would stay and await their fate.

All were arrested, six publicly executed. One, like Chu Yuan, secreted a manifesto in his clothes, so that after the fourth day, when the family could recover his body, the message was found and read to the watching crowd. It protested that there was no intention to assassinate the empress, only to reform the monarchy with her approval for the welfare of China. His wife and son committed suicide.

The blood purge of the reformers horrified the nation. With constitutional monarchy no longer a possibility, reformers like my father were driven to join hands with the revolutionaries seeking to overthrow the Ch'ing dynasty and establish a republic. It was this course of events which brought Sun Yat-sen to the forefront as an alternative and started his rise to power.

Even our sleepy little town was awakened by the fast-moving national shock waves which were coupled with strongly antiforeign sentiments and demands for the recovery of our rights and territories as a sovereign state. Our school began to admit students of other clans, and the enrollment jumped to sixty students, with more applicants waiting because we lacked facilities for them. Father negotiated with the Anglican mission, which agreed to appropriate funds from the Boxer Indemnity* to build a new and larger school with a playground. All went well with the new school until an incident on the playground that involved an Englishman and the English game of football.

A young missionary had come to teach English and introduce us to football. He told us, among other things, that his nation prided itself on developing the game and the playground spirit, and that he had been a varsity player at Oxford. One afternoon there was a demonstration game for the students, their parents, and the community. The coach played center on one team. The center of the opposite team was Chu San, a fifteen-year-old boy. The Englishman was tall and husky; he was wearing his colorful uniform and leather boots with cleats. All the other players wore everyday short jackets and

48

* For damage done during the Boxer uprising, China was saddled with an excessive $330 million payment. Some western nations returned their shares in the form of scholarships or capital improvements, like Father's school.

trousers, and homemade cloth shoes. Somehow Chu managed to wring the ball from the coach several times to the amusement and cheers of bystanders. Finally, when it became clear that Chu's team would win, the coach became enraged. He kicked Chu on the chin while the latter was bunting the ball with his head. Chu was badly injured. He bit his tongue deeply and his neck was lacerated and bled profusely. Fortunately, the head of the local Anglican mission was there. In fluent Chinese he assured the assembly of angry students and parents that it was an accident and that he would see to it that Chu got the best medical care. The next day twenty-three of us students held a meeting and demanded the dismissal of the coach and an apology. The mission did send the coach away and provided treatment to Chu, but refrained from offering an apology. All of us refused to go back to school.

The students' meeting in itself was unprecedented. The parents of the students who struck were at a loss what to do about this unheard-of, indeed unthinkable, disobedience to authority. They dispatched a messenger to request help from my father, who was in Tientsin.

Father returned and managed to convince the parents that the students had just cause for their action and that he would be glad to help them enter other schools. But the news he also brought electrified us all. It was about October 10, 1911. He reported that the republican revolution had won a great victory at Wuchang, and that all southern provinces had gone over to support Sun Yat-sen's newly formed Government at Nanking, called the Republic of China. Negotiations were going on to bring about the abdication of the new emperor, the infant Henry Pu-yi, in Peking. "Most important," Father told us students, "is the need for modern trained men in all lines. You should go to good schools and get prepared." For me he had already a plan in mind. He took me with him to Tientsin to be tutored for the entrance examination to Nankai Middle School.

In several ways my father had been preparing me to leave home, as well as teaching me what home stood for. For five years I had been

49

in the guest room of the front quadrangle, where I did my homework and slept alone. It was not bad for me to study alone, but it took a long time for my parents to train me to sleep alone. Just think, I was the only person in the quadrangle at bedtime—I who had been accustomed to living in a quadrangle full of people, and who had been learning ghost stories all my life! At first, someone stayed with me till I fell asleep. Father tried to debunk my superstitious fears.

Getting ready for my going away, my mother sewed new clothes, packing and repacking things she thought I would need. She kept telling me that in order to distinguish myself and bring glory to the family, I must go to the cities to seek honor and fortune. As often as not, her feelings overcame her conviction.

Finally, the day came. I was to leave my ancestral home for the first time. Even though my mother was a seasoned stoic, she had great difficulty concealing her tears. My own heart was on the verge of breaking. Two factors helped to sustain me: the company of my father and the solid sense of my family, the firm foundation and root of my being, the place of my apprenticeship for life and the source of my knowledge that it is all for one and one for all, and we are all in the same boat, on this earth and beyond.

Part 2

Contacts with the West

Two Schools Modeled after Phillips Academy

Revolutions: Cultural and Political

Two Schools Modeled after Phillips Academy

Tientsin, the great seaport in northern China and the gateway to our national capital, Peking, had become an important international center. About the middle of the nineteenth century, after we suffered a series of defeats by western powers, the city was dominated by foreign concessions and garrisons. The old city was actually destroyed in 1860 by British and French forces. Hence, the people of Tientsin became sensitized quite early to the forceful invasion of China by the West.

It so happened that two old Tientsin families, Yen and Chang, each produced a man whose collaboration opened the way for new educational directions in our generation. The elder, Yen Hsiu (courtesy name: Yen Fan-sun*), had attained cabinet rank in the Imperial Government, but chose to retire when Emperor Kuang Hsü failed in his attempt at political reforms. Chang Po-ling, the younger, was among the first group of modern-trained naval cadets, and had witnessed our defeat by Japan in 1894-5, in spite of our apparent superiority in numbers and armaments. Our navy was not only larger than Japan's, but our ships were more up-to-date, having been purchased recently from England. We even had some thirty British naval officers as advisers. Yet we were badly defeated, Chang and his contemporaries were convinced, because our sailors were mercenary and had no will to fight.

After this disaster, Chang resigned from the navy and made up his mind to do something about creating a generation willing to die for their country, like the Japanese, who had studied the West and adopted reforms. Yen offered Chang the tutorship of the Yen clan school, with the understanding that they would visit Japan to observe the new educational methods and systems.

In the Japan of 1903 they found that the Japanese had made tremendous progress in modernizing their armed forces. Students had been sent to England and Germany to study systematically their military, industrial, and scientific methods and organizations. What made the Japanese good fighters, however, was their fanatical religious belief

---

* A "courtesy name" is friendly and informal, rather like a nickname. For any but peers and intimates to use it is impolite.

in the manifest destiny of their race, which was indoctrinated in them from childhood.

Returning in 1904, Yen and Chang established a school for boys, the First Private Middle School. Yen, the eminent scholar and elder statesman, was made trustee and Chang was appointed principal. They based their school on the Japanese educational philosophy that political and military power should derive from citizens indoctrinated in emperor-worship, the emperor representing both the divine beginning and the destiny of the race. Using this powerful motivation, Japan had been able to carry out universal conscription and universal physical education, which provided her with fighting men thoroughly fit and ready to glorify the Rising Sun.

Yen and Chang's combined prestige and energy met with favorable response from the gentry of the community. They received generous donations of funds and land, and boys of the best families applied for admission. In less than three years they were able to build on a new campus located in the Nankai section of Tientsin and took a new name: the Nankai Middle School.

Though the school prospered and won wide recognition, Yen and Chang themselves felt uncomfortable and were not sure that they were on the right track. For one thing, it was no longer possible to inculcate emperor-worship in Chinese students. Secondly, there was the long-standing cultural downgrading of the soldier in China. Third, but not least, was the traditional prejudice against physical work and exertion by intellectuals. On those and other problems Chang wrestled with his associates and friends, one of whom happened to be Robert Reed Gailey.

Bob Gailey was an American who, while a student at Princeton, volunteered for missionary work in China and became one of the founders of the YMCA in Tientsin. He suggested that Chang visit the United States to see how American schools prepared their students to love and defend their country with a different kind of motivation. Gailey was the personification of physical fitness, a husky giant of six foot four, a football star—he was the center on Walter

American friends of China—and of young
Chih Meng—were these Princeton graduates
who ran the Peking YMCA in 1918. Bob
Gailey, a Walter Camp All-American, is at
center, seated. In back, from right,
are Dick Ritter, Sidney Gamble (3rd), and
Sam Shoemaker (5th). At bottom is
Princeton Court, a hostel for bachelors
and student volunteers engaged
in Y work, where modern-minded Chinese
encountered the exciting ideas underlying
western faith and progress.

Camp's 1896 All-American team—and a most congenial and cheerful promoter of things American. He soon became Chang's close friend and his adviser on western affairs. In 1908 he succeeded in arranging for Chang to visit the United States.

America was ready for Chang Po-ling. The anti-Chinese acts and sentiments generated by resentment of imported Chinese laborers and by the Boxer Uprising were things of the past. The orientation of Sun Yat-sen's revolutionary movement led Americans to feel that young Chinese were apprentices of the American republic who deserved help and guidance.

Chang, too, found the American philosophy of education congenial. The way private schools had evolved in New England attracted his attention because the circumstances of their early beginnings paralleled those he saw in China. He particularly admired the Phillips Academy at Andover, Massachusetts, for its integrated programs which dealt with students not only in their studies, but also in their recreation and behavior, for almost twenty-four hours of the day. His ideal principal was Endicott Peabody, of Groton, a pioneer educator who inspired his boys in his roles as parent, teacher, and confessor.

The American visit provided a foundation for Chang Poling's own educational philosophy. From then on he became increasingly an advocate of his chosen kind of modern education. Soon the whole nation began to notice the effectiveness of Chang's leadership and the high caliber of his students.

During these prerepublican years, Father had gone through similar experiences with his study of modern forces as demonstrated by Japan's rise as a modern power, capable of warding off western aggression, while graduating from the posture of our country's younger brother and imitator to that of its threatening tormentor. Though father was especially interested in governmental reorganization, he recognized the importance of educational reform and was an admirer of Chang's now-famous Nankai Middle School.

56   Nankai was a private boarding school for some four hundred and fifty

boys, located in the southeast corner of the city, and housed in western-style buildings on a spacious campus providing playgrounds and athletic fields. The dormitories were rows of one-story rooms with verandas, and the students were assigned two to a room according to their academic classes.

Daily life was well ordered and fully scheduled. When I was there, monitors saw to it that we rose on time, exercised, breakfasted, attended classes, lunched, had a physical-education period, ate dinner, studied, and exercised until bedtime again and lights out. Regularly, Chang Po-ling brushed his teeth and washed with us in our common washroom, and took part in the afternoon physical education. Every Wednesday afternoon he talked to the whole student body in the auditorium on self-cultivation and national and international affairs. Frequently, he had breakfast with us, especially on Saturdays and Sundays, when some students were at loose ends or felt homesick.

Extracurricular activities were required and were conducted by faculty members. In my time, track and field were already well established. We were quite good at basketball and soccer, but had little tennis and no swimming. We had a discussion society (Ching Yeh), and a drama club (Hsin Chü). Our lives were so full, and our teachers and monitors were so close to us, that the school was truly a community bent on developing a common devotion to the cause of serving our nation. School rules of conduct were strict. Smoking, visits to the theaters, and marriage were major offenses. In all my years there I never heard of any violations. In fact, we all felt proud of our responsibility to set examples for those who could not go to school—so much so that we behaved scrupulously and often self-consciously to let others see how good we were.

A number of promising students received special attention from our principal. Chang openly extolled them for their behavior and achievements, and held them up for others to emulate. Off and on, there was some jealous grumbling about favoritism, but on the whole his choices were regarded as wise and were respected. In ensuing years and events most of his favorite students distinguished themselves. Kuo

Yu-pin and Wei Wen-han, for example, won first place in track more than once in Far Eastern Olympics. Wan Chia-pao became a noted writer. James T. C. Yu and Chang Ping-chuin became consuls general in New York, and Tuan Mao-lan ambassador to France. Five attained high offices of cabinet rank. Two brothers became well-known educators and university presidents, Y. C. Mei of Tsing Hua, and Y. P. Mei of Yenching.

Perhaps the best known of all Nankai alumni was Chou En-lai, the longtime Communist revolutionary who was premier of the People's Republic from its establishment in 1949 until 1976, when he died in office. Chou En-lai was one year below me in class, but one year older in age. He had been born in south Kiangsu, but was orphaned early and sent to his uncle in Fengtien (Mukden), where he received elementary schooling. Chou not only enrolled as a student from Fengtien, but his sentiments were those of a northeasterner. He reacted emotionally against the Japanese as the worst of all the foreign powers that threatened our nation's existence.

Chou failed to qualify as an athlete. He was among eight of us who trained for the five-mile run, and in the final tryout he finished next to last. Nor was Chou a top student, having difficulty passing English and physics. He stood out, however, in his loyalty to Nankai, its principles and its tenets. Usually, Chou spoke in a low key, blushed when teased, and was regarded as a bashful loner. But when aroused by a discussion in the Ching Yeh society, he could be quite forceful and eloquent.

Because of his fair complexion and girlish air, Chou was selected to act female parts by the faculty adviser of our drama club, Kang Nai-ju. His acceptance naturally led to all kinds of razzing whenever plays were being rehearsed or performed, but he acted his parts well, and, of course, males in female roles was an old theatrical tradition in China. Kang and Chou became fast friends. Later, when Chou had become a Communist and gone underground, Kang once saved his life by hiding him in the family lavatory at great risk to himself.

Chang's American friends, especially Bob Gailey, had by

this time sold him on the American way of life. Physically, Chang was as tall as Gailey. Both were athletes and both believed in health and physical education for boys as an essential element in their package of three. The second element was mental: Chinese students must learn modern subjects, such as the sciences, as well as the traditional classics. Third and most important was motivation. Here neither familyism nor emperor-worship would do. For Bob Gailey it was the Christian faith that had moved him to love not only his country but his fellow-men everywhere, and had led him to come to China as a volunteer to spread that religion among the Chinese people. Chang shared Gailey's faith. His visit to the United States had convinced him that Christianity was the motivating force underlying America's democracy and humaneness, and in 1909 he announced his conversion. However, he felt that Christianity must take root in Chinese culture and must rise above western sectarianism. Not long after, he and a few other Chinese Christians founded an independent China-for-Christ Church. He lectured frequently on Christianity, but refrained from holding evangelical or worship services on the campus.

In order to promote better understanding of America, he employed an American teacher to teach us English. This American's appearance at first reawakened all my prejudices against "foreign devils." He was very tall and husky, with red hair, blue eyes, and a deep, resonant voice. In other words, he looked and sounded inhuman to me. All I had heard about "foreign devils" and all that had been done to my home town came immediately to mind.

However, it did not take long to still my misgivings. Most of my classmates were more or less accustomed to meeting westerners. Our principal spoke favorably about America and Americans publicly and privately. He also brought American visitors to the school, among whom, of course, was Bob Gailey. Bob talked to us about America and American sports, and his cheerful voice would shake the whole basketball court. Moreover, my "foreign devil," the American teacher, Bayard Lyon, went out of his way to know us personally and to learn Chinese language and customs. During my fourth year he began to court a Chinese woman who had returned recently from studying in England. She came from a well-known and well-to-do Chinese family. It was then prestigious and in high fashion in Tientsin to wear western clothes, and more often than not she dressed in the up-to-date western fashion which featured a low neckline and a tight skirt. My whole class was invited to the Lyons' home shortly after their wedding. To our surprise—since it violated old Chinese etiquette—the bride stayed with us throughout the tea party. We were entirely unprepared to sit down with her, or to observe—as it seemed to us—her inordinately exposed bosom and ankles.

The new Chinese Republic, established on October 10, 1911, needed trained men in all walks of modern life. Those few who had been educated abroad were in great demand. Alliances and rivalries ran riot among Chinese students returned from Japan, France, Germany, England, and America. Politics created strange bedfellows.

A number of historical factors and circumstances enhanced and increased American influence. Sun Yat-sen and the advent of the republic profoundly impressed my student generation. Sun proudly acknowledged the American way as his inspiration and model. The American people frankly and affectionately welcomed the infant republic as their protégé and set about enthusiastically helping to educate Chinese students for the new order in China, as well as in the United States.

The whole Nankai school community went wild with joy at the establishment of the republic. When Sun Yat-sen, the head of the Kuomintang—the National People's Party—and father of the republic, came through Tientsin in 1912, on his way to Peking, tens of thousands of people went to the railway station to greet him. Now that the dynasty had been overthrown, he told the crowd, they must assume the responsibilities of citizenship based on his San Min Chu I—the Three Principles of the People—nationalism, democracy, and the people's livelihood. He explained at great length how he had arrived at these through a study of the American Republic and Abraham Lincoln's nation of, by, and for the people.

By 1916, the year of my graduation from Nankai, admiration for American democracy and the American people was at its highest point among Chinese students. Our country had decided to modernize itself not in the European or Japanese styles, but in the American way. We believed American education would help us to solve all our problems, personal and national. While an education in America was very costly and required long preparation, opportunities were open. One of the best was to get admitted to Tsing Hua (Junior) College and try to earn a scholarship.

That summer more than two thousand students from all over China competed in the entrance examination for Tsing Hua. Only fifty were admitted, of which I was fortunate to be one.

Tsing Hua was located in the west suburb of Peking, which I was about to see for the first time. I was greatly excited. Peking was so much talked and read about that everybody wanted to visit it. The reality was much more grand and colorful than I had dreamed. On my way from the train, through the south city gate, I had to traverse from the east section to the west, then out of the city and about seven miles by rickshaw or donkey to my school. The city wall looked so tall. Even taller and more majestic was the entrance, topped by a multistoried watchtower of curved roofs and rainbow-colored eaves. The streets were wide and straight. Main intersections were embellished with *pai lou*. The traffic of people, rickshaws, carriages, donkeys, and camels seemed endless.

The cheapest form of passenger transportation was by donkey. The Peking variety of the species ranged down in size from pony to Great Dane. It was more spirited and tougher than a horse. The fare was ten coppers (five cents) an hour. An experienced rider could travel very fast. Even a novice had no trouble making at least four miles an hour (if he tipped the tender well), without much danger of falling off, because he could use his feet as brakes to maintain balance. But the poor donkey tender had to walk or run with his charge, so he could collect his animal and the fare at trip's end. A rickshaw cost more and was much more exhausting for the puller. Not many could afford carriages, and only a few high officials and the very rich rode in motorcars. The train ran on unreliable schedules.

The broad streets were lined with old trees. As I crossed from the outer city into the inner city and passed the Imperial City, also known as the Purple Forbidden City, the conviction grew in me that Peking had been conceived and planned by great minds who comprehended the grandeur, the dignity, and magnificence of the empire and had constructed this metropolis as its architectural expression. The Imperial City, the official residence of the imperial family, was its heart. The audience hall was the largest single hall in the Chinese empire. It was supported by eighty-four pillars covered by two tiers of glazed yellow tiles, and adorned with rainbow-colored pendentives. It was sited on a high square in the center of a great quadrangle paved with white marble, with three approaches of twenty-seven terraces, nine balustraded steps, and then nine more balustraded steps of sculptured, five-clawed-dragon design. Rising from and framed by the surrounding moat and lacquer-red walls were the three Ching Hills and their pavilions.

As I went out the west gate of the city, the shadow of the empire loomed long and heavy, while that of the republic, by comparison, felt fresh and slight.

As the city wall was receding from view I passed the verdant Botanical Garden. In the distance, emerging from the horizon, I could see shadows of distant mountain peaks in light and deep shades of gray and blue. I passed villages and temples and farms of fertile and flat lands; and about halfway on my journey I encountered a scene straight out of a Chinese painting: a glazed porcelain pagoda perched atop a hill bordering a lake of turquoise water. It was my first view of the famous Jade Fountain Hill and the Yi Ho Yuan summer palace.

The city of Peking and the scenes along that seven-mile country road impressed me with the continuity, the splendor, and the strength of my heritage. Frequently I alighted from my donkey and lingered, overwhelmed by the beauty of the senses and almost drunk with the sense of history.

Suddenly, at the end of my journey I was awakened by something absolutely foreign—the Tsing Hua campus. The main entrance both jarred and excited me. It was a huge gateway constructed of white masonry and supported by two pairs of tall round columns (half Doric, half Corinthian), the whole entirely out of harmony with its surroundings and with my reverie.

The gateway opened on an expanse of green lawn and a wide, smooth gravel road, leading to a large whitewashed, three-storied, L-shaped building. As I later learned, this housed the offices, laboratories, and classrooms. Beyond were three rows of dormitories, the dining hall, and quarters for the kitchen and services. All these foreign-style buildings constituted the school's "high section," somewhat equivalent to an American junior college. To the rear was another and similar group of buildings for the "lower section," about seventh grade to senior high. In between the two groups was the library, built of red brick in New England colonial fashion. Even more imposing was the gymnasium, the front of which was graced with eight Corinthian columns, and which was named the Theodore Roosevelt Memorial. To the northeast was a settlement of faculty houses, some twenty western cottages, each with its front and back yards, resembling very much an English village. At the northwest corner of the spacious campus I found the only Chinese-style buildings, a remnant of the original palace of Prince Tun, with its garden quadrangle, moon gate, lotus and goldfish pond, and camel-back bridge, connected with an octagonal pavilion of lacquer red. This quadrangle housed the Chinese faculty members.

Naturally, I compared Tsing Hua with Nankai. Both schools had frankly adopted Andover as their model. The same Chang Po-ling was responsible for this, and also for introducing the emphasis on athletics, school spirit, songs and cheers, and the school colors of purple and white. The two student bodies were cosmopolitan, Tsing Hua a little more so because it had a sort of quota system for admitting students from all of the eighteen provinces and five territories of China. The chief differences resulted from the fact that Nankai depended on

63

voluntary contributions for its maintenance, while Tsing Hua could count on funds guaranteed by the Government; the former had to live thriftily and charge high tuition while the latter could live lavishly and yet charge only minimal fees. The faculty of Tsing Hua was the best paid in all China and provided a ratio of one teacher to eight students. Classroom and laboratory facilities offered particularly sharp contrasts, Tsing Hua having the most lavish and up-to-date of everything, including Italian marble paneling in the library and gym.

It took me time to get accustomed to the western style of Tsing Hua. Classes in the four morning periods were taught a curriculum almost identical to Andover's. Courses were taught in English, French, or German by eighteen Americans and thirty-four Chinese teachers who were graduates of American and European universities and wore western clothes. Two periods of Chinese studies were given in the afternoon, taught by eleven old Chinese scholars wearing Chinese clothes. Inevitably, the pro-western bias rubbed off on the student body. It was fashionable to use English words in our conversation, the more the merrier. We imitated western walk and talk. Many of us patronized the school store and indulged in western pastries and ice cream.

What was a new and startling experience for me was the gamut of extracurricular activities and the enthusiasm and ingenuity of the teachers who conducted them. They made us see social problems and feel responsible for doing whatever we could to alleviate them. As a group they gave their time and resources freely to help us become activists. Several American teachers offered Bible classes and arranged for missionaries to preach the Christian gospel.

Such extracurricular activities caught my imagination. Coming from a rural community I felt close to the farmers. Our farmers were most hard working, dedicated to Old Heavenly Grandfather, and had almost an unmitigated reverence for scholars, who had been their mentors in behavior and leaders in social action from time immemorial. Unfortunately, being uneducated, farmers could be easily misinformed and misled by unscrupulous demagogues. A historic difficulty was that we had never developed effective communication between the learned and the masses. One of our English-language courses, that in public speaking, gave us fresh inspiration to tackle this problem. I was among those who recited passages from Shakespeare and American orators with delight, and imagined myself someday a Chinese Cicero, Brutus, or Patrick Henry.

I was rethinking my whole philosophy. I had been brought up to regard the ultimate end in life to be self-cultivation and the achievement of glory and honor for oneself and one's family. Nankai had enlarged my horizon from familyism to nationalism. Chang Po-ling's personal life had raised the question of whether there was a more adequate way of life than that of personal ethics and agnosticism.

I was able to organize two associations, the Social Research and Service Club (fifty-five members) and the Ming Teh Shê (twelve members). The Club aimed to do field investigation in nearby villages and to render what service we could whenever need or opportunity arose. Shê was more of an honor fraternity, the members of which were voted in and all members required to pledge to help one another in searching for the highest good in life. The name Ming Teh meant "self-evident virtues" and was taken from *Ta Hsüeh,* one of the four Confucian books.

One of my faculty advisors was Mei Yi-chi (Y. C. Mei), a graduate of Nankai, Tsing Hua, and Worcester Polytechnic Institute, a former YMCA secretary, and now an instructor in physics and mathematics. He suggested that I do something of service to the students of the orphanages in Peking. The project agreed upon was for me to hold regular weekend meetings at the orphanage for the purpose of teaching the youngsters some general science. Those institutions did not have such instruction or the necessary equipment. Many evenings Mei would stay with me in the lab and guide me in how to explain and demonstrate scientific phenomena, such as electric light, telephony, and so on. He also let me take what apparatus I needed from our lab.

Mr. Clarence Dittmer, teacher of social sciences, advised us how to gather data and make statistical tabulations—in effect, the methodology of modern research. He thought the drug problem among laborers deserved priority, and we investigated the plight of Peking's many young rickshaw pullers who became invalids or died at around twenty-five from opium or morphine addiction. Our efforts made us realize how much grass-roots research needed to be done on China's social problems. For me personally, I was cured forever of thinking of using devious means of getting high, even including cigarette smoking.

Nearly all foreign visitors to China gravitated to Peking sooner or later. The American Student Volunteer Movement was gathering momentum and the Ivy League colleges were sending young graduates to student centers of their choice in China. Princeton University's student volunteers adopted Peking as their missionary base and established the Princeton Court, a hostel for Princeton students who wished to prepare for YMCA work in China. They and other young American students usually visited Tsing Hua, and quite a few of us got to know them. Among my special friends were Sidney Gamble, Larry Sears, and Dick Ritter. They invited me to parties at Princeton Court and at the YMCA, which attracted students and other modern-minded men who wanted to take various courses of study and classes for physical fitness. Its dining room was also very popular because one could sample western dishes there at modest prices. Incidentally, the chefs at the Y, being Chinese, blended Chinese flavoring into cooking western dishes and introduced western vegetables into Chinese cuisine. It was here that I first tasted *ping chi ling* (ice cream), "dragon beard" (asparagus), and "western red persimmon" (tomato).

  The three years I spent at Tsing Hua, from 1916 to 1919, brought many sharp contrasts and rapid changes. Events, and my involvements in them, constituted a succession of family and national crises, placed against a backdrop in which traditional and modern life styles were fantastically juxtaposed.

  Our republic had a sick and turbulent infancy. Within months after Sun Yat-sen and Yuan Shih-kai, his successor as president, had cooperated in establishing the Republic of China, disagreements between them degenerated into terrorism and civil strife. By 1916, Sun had bolted, declared his opposition to Peking and his intention to organize a Kuomintang Government in Canton. Yuan proclaimed himself emperor and founder of the Hung Hsien dynasty, which lasted exactly eighty-three days. This shortest dynasty in Chinese history owed its occurrence at least partly to American-managed public relations. Yuan Shih-kai, Napoleon-like as a soldier and a shrewd and ambitious politician, could not get along with China's American-oriented Senate and House of Representatives. He tried to organize his own political parties, but could not stand the slow and quarrelsome processes of advise and consent, and of campaigns and elections. At bottom, he thought the newfangled scheme of governing was nonsense and that a traditional, benevolent, fatherly monarch could better serve his country.

Yuan had quite an impressive group of advisers, at least two of whom were Americans: Upton Close (Joseph Washington Hall) and Frank J. Goodnow. Close was the Associated Press correspondent who scored a beat on the story of Japan's infamous Twenty-one Demands, a secret ultimatum served on President Yuan in 1915 which exacted political, economic, and military concessions. Dr. Goodnow, a distinguished scholar, was professor of government at Columbia and later president of Johns Hopkins University. The first premier, Tang Shao-yi, who had studied political science at Columbia, introduced them to Yuan, the journalist as an expert on publicity, the professor as an authority on government and constitutional law. Both seem to have been convinced that China was not ready for democracy and that the best solution was to revert to a constitutional form of monarchy. They helped launch a vigorous public relations campaign in China and the United States. In China it created an artificially popular appeal for Yuan to become emperor.

My father was discouraged and depressed. His old comrades in the revolution split in four factions. As a Commissioner of Self-government in the western sector of Hopei province, he could accomplish nothing because of the interference of local warlords. He resigned,

67

returned home, and devoted his remaining years to calligraphy and horticulture. But my mentors at Tsing Hua were not at all discouraged. The American-style campus exuded newness, youth, and optimism. American friends in the city were equally encouraging. At a discussion at Princeton Court some of us, reporting what we had witnessed on a visit to China's Senate, expressed shock at the violent arguments and rude language we had heard. They assured us that their own senators in Washington did the same and sometimes worse, and that in time the Chinese would learn to carry on government in accordance with the will of the people.

Gradually, modern things and manners were taken for granted. We wore leather shoes and sneakers, shook hands, mixed English words in our conversation, and adopted Christian names. We were David Hung, James Wang, and Lincoln Cha. Our teacher of English literature used the bilingual name John Wong-Quincy, spoke with an Oxford accent, and always was seen in tweeds and with a pipe in his mouth. Mr. Tsui, on the other hand, was a Sinophile. He was an American who had abandoned his western name, wore Chinese clothes, spoke Chinese, ate Chinese food, married a Chinese wife, raised five children, and settled permanently in China.

Summer vacation was another innovation. Our traditional schools were in session every day of the year. Modern schools like Tsing Hua adopted the American practice of scheduling, but neither the schools nor society made any provision for the students to use the long summer gainfully or beneficially. Almost all of us returned to our families to do what we could on our own initiative and resources.

In my case, I traveled home by train from Peking to Lang Fang, halfway to Tientsin. At the station Old Li, our family coachman, waited for me with our mule carriage of ancient design, a two-wheeler without springs. As soon as he greeted me, placed my baggage in the back, and started moving, all things modern disappeared. We were engulfed in a different world. The road we took had been there from time immemorial. Our faithful mule pulled doggedly and we rode bumpily along at perhaps three miles an hour. At the inn, the friendly hereditary hostel run by the same family for as long as anyone could remember, we had our lunch, always the same four dishes—two of pickled vegetables and two of smoked meats—and the same soup— noodles with poached eggs.

We had to surmount the dike to get the ferry across our muddled Yung Ting river. The same hereditary ferryman placed the same planks so we could board his ancient flat-bottomed boat. As usual, our mule pretended fear of the stream both at embarking and disembarking, and Old Li had to do the usual cajoling of his animal friend.

This journey, which took almost a whole day, always impressed me with the more deep-rooted reality of our profoundly sentimental ancient world. Here were intimate and familiar identities and relations. Communities were named Chang Chia Tsun (Chang Clan Village), Wang Shih Chen (Wang Name Town), Han Chia Tien (Han Family Inn). Even road crossings had their historical designations, such as Kuo Hero Mouth (intersection). When travelers met on the road they were likely to be cousins or cousins of cousins, or acquaintances of acquaintances. A total stranger was as rare as something modern. To the south of the railway there was no electricity, no telephone, nothing new that I could think of.

When strangers met they introduced themselves by exchanging family and given names and their native places. More often than not the introduction disclosed some friendly connections. We placed great value on being from the same place of birth, the same clan, and the same generation of the same name. My clan headquarters was in Tsou Hsien, Shantung province, the birthplace of Mencius. Every twenty years, each Meng family, no matter where it was located, was required to send a representative to Tsou Hsien to file a written report on the vital statistics of his family and to receive an updated list of the twenty auspicious characters which had to be used as the first word of the two-word given name of the next twenty generations. Thus, when two Mengs met they would know what generation each belonged to as soon as they exchanged information on their names.

About a thousand years ago, moreover, the Mengs, the Kungs, the Yens, and the Tsengs, the recognized primary families of the Confucian school of philosophy, had all agreed to adopt the same words or characters for their given names. It was a sign of my father's radical leanings that he gave me a name which did not follow this formula; clan headquarters recorded my name as Meng Fan-li, "Fan" being the proper name for my generation.

I always have been aware that my roots lie in Shantung. Psychohistorically speaking, I derive from its economy of scarcity, of recurring floods and famine, and I carry within me the subconscious insecurity it breeds, as well as the compensatory instinct of thrift. The people of Shantung always have had to struggle to survive. For many centuries, because of the area's dense population, large numbers of them have had to migrate to other parts of China and to Japan in order to earn a living.

Fortunately, they were welcome wherever they went. They grew taller than their countrymen, according to tradition because they ate raw garlic three times a day! They made the best soldiers and policemen, whom local authorities—and warlords—eagerly sought out and employed. Shantung also produced China's most admired "Robin Hoods," as we know from the classic, *All Men Are Brothers*. And it gave birth to the sages Confucius and Mencius. It is a heritage I am proud to partake of. In my life and in my business, I think I instinctively behave like a Shantungese.

Homecoming always took me back into history. Our house was early Ming (fifteenth century) and our family traditions, as I have said, went back to the teachings of Mencius. The few modern or western things I had acquired at Tsing Hua became incongruous and out of place as soon as I arrived home. Though I loved all members of my family dearly and was happy to be reunited with them, I could only bow to them and inquire how they were. Our custom did not provide for kissing, embracing, or handshaking, or any other outpouring of emotion. I had to put away my leather shoes because they made too much noise, and to dye my tennis sneakers black, because white shoes were worn in mourning.

By tradition, the relationship of father and son was rather formal, especially after the son came of age at fifteen. I hardly knew my father, since he had been absent from home a great deal. For almost the first time, in the summer of 1917, we lived for more than two months together. Father was now head of the family. He even sought my companionship. He began by asking me to assist him in making ink, cutting paper, and cleaning pen-brushes, and to comment on his calligraphy. He expressed approval of my practicing modern calisthenics, but insisted I should also know something of our own exercises. He searched out several books on boxing and fencing, and even tried with me some basic tactics of Tǎi Chi and Tüng Pei boxing. He took out from the old storeroom two antique weapons, one of steel and one of bronze, twelve feet long, modeled after the one used by Kuan Yü, a great hero in *The Romance of the Three Kingdoms.* Soon we developed a comradeship and were able to carry on a give-and-take conversation. He wondered what I thought of the kind of education I was getting and what my opinions were on the new Peking Government. My impression was that Father was having second thoughts about some modern innovations and importations. He was particularly disillusioned with the nationalism of Japan and regarded Japanese policies as being dangerous to our future.

He also wanted me to be more successful. He took me to visit both my granduncle and our nextdoor neighbor, Chu Shen, who had been one of his colleagues in Government service. Our town looked up to these two as our most successful elder statesmen.

Granduncle, a younger brother of Grandfather, had served the empire all his life, rising from magistrate to governor general of the Northeast (Manchuria). He remained a monarchist and a loyal and faithful servant of the Ch'ing dynasty. Even his friend President Yuan Shih-kai could not persuade him to serve the Republic. Granduncle had no use for modern reforms. He thought the West's only superiority lay in science and technology. He was preparing both of his sons to study engineering in America and urged me to do the same.

Father's old associate, Chu Shen, had been a brilliant student and had graduated with honors from the Imperial University of Tokyo. He joined Sun Yat-sen's political party in Japan and later was appointed Minister of Justice (attorney general) in the first cabinet of the Republic. He resigned because Yuan reneged on the terms of his presidency and proclaimed himself emperor. He remained faithful to his ideology and his belief in judicial reforms, but was thoroughly disgusted with modern politics and politicians. He warned that western society would not last because it was being corrupted by universal voting and majority rule.

A Mr. Davis, an advance salesman for the British-American Tobacco Company, came to town to distribute free cigarettes. He made my acquaintance after hearing that I knew English and was a member of a well-known family in town. I was glad to meet him, show him the town, and otherwise make his stay pleasant. One day we were watching an elaborate funeral procession. It was led by a group of nine Buddhist monks in saffron robes playing Buddhist music, followed by a group of nine Taoist monks in blue caps and gowns playing Taoist music, and then a modern band in western military uniform playing "Onward, Christian Soldiers." Looking puzzled, Mr. Davis asked, "Why do they engage three different religions?" My answer was, "The family is not taking chances with just one."

During the long, warm days of summer I enjoyed the freedom of browsing in our large library. Since I no longer needed to ask permission regarding what books I could read, I naturally or naughtily gravitated to fiction, which was strictly forbidden to young students. I devoured with pleasure *Dream of the Red Chamber* and *West Chamber Romance,* but was disgusted with *Chin P'ing Mei,* or *Golden Lotus,* a notoriously pornographic novel. Reading those love stories revealed to me an entirely different type of literature which I thought it unwise for young people to read. As Mencius pointed out, "When young, restrain the sex impulse; when adult, restrain violent behavior; when old, restrain tendency for gain."

72   Finally, the day came when I had to return to school. The

same mule cart with two wheels and no springs took me along the same road to the same railway station. When I got on the train I felt I had shed a millennium of time and tradition from my shoulders. I did not realize that the summer of 1917 was the watershed of my life. I was to be swept away by irresistible tides, never to return.

When World I broke out in 1914 and the western powers became locked in a death struggle in Europe, Japan seized the opportunity to expand in East Asia. Her ultimate objective was to dominate and eventually to subjugate China. She made secret deals with the Allies and took by force the German naval base at Tsingtao in Shantung province. Aware of Yuan Shih-kai's need for funds, she made huge loans to Peking, exacting in return secret conditions, which came to be known as the Twenty-one Demands. When revealed to the world by Upton Close, they were ostensibly withdrawn, mainly because of strong American objections. Actually, many of them were accepted by Yuan under threat of further Japanese invasion.

In 1917 the United States entered the war on the Allied side, with the aim—as Woodrow Wilson said—of "making the world safe for democracy." For the first time in history a national leader attempted to inspire the peoples of the whole world by proclaiming aims of outlawing war, enabling small and weak nations to determine their own destinies, and setting up a League of Nations to enforce peace. Wilson urged China to join the Allies chiefly because he wanted her as a showcase for working out his ideals, but partly because the Allies needed laborers, which China could easily supply. Our whole nation felt uplifted and responded with enthusiasm. Thousands of laborers from Shantung, the most densely populated part of China, were quickly transported by American ships to southern France. We even sent a token battalion of infantry. During the final years of the war, American influence in China increased and American-trained students began to rise to positions of dominance in Chinese education, business, and government.

Revolutions: Cultural and Political

Meanwhile, Chinese students in the United States were helping to make history and earning the attention of both governments. As a group, they were sold on the American way of life and vigorously supported Sun Yat-sen's republican revolution. The young Republic of China used American-returned students to inaugurate a number of vital functions of government. The most difficult job was to acquaint four hundred million people with entirely new systems and train them to participate. One man, in particular, recognized this problem and devoted his energies to correcting it.

While a student at Cornell, Hu Shih had cultivated a faith in democracy and first perceived the problem of communication between Chinese intellectuals and the common people. He started a movement among his fellow students to revolutionize traditional or elitist writing and speaking, so they should be plain and intelligible to the masses. He graduated from Cornell in 1914, got his Ph.D. from Columbia in 1917, and returned to China to teach at Peking University. From that platform he launched his literary revolution, which has been called "the Chinese Renaissance."

Hu Shih was an eloquent speaker and a persuasive writer. He campaigned vigorously with voice and pen. At first he encountered opposition from students and faculty. When he lectured at Tsing Hua, there were more boos than applause from the audience. This in no way deterred him.

His second cause, not so well known, but cherished by him, was birth control, another American inspiration, from Margaret Sanger. He founded a "No Offspring Club." To publicize their intentions and to inform the public, the members placed plaques, "No Offspring Here," on the front door of their houses.

Hu was an ardent and uncompromising reformer who did not mince words in condemning the old and advocating the new. He wanted to abolish overnight all obsolete thinking and social aberrations, such as Confucianism, foot-binding, mule carts, and rickshaws. He advocated total adoption of western culture, not only science and rapid transportation, but free marriage and birth control. Yet his devotion to his widowed mother (his father died when he was two) obliged him to marry the woman of her choice, and, to please her, he violated his club pledge and begot two sons. His fellow members summarily ousted him from the "No Offspring Club" and took the plaque down from his door.

Hu Shih put his heart and soul into his cause. His biographers and other writers on this period have credited him with intellectual leadership of the Chinese Renaissance and have called him its father. Actually, Hu behaved more like a fanatic. In his writings, and especially in his public addresses, he spoke with intense emotion and extreme rhetoric, much like an American evangelist, so much so that he soon exhausted himself physically and had to take a leave of absence for rest and medical treatment. He adopted his life style because, as he repeatedly told his intimate friends, history had convinced him that only extreme measures and shocking tactics could jar loose masses of people from the inertia of conservatism, and that radical protests against evils or grievances united people more effectively than passive ones. Hence, he declared himself an atheist and a pragmatist-in-action. He confided to some of us that to comment on Confucianism and traditional ways of life in detail, and to criticize with moderation, would not awaken anyone forcefully or quickly enough. Instead, he started his jarring process wholesale, condemning all that was traditional and praising all that was modern. Chinese intuitive thinking was nonsense. Western science could do no wrong.

Hu's strategy and tactics brought a divided response from students and faculty members. But my fellow students and I were awakened intellectually and, even more astonishing, quite a few of us were stunned into action. To begin with, we became convinced that religion was superstition and that filial piety was enslaving. I and practically all my Tsing Hua classmates served notice on our parents that we would not marry the girls of their choice and most of us actually carried out our determination to choose our own wives. Naturally, such

75

unheard-of behavior engendered all degrees of conflict in our family relations. Among the casualties of our activism, not least was the neglect of our own arts and classics.

On the national scene the processes of change went forward with tremendous speed and extraordinary unanimity. We were united against foreign aggression, Japan replacing Britain as our public enemy number one. We had downgraded familyism and embraced nationalism and democracy. In our attempt to stamp out official corruption and warlordism we looked to the United States and our American friends in China to guide and help us.

In spite of my repudiation of family domination, my mother's death in the spring of 1918 brought on a long period of depression. Deep and close was the tie which bound us. She was my sanctuary of absolute love and trust, and I was her only son and the carrier of all her hopes and expectations. My depression was deepened and made more painful because of my sense of guilt. I could not shake off or rationalize away my acts of disobedience, of renouncing the parental betrothal, and of refusing to accompany her to the Buddhist temple to burn incense and to pray. Her funeral was such a contrast to that of my grandfather. Going through the traditional formalities was agony for me. I felt such a hypocrite, and at the same time felt betrayed by the old and the new ideas and beliefs which were rumbling and clashing undigested in my mind.

Father fell into an equally deep valley of sorrow. He did his best to comfort me and succeeded in persuading me to return to school and to do my best, so that Mother's spirit would be gratified. We agreed that my third sister should go to a boarding school; fortunately she was admitted to Keen School in Tientsin. Upon graduation she trained at Isabella Fisher Hospital, became a modern RN, and achieved a fruitful career at Rockefeller-founded Peking Union Medical Hospital, first as a specialist in pediatrics and then in the pharmaceutical laboratory, dealing with polio antibiotics.

When my spring semester was drawing to a close, Father

urged me not to return home, but to make plans to spend the summer elsewhere with my sister. He sent word that banditry was rampant in our county. Brigands were terrorizing well-to-do families with daylight robberies and kidnappings. First Sister's family was moving to Peking. Father was turning over our home and affairs to Uncle Chou, my mother's younger brother, and would be traveling.

The headmistress at Keen arranged for Third Sister to attend a YMCA summer camp located at Ssu Wong Ting (Four View Peak) in the Western Hills, near Peking. It so happened that Tsing Hua was inaugurating its first summer camp at Wo Fo Ssu (Sleeping Buddha Temple), also in the Western Hills. I immediately enrolled.

For more than a thousand years the Western Hills have been treasured as one of the natural beauties of China. They stand some sixty *li* (twenty miles) from Peking and are reached by an ancient, well-traveled road. They are modest in elevation; the highest is perhaps 5,000 feet (1,524 m). But they offer entrancing views, especially after the atmosphere has been washed clean by a violent thunderstorm. The mountains are cloaked in purple shadows, their peaks in sharp outline against the turquoise-blue sky. It is easy to believe that immortals have their home in these hills and that westward is the way to Heaven.

Ever since Peking emerged from its primitive beginnings, its people have been coming here to enjoy the forested slopes, the ponds and streams, the long views, the deep quiet and serenity. Temples abound, some set among open fields of wheat or *kao liang*, some nestling in a fold of the hills, some sitting foursquare on summits, a few clinging alarmingly to precipitous slopes. All of them are exemplars of classical Chinese architecture, with long avenues approaching green-and-gold-tiled *pai lou*, and quadrangles embellished with rare plants, lotus ponds, and rock gardens. Lining the avenues and shading the temple walls are tall old cypresses, pines, and cedars which make these compounds spectacular oases in the barren landscape of North China.

On closer acquaintance the temples disclose their individuality. The casual western visitor considers all of them Buddhist, but Chinese religions are traditionally eclectic, and Buddhism has been so

adapted and modified since its importation from India that it is doubtful whether its founder, the Enlightened One, would recognize—or
approve of—our permutations. Initially, Buddhism met with opposition
from Chinese scholars, who were practitioners of Confucian thought.
Gradually, in the course of becoming Sinofied, it departed widely from
the original both in theory and practice. China evolved its own Buddhist rituals, art and architecture, and cosmology, including our special conception of thirty-three heavens and eighteen prison hells.

Originally, Buddha taught that life on earth was a sea of
sorrow. Nirvana, or perfection, could be achieved only through the
sublimation or negation of earthly passions, such as sex, greed, power,
and vanity. For the masses such cravings were to be curtailed through
the Eight Prohibitions (not to kill, steal, drink alcohol, dance, sing, use
cosmetics, sleep too much, or eat meat or animal food); this was called
the Hinayana or Lesser Vehicle. The chosen few were exhorted to
undergo more difficult discipline. They must go beyond the Eight
Prohibitions and try to annihilate passionate thoughts, even to banish
all thoughts, all ego identity, so as to achieve oneness with the cosmos.
This Mahayana or Greater Vehicle led to Ch'an, or Zen, Buddhism.
However, our Chinese cultural background of humaneness and moderation evolved also Kuan Yin, popularly known in English as the
Goddess of Mercy, a celestial matron saint who neutralized Gautama's
aversion to marriage and to whom wives could petition for domestic
bliss, fertility, and for protection during pregnancy and childbirth.

Chinese Buddhists prayed in highly fanciful and musical
liturgies and rituals, and wore ornate costumes rather than the originally ascetic ones. They produced paintings, sculptures, and buildings
far more beautiful than their Taoist and Confucian counterparts. In
the Western Hills we had one Buddhist sect living at Ta Chueh Ssu
(Great Awakening Monastery) whose five hundred monks vowed to
observe absolute poverty, celibacy, and isolation from mundane people.
In contrast, at Wo Fo Ssu the monks followed a Buddha who, they
believed, had slept comfortably lying down on a bed, had eaten well
and acquired an ample physique, and had been gifted with humor and

so laughed abundantly. "Sleeping Buddha" wanted his disciples to take an interest in mundane affairs and to save people from sorrows.

During years of disturbance or famine, some temples resorted to leasing buildings and grounds for revenue. The best tenants were foreigners, who could afford to pay generous rents and could also extend extraterritorial protection. There were fourteen such summer resorts leased by foreign individuals or organizations in the Western Hills.

My favorite haunt was Pi Yuin Ssu (Temple of the Azure Clouds), whose main quadrangle was perched upon a summit, but whose minor halls and gardens flowed to all slopes. Standing on its Moon Patio I could see Pa Ta Chu, the Eight Great Places—eight equally proportioned hills bedecked with smaller temples—and the Hunting Lodge at ground level, near the foot of Fragrant Hill. Pi Yuin Ssu was noted for its hall of five hundred *lo han*, Buddha's helpers (Bodhisattra), represented by slightly less than life-size gilded figures, each face unique and individual, contemplating eternity in the pale, dim light. It was also appreciated for its extensive lodgings for pilgrims and vacationers, and for its excellent vegetable cuisine.

Wo Fo Ssu, my summer home, was on level ground at the eastern access to the Hills. Like the other temples it occupied a spacious compound nestled against a foothill, but being the oldest of them all it was most Chinese in appearance. It had the traditional *pai lou*, an east hall with wall paintings of the thirty-three heavens and a west hall with representations of the eighteen hells. There was a series of quadrangles enclosing lotus and goldfish ponds, a main hall for the Sleeping Buddha, another of equal splendor honoring Kuan Yin, plus a dining hall, kitchen, and dormitories for the monks and novices. A special hall was reserved for visiting scholars; through the ages they had inscribed samples of their calligraphy on stone tablets, among them the illustrious Chien Lung. The American secretaries of the YMCA leased the quadrangle with the lotus pond. Under the empire it had been reserved as the Great Travel Hall of the emperor. My school rented a huge hall with a high ceiling and thick walls. Parts of this temple had been

Tsing Hua and YMCA share a memorable
summer at Wo Fo Ssu, the Temple of the
Sleeping Buddha, in tranquil Western Hills.
Below: Tsing Hua group includes some who
will be "dare-to-die" members of May
Fourth Movement. Author is fifth from right.
Bottom: Morning exercises around pool.
Roof of temple containing Sleeping Buddha
can be seen through trees at right.

Ranged in front of Wo Fo Ssu's pai lou
are leaders of Y conference for North China
students. Sam Shoemaker is second from
right at rear. In same row, with bow
tie, is Chang Po-ling, innovative head of
Nankai Middle School. Author is seated,
arms on knees, at left of second row.
Bottom: Contemporary photo of changeless
beauty and serenity of Wo Fo Ssu.

demolished by French troops in the invasion of 1860, and the abbot leased the unrestored parts to individuals and organizations, who brought their own equipment and managed their own housekeeping. We cleaned it and set up our cots and mosquito nets. Daytime we spent outdoors or in pavilions. The YMCA, which had much larger quarters, let us rent part of their kitchen and dining room and use their lotus pond, which had been converted into a swimming pool. We found the nights pleasantly cool.

During the last week of June, the Y held a conference for students from all North China. More than two hundred middle-school and college boys from missionary, Government, and private institutions attended. Most of us joined them at this ten-day conference, managed and led by American secretaries. The daily conference schedule consisted of morning watch, breakfast, worship, and discussion. After lunch the afternoon was free for personal or interest-group gatherings, sports, or picnics. Dinner was followed by evening worship and discussions. The surroundings were conducive to meditation and fellowship. Leaders and subjects chosen for discussion were inspiring and timely. A most dynamic speaker was Sherwood Eddy, the American Y official and writer, who challenged us: How much did we care for the common people, and why did corruption go on unchecked for so long? Sidney Gamble, my Princeton friend, advised us that before we could carry out social reforms effectively we had to know the facts. He was conducting social research in Peking and invited students to do field work. Chang Peng-chun (Clark and Columbia), one of my teachers at Nankai, emphasized the importance of performing arts as a vehicle for arousing people to face their problems and responsibilities. A quick and effective way, he believed, was the use of the community theater with performances by students. Mei Yi-chi of Tsing Hua urged the scholars to participate in voluntary charity work, an American practice, and to contribute their time and money faithfully. Quietly and untiringly, the Princeton contingent—Sam Shoemaker, Jack Childs, Dick Ritter—and Dr. W. B. La Force, Tsing Hua's physician, did personal work, persuading individual students to embrace the Christian faith for their own good and the good of the nation. The climax came at the farewell session when Jack Childs spoke of the love of Christ, quoting His compassionate words, "Father, forgive them, for they know not what they do," and a Princeton quartet led the singing of "Lead, Kindly Light," and, joining hands, "Blest Be the Tie That Binds."

I had arrived at the conference feeling and looking dejected and lost. My pitiful appearance attracted the attention of a young medical missionary from Harvard, W. G. Hiltner, who tried to help with professional advice. By the end of the conference I had become a different person, so much so that many people noticed the contrast. Years later Hiltner and I met again in Seattle, at a China Club meeting. Reminiscing, he joked that although the 1918 conference had been run by Princeton, it took a Harvard man to get the sick Meng back to health!

Actually, spiritual uplift had preceded and made possible my physical recovery. My original religious background was composed of Confucian agnosticism and the usual family-engendered mixture of Taoist and Buddhist folklore and cosmology. I had visited all kinds of temples and attended their rituals. But the unique experience given me by the Americans was what I called "participatory worship." The partnership of leaders and congregation in prayer, in singing hymns and in responsive reading, was entirely new to me. Our ancient concepts— "under heaven all is one family" and "within four seas all are brothers"— coincided with the Christian "brotherhood of men" and "fatherhood of God." But our religious leaders had not developed the rituals or exercises with which their followers could put these concepts into practice. At the conference there were opportunities for personal consultations on such philosophical matters, as well as on practical problems.

The Wo Fo Ssu Conference gave me a tremendous new motivation. My fear and hatred of foreign devils had dissipated because of my growing acquaintance with and understanding of them. I had not been able to reconcile the teachings of the *Four Books,* however, with those of the Bible. The prevalent opinon among missionaries was that the two systems of teaching were incompatible. I was now pleased to find quite a few American student volunteers who had studied our classics and thought highly of them. Thomas F. Carter (Princeton 1904), after working as a missionary, decided to study Chinese history and later taught it at Columbia. Among us students he made a lasting impression by announcing, "I came to teach but will stay to learn." He, L. Carrington Goodrich, and Lucius Porter, China-born sons of missionary families who later taught Chinese at Columbia, could be called America's early "returned students from China."

Other missionaries also stayed on and befriended our students and scholars, especially because of their knowledge of our language and cultural background. Among them I got to know well J. Leighton Stuart, the president of Yenching University, Edward H. Hume, founder and president of Yale-in China's Hsiang Ya Medical School, and Henry Winters Luce, the father of Henry R., the founder of Time. I was especially attracted by Luce (Yale 1892), because he had studied the teachings of Mencius and had come to the conclusion that they were complementary to the teachings of the New Testament. He argued convincingly that for the Chinese the *Four Books* might be considered to have the same relationship to the teachings of Christ as the Old Testament for the Jews.

I found that I had something to live for, that there was something worthwhile I could do, and that I had with me many people of the same mind in my country and the United States. The "Go ye into the world" spirit seized me. Immediately after the conference, I ventured into the villages in nearby valleys to see what I could do for my fellowmen. I tried to start conversations with farmers resting in the shade and with children playing on the threshing floor. Usually they were polite, but I found no way of talking to them on any subject for any length of time. I wanted to tell them about our new Republic, about citizenship, elections, and so on. But we did not have any common background, even in terminology. The shorts I wore and the bicycle I rode sometimes aroused their curiosity and sometimes their antagonism. They invariably asked me who I was and then, after an interval, dispersed. I did not give up. I even succeeded in securing companions to go with me on some of these excursions which I undertook almost daily and sometimes late into the evening. Occasionally, my companions would be "big shots," such as Chang Peng-chun—P. C. Chang—the Reverend Bentley from Oxford, England, or my Princeton friends, Sam Shoemaker and Larry Sears.

One day after bicycling about two hours from Wo Fo Ssu, I found Ssu Ping Tai (Four Level Terraces), the camp of the Peking Orphanage. Director Chang Wen-tou was most hospitable. He invited me to stay for tea and to meet some forty of his adolescent orphans. Hearing that I was interested in giving talks, he suggested that I make regular visits and speak on various subjects. It was here that my regard for Dick Ritter (Richard Henry Ritter, Princeton 1917) deepened. I acted as his interpreter when he talked about America, and our common devotion to the orphans bound us in a lifelong friendship. He and Henry W. Luce did most to make 1918 a landmark year for me. Because they hoped that someday I would go to America to "preach" the gospel of good will and understanding for China, they offered me, and I accepted, the Christian name Paul.

My final year at Tsing Hua, 1918-1919, was anything but normal. Most weekends I spoke at the orphanage. I was assisting Dr. Dittmer in his investigation of narcotic addiction in the western suburbs. But the most exhausting work was the undercover organization of demonstrations against Japan's designs on Shantung province.

After the conference six Chinese students arrived from Tokyo bringing us the ominous news that Japan had succeeded in intimidating the Peking Government into agreeing to turn over to her all of Shantung province at the coming Peace Conference in Paris. These six had been sent by the Chinese Students' Association in Japan to alert and organize their fellows at home to prevent such an eventuality. After a number of discussions, we decided that the time had not come for us to do anything openly, but that we should enlist, secretly, a small group of dare-to-die members who would keep in touch with the Tokyo group and watch for opportunities to act.

During the fall semester I was assigned the project of organizing street speakers to arouse popular support. I had to visit twelve other schools to find qualified student speakers. A desirable student speaker should be enthusiastic, have a strong voice and a fair command of the Peking dialect. At each school we had a local leader, and all local leaders met periodically for consultation on the content of our intended speeches and wall bulletins. By the second semester Japan's designs on Shantung had been exposed at Paris and in the public press.

As one of the Allies, China had sent a delegation to Paris hoping to benefit from the realization of President Wilson's idealistic Fourteen Points for international peace and development. Instead, it found Japan pressing to legitimize its takeover of Germany's possessions in Shantung—the Kiaochow Peninsula and its important naval base at Tsingtao—as well as to some additional rights and concessions of its own devising. Further, the Chinese were shocked to learn that treaties acknowledging these claims had been signed by Great Britain and France in the difficult days of 1917 as the price of keeping Japan— and her considerable navy—on the Allied side. Feeling betrayed, China's delegates refused to sign the Versailles Treaty and returned home, angered and embittered.

Since word had preceded them, and since corrupt and unscrupulous Chinese in positions of power had already been playing Japan's game, feelings of shame and outrage were intense among urban Chinese. Our working association of thirteen colleges and universities was formally organized into the Peking Students' Alliance. It began to hold meetings openly and to make official declarations of its objectives, which were presented to the Government, to school authorities and newspapers, and to eleven other educational centers. Our principal objectives were to recover the Kiaochow Peninsula for China, to reject the award to Japan of rights and privileges in Shantung, as the Peace Conference proposed, and to punish the traitors who had agreed to these depredations and were helping Japan to achieve them.

Two delegates from our student association in Tokyo arrived bringing news that the Chinese minister to Japan, Chang Tsung-hsiang, was returning with an agreement for signature by the Peking Government which would convey China's consent to surrender Tsingtao. The signing was to be done in secret and would probably take place some Sunday early in May. From that time on we hardly studied at all, and we had the sympathy of our teachers, who made it possible for us to make hundreds of placards and *ta tze pao* ("big-character newspapers," or wall bulletins).

At ten o'clock Sunday morning, May 4, students grouped by schools began to assemble at Peking's tremendous central plaza, Tien An Men Square. In two hours there were at least two thousand students carrying placards and flags. Some mounted the steps, some climbed the pedestals of statues shouting slogans at the top of their voice: "Give us back Tsingtao," "China has been betrayed by the Allies," "Down with the traitors." We demanded that the current president of the republic, Hsu Shih-chang, appear in person to explain the Government's policy. A weak and vacillating man, an old-school mandarin and intriguer, Hsu would not show himself. Various secretaries came out and offered all kinds of excuses.

At about 2:00 P.M. mounted police arrived and began to arrest our speakers. We were angered and frustrated. The "dare-to-die" members rallied and decided to dispatch one group to demonstrate before the legations of the Allies and another to search for the traitors, namely Minister Chang and his patron, the head of the pro-Japan clique in the Government, Tsao Ju-lin. I went with those determined to confront the traitors.

Our small band of volunteers knew that Chang was staying at Tsao's home and we rushed there first. A cordon of policemen blocked our way. In spite of our pledge of peaceful intent, they stubbornly refused to let through even one representative. Meanwhile, the group that had gone to the legation area arrived with the report that they had been forestalled by foreign armed guards. Their arrival more than doubled our number, which must have been several hundred. While time dragged on and tempers mounted, one of the delegates from Tokyo mounted on another's shoulders and shouted that he had seen the traitor Chang entering the rear gate with a Japanese escort. That triggered an instant emotional explosion. We rushed both front and rear gates. Tsao's was a western-style house with only a picket fence instead of the usual high wall and we were too many for the forty-odd policemen. Minister Chang, instead of facing us and offering some statement, turned and ran, while his Japanese escort gestured at us threateningly. This sparked us to violence. We beat both of them and set the house on fire.

The police finally fired some shots and arrested thirty-two students at the scene. Some twenty students were wounded, one of whom died the next day.

The Students' Alliance declared a general strike to protest the arrests and telegraphed the eleven other student centers to take similar action. Support came quickly from most Peking school faculties and newspapers and some labor unions. The eleven additional centers struck. In Shanghai, on June 5, the powerful guild of merchants and the labor unions also struck. Stores were shuttered. Public services were halted. Two days later the Government apologized to the Alliance and released the thirty-two arrested students. But the Alliance refused to end the strikes and kept demonstrating in the streets, particularly around the president's office. Many brought their bedding and picketed day and night. At last, on June 28, the Government accepted our demands and instructed the Chinese delegation to reject the Paris treaty. It also dismissed the traitors from office.

Looking back on the May Fourth Movement, I realize that, like the soldier in battle, I knew little of what was happening at any given moment, although later, as the day gained in historical significance, many details were filled in.

I remember that we planned originally a confrontation only, not violence. We were incensed, however, by the presence of a seemingly authoritative Japanese at Tsao Ju-lin's house, and when one of the "dare-to-die" corps recognized the traitor Chang there was no holding us.

88 How many students actually were arrested or wounded and

whether more than one died, no one can say. The total of thirty-two arrests probably is close to the fact, although after the event, when there was credit to be taken, people unknown to me came forward, claiming to be among the heroes arrested. In truth, most of us insiders tried our best not to be identified for fear of retaliation by Japan's secret police. There were no reporters at the scene and no exact figures were known or published at the time.

We had no complaint about our Chinese police. In those days students were regarded as among the elite and the police treated us very gently until the violence escalated. This brought the chief of Peking's police and the commander of the Security Corps to the scene, and it was at their urging that the police waded in to break up our demonstration.

I was among six taken to the East City police station. Because I spoke the Peking dialect I could discuss my situation with the police; those who could not were less well treated. I was permitted to phone my relatives, who soon arrived with food and bedding. Even so, I slept little and worried a great deal. Our cell was crowded, filthy, and overrun with vermin. In exercise periods we discussed our situation among ourselves and tried to explain the incident to our guards. Some of our fellow students demonstrated outside the jail to show their sympathy for us and, of course, we had increasing public support. Emotionally, our spirits were high, but physically we suffered from indigestion and lack of sleep. I suffered from insomnia for many years afterward.

The May Fourth demonstrations awakened students and intellectuals throughout the nation. Victory over the Government heightened our morale, earned us wide support, and spurred us to further action. We demanded and got graduation or promotion without final examinations. We managed to oust practically all the teachers who had openly opposed or criticized the demonstration. We established the custom of expressing collective disapproval of particular school actions or personnel of whom we disapproved. We started our own organizations and publications, often without faculty advice and consent. In July, six new organizations sprang up, including the Marxist Club, and eleven publications, including the *New Woman Monthly*.

For the first time in our history men and women students came together at meetings. The Women's Normal College joined the Alliance and sent representatives. One of the girls, Hu Ying, a sophomore, volunteered to do street speaking in the West City. At my graduation exercises I invited her as one of my guests; my first date.

The students of Peking emerged from the experience of the May Fourth Movement dazed and confused but determined. Dazed, because we had committed violence against our own inclination and tradition as scholars. Confused, because of the way the United States acted at the Peace Conference and the United States Senate's later rejection of the Versailles Treaty, and because Soviet agents in China had ably preached the emancipation of all oppressed peoples of the world and the international brotherhood of the proletariat for the overthrow of the imperialist and capitalist powers. But also determined, because we had awakened to the fact that the masses of the people were the backbone of the nation, and knew that we must learn how to work with them to achieve our common destiny.

The literary revolution fathered by Hu Shih received a great boost from the student demonstrations. We all believed that when the people understood the issues they would know how to decide. It was essential, we thought, for scholars to enlighten the people not only on foreign relations but also on the duties of modern citizenship, on modern life, and on developments in science and technology. About eighty-five percent of our people were illiterate and uninformed. They spoke a number of dialects, some of which were mutually unintelligible. The tremendous task before us was to evoke a national way of talking and writing, so that scholars and the masses could communicate effectively.

To evolve such a medium it was necessary to make a nationwide linguistic survey. Under the leadership of Hu Shih and with the expert direction of Dr. Chao Yuan-ren (Cornell and Harvard)—known in the States as Y. R. Chao—such a survey was launched. One interesting part of the research was the collection of folk songs.

Specialists and students were sent into the countryside to collect folk songs. We did not have any recording equipment, but we wrote down the lyrics and some of us were able to memorize our favorite tunes. The result exceeded our expectations. The folk songs of China reflect not only local flavors and colors and a wide range of expressions, ranging from lullabies, work chants, and songs of war and revolt, but also present vivid evolutionary accounts of how common people talked through the ages, while scholars were clinging tenaciously to an archaic style of expression crystallized during the Han dynasty.

One lullaby's melody was so beautiful that its popularity has been spreading steadily in the United States since its introduction about sixty years ago:

"Purple Bamboo" *(Tzu Chu)*

> Purple bamboo, graceful and straight;
> To my bao bao for a flute
> Flute up to the lips, lips against the flute,
> And then out flows a new melody.
> Dear little one, yii-dee, yii-dee!
> Yes, he blows! Hsia bao bao, yii-dee, yii-dee!
> Ah, he knows!

Chinese culture always has given a high place to the mother and the utmost importance to the begetting of children; hence, the code of parent-child relations. *Woo Yah* ("Black Crows"), we thought, set a good example for us humans, and we sang their praise:

"Black Crows" *(Woo Yah)*

> Woo-Yah, Woo-Yah, they are good,
> Help each other Woo-Yah would.
> Mother too old, cannot fly,
> Little Woo-Yah they will try.
> Day after day they hunt food.
> At home they first feed Mother.
> Mother worked once to rear us,
> We now take good care of her.

91

The following spring song was evolved to fit a piece of traditional instrumental music used for weddings, when the bride was being conducted from the sedan chair to the family altar:

"Spring Tidings" *(Chun Hsun)*

Spring permeates east meadow.
Spring expression in her eyes.
Moon casts shadows in the garden.
Fantasies play in dreams.
Blossoms look intoxicated.
Longings stretch like weeping willows.
Wishful desires ascend higher and higher,
Far up beyond the Bridge of Magpies.
Tears of frustration flow on lonely nights.
Time growing old, beauty wasted.
When will meet again youth, full moon in
    springtime?

Our country folk sang at work, women at their outdoor laundries, men in the fields, and along the great rivers the boatmen:

"Yang Tze Boatmen" *(Yang Tze Cheng Chuan)*

Pole and pole, wey yoh hey yah!
Pole harder, wey yoh hey yah!
Slow down now, wey yoh hey yah!
Speed up now, wey yoh wey tzo hey!
Upstream go, oy yee yoh weh!
Downstream come, wey yoh hey yah!
Against the wind, oy yee yoh wey!
Now with the wind, wey yoh hey yah!
Pull up sail, wey yoh hey yah!
What good wind, wey yoh hey yah!
Ah wey wey sah wey dih wey yah!
Wey hey hey wah, wey woh, wey wah!

Peddlers, barbers, blacksmiths, and repairmen all announce their presence in the streets by their distinctive singsong chants. We could tell inside our houses who was passing by and decide whether we wanted to buy candles, roast chickens, haircuts, knives, or repair services. Every home had at least one large earthenware vat—*kang*—for storing water, very costly and difficult to replace. Hence, any crack or leak that happened to the water vat was a domestic crisis which must be attended to at once. Kang repair was thus a specialty, and the repairmen commanded high pay and consideration. Usually, they had to drill holes along a crack in order to sink in staples to prevent it from opening wider, an operation which always attracted a crowd. Perhaps that was the reason why the kang repairmen evolved as their work chant a satirical song on life in general:

"Drilling Large Vat" (Ding Da Kang)

Once there was a maiden Wong
Determined to marry Liu Ehr Kuang Dong.
Betrothed in First Moon and wedded in Second,
In Third a son was born.
He learned to crawl in Fourth and to walk in Fifth.
In Sixth, he was talking to his parents.
To school he was sent in Seventh.
In Eighth he completed his studies
He went to the Capital in Ninth to take the exam.
In Tenth Moon he won top honors.

Appointed governor, he assumed office in Eleventh.
At the end of Twelfth he retired and returned home.
New Year's eve he suffered a stroke.
His soul went back to its Maker on New Year's Day.
This was exactly:
     Quickly come, quickly go
     Known as "Busy at both ends."

During the Northern Sung dynasty, toward the beginning of the twelfth century, the Hsiung Nu tribes became strong enough to penetrate the Great Wall, invade the capital and capture the emperor. The Chinese Government moved south and split into two factions, one wanting to fight and drive out the invaders while the other advocated appeasement. The appeasement faction got the upper hand and ordered the commander at the front to retreat. The commander was Yao Fei (1103–1141). Before he committed suicide, he put his feelings into words to be sung to a folk melody which came down to us as a most admired folk song:

"Full River Red" *(Man Chiang Hung)*

> Angry hair raises my helmet.
> Command post wet with depressing rain.
> Eyes looking up I cry to Heaven,
> Swelling heart swelling in my breast.
> Thirty years' campaign becomes dust.
> Miles of defense goes like fleeting clouds.
> My head of hair turns white with grief.
> Despair fills the air.
> Ching Kang shame not yet avenged.
> Pent-up hatred burning to be quenched.
> For us to drive our train of chariots
> Through Ho Lan mountain pass.
> We would appease our hunger and thirst
> With Hsiung Nu's flesh and blood,
> And then repair their ravages
> Within Chao Tieu Pass.

Appeasement only worsened matters. Soon the people took things in their own hands and one hundred and eight popular heroes began to exhort others to join them in making their grievances heard by the throne. Out of this movement came this unique folk song:

"Water Fairy Flower" *(Shui Hsien Hua)*

> What lovely lily blossoms.
> Some of these fresh blossoms

Will drop in your home or mine.
When the king rules justly,
The people live happily.
When the king rules justly,
The people live happily.

Toward the end of the Yuan dynasty (Mongol or Tartar dynasty, 1206–
1368), when the Chinese people could bear no longer the brutal alien
rule, they produced a most violent and blasphemous song:

> "Old Heavenly Grandfather" *(Lao Tien*
> *Yeh)*
> Old Heavenly Grandfather,
> you are old:
> You are old, deaf and blind.
> You are so old, deaf and blind,
> You no longer see and hear your people.
> Murderers and arsonists
> Are wallowing in glory and wealth.
> Vegetable-eaters and scripture readers
> Are starving to death.
> Old Heavenly Grandfather,
> You no longer know how to rule.
> You had better fall down!
> You don't know how to behave like Grand-
> father.
> You had better fall down!

Most commentators on Chinese culture had observed that romantic
love did not occupy an important place in Chinese poetry and folk
songs. This observation resulted from a scrutiny confined to published
Chinese literature. But to circumvent the puritanical restrictions of the
T'ang and Sung dynasties, authors of romantic drama and fiction who
did not withhold publication used pseudonyms, or circulated their work
privately or orally. Hu Shih's 1917 *pai hua* (common speech) movement
unearthed quite a number of folk songs of love, quite as romantically

expressed as western love songs. It was my good fortune to discover one of unusual beauty in its melody and lyric:

"Longing" (*Wong Ching Long*)

Longing for him, could I but see through obstacles!
Regretless Heaven, sorrowless Heaven,
Quench not my heart's yearning.
Could I grow two wings, to him I would fly!
"Hard-hearted you!" I would scold.
"Why have you forsaken me?"
"Have you found new love and forgotten old romance?"

Home, away far, my returning is like an arrow.
Dreams of meeting; words unspoken;
Likely she suspects and resents.
Thinking affairs cause delay.
"You should know my heart well, Love!"
But long separation breeds frustration.
East Wind, pray help speed my sailing home!

Peking University and Tsing Hua took the initiative of inviting prominent American and British scholars to lecture on western intellectual trends as a means of combating the inertia of traditional Chinese thinking and opening avenues to modern scientific attitudes and methodology. A Harvard astronomer was asked to speak on the solar system and the roundness of the earth (quite a few of my generation still believed the earth was flat); an MIT physicist talked about atoms; chemical engineering was the subject of a professor from Purdue. These extracurricular public lectures were well received and met the popular aspiration for adopting western solutions for our problems.

It was at this point that I got to know well the philosophers John Dewey and Bertrand Russell, who were among our visiting lecturers. Each of them wanted to know something of traditional Chinese culture and the life of the common people. I acted as a private guide and interpreter for Dewey. Upon learning that I was from the country and an old clan school, he asked me a number of questions about traditional Chinese education and the *Four Books,* which I still could recite from memory. He seemed to think quite highly of Confucius' philosophy of education as summarized in the first paragraph of *Ta Hsüeh:*

"The Way of Great Learning lies in understanding evident virtues, in renewing the people, and in aiming at utmost excellence. Knowledge of the aim produces determination; determination produces calmness; calmness leads to peace; peace enables thinking; thinking makes possible begetting something.

"T'ang's (emperor, 1766–1753 B.C.) engraved plaque in his room says, 'Assume each day brings something new; try to find new things day after day; renew yourself and your fellowmen.' "

Russell surprised me. He disagreed with Hu Shih on the total adoption of western culture by the Chinese. He favored more science and technology for China, but decidedly not the western way of life. He had that somewhat ruthless British wit and appeared to enjoy casting barbs at missionaries, or anyone who believed, as many westerners did, that the Chinese were an inferior people incapable of self-government. Russell urged retention of our intuitive approach, applauded our familyism and abhorrence of war, and spoke and wrote forcefully in support of our traditional approach, somewhat to the embarrassment of Hu and his associates. He even thought that our parent-dictated marriages were not necessarily bad compared with British marriage customs. "With the Chinese," he said, "romance begins on the wedding day, but with the British romance ends with marriage." He also said that "filial piety is far superior to patriotism and militarism," and that "the Chinese have discovered and have practiced a way of life, which, if it could be adopted by all the world, would make all the world happy."

At Princeton Court I met Norman Thomas (Princeton 1905), a past minister of the Brick Presbyterian Church of New York

City. He was a pacifist and a socialist whose antiwar activities had aroused criticism from fellow ministers and some church members. He had resigned from the ministry and was on a world tour in preparation for his new cause—promotion of world peace through socialism. In China he found kindred spirits among the intellectuals. He discovered that, historically, Chinese thought and thinkers overwhelmingly condemned force and war and extolled virtue and the benevolent rule and ruler. Mo Ti (470–391 B.C.) was a militant pacifist and socialist. Mencius devoted his whole life to an attempt to convince the feudal rulers of the day that *jen,* or humaneness, rather than *pa,* or force, was the only way to achieve national and international peace. When Thomas learned that I was going to the United States, he asked me to promise to join the antiwar crusade he was carrying on among American students.

At the 1919 Tsing Hua commencement I was awarded a five-year scholarship to study in the United States. It was a signal honor and I was overjoyed.

Father attended the exercises. We spent two days together. He appeared cheerful for the first time since Mother's death. My conscience felt more at ease, since I had fulfilled some of his expectations. At parting we did not express but knew well our mixed emotions: joy at a step forward for me and sorrow at not knowing when we might meet again.

My class went to Shanghai to get outfitted and to sail. Sun Yat-sen gave us a reception at his home on July 30. A man whose eye was bright and whose enthusiasm bubbled out of him, he was eager to know more about the May Fourth demonstrations and our ideas about current affairs. He had heard about my participation and imprisonment. He took me aside in the garden, commended me, and advised me to continue my activism. But, he warned, "in your enthusiastic pursuit of the new American education, be sure not to neglect our own cultural heritage, including the teachings of your ancestor, Meng Tze. I have been trying to make up for my own neglect. Whenever possible I review the classics and practice calligraphy."

1919: Protest group in Peking burns
Japanese goods. Young Republic of China was
sorely beset by Japan's encroachments,
particularly the seizure of Shantung,
and boycotts and demonstrations were among
the few available expressions of
outrage. Author, newly graduated from Tsing
Hua, departed at this time to begin
a new life in the United States.

That was a year of vigorous anti-Japanese activity, including intensification of boycotts of Japanese goods. We had booked passage on a large Japanese steamer months ahead, but decided to cancel it. The only space we could find was on a small American ship, the S.S. *Colombia*. We had to draw lots for the few cabins available. Many of us had to take steerage. All of us refused to go sightseeing in Japan when the ship stopped at Nagasaki and Yokohama.

On the *Colombia* were some one hundred and forty Chinese students, fifty of them from Tsing Hua, the rest from missionary or private schools and traveling on Government scholarships. We Tsing Hua students were accompanied by two faculty members, one of whom was Lin Yutang. He had been born and brought up in Amoy, in a Presbyterian family, and received his college education at St. John's University, an American Episcopalian-supported school in Shanghai. At Tsing Hua, Lin was an instructor in English. To us, he seemed to behave more like an American than a Chinese. He wore western clothes, knew how to use knife and fork at dinner, and even walked on deck with his bride, arm in arm.

Our sixteen days on the Pacific were a delightful interlude amid the pressure of our constantly changing lives. We were isolated on the high seas; we were tourists; life on the ship was designed to be fun, with all sorts of games, three meals a day supplemented by teas and snacks, and (for the very bold) dancing to western-style orchestras. For sixteen days we could lead—or at least watch—a life that most of us had never seen, let alone experienced.

On landing I learned that Father had died during my voyage. As a dutiful son I would have returned for the services honoring him, but he had left strict instructions that I should continue my studies abroad without interruption. In the end, my dear forward-looking father preferred that his son continue on his way into the future, rather than re-enter the world of Chinese tradition.

Part 3

A Chinese Activist in the United States

From the South to New York

Chinese Students in America and Europe

From the South to New York

Our first glimpse of the New World was at dawn, with an early September sun rising over San Francisco's Golden Gate. What a skyline! How different the noises and the crowds! We were immediately self-conscious at being Orientals. This feeling was aggravated by the immigration inspector. Chinese were herded to an isolated spot on deck and lined up for a physical examination. We were the last passengers to be released. However, the warm welcome showered upon us by friends and fellow countrymen once we were cleared immediately made us feel at home. Chinatown, the Dollar Steamship Line, and the University of California at Berkeley had arranged several days of sightseeing, parties, and banqueting for us.

About half of us could speak English fairly well. The rest had to depend on us to interpret and explain things. Some of the Tsing Hua fellows had fun showing off their superior understanding of things American. At an evening concert in the Chinese YMCA auditorium, a Chinese student was much enchanted by the melody of a cello passage. He asked his Tsing Hua friend, S. T. Shen, a music major, for the name of the tune. Shen said, "It is posted at the side of the platform. Let me go up there and find out." When he returned he proudly whispered, but loudly enough for others to hear, "The name of that melody is 'Refrain from spitting.'" Another time one of our English Lit. majors, H. H. Chang, shouted to a cable-car conductor, "Please procrastinate me at the next street corner."

In California we had our first experiences with racism. Three barbershops in the Bay Region refused to cut our hair because we were Asiatics. What hurt most was that the YMCA in Los Angeles declined to rent us transient rooms for the same reason.

George H. Danton, one of my German professors at Tsing Hua, had warned us that there was anti-Chinese prejudice in the United States, especially among Americans who had never met any educated Chinese. He hoped that Chinese students would work to overcome such prejudice and urged that some should be adventurous enough to go to schools where there had never been any Chinese. I immediately volunteered, and he arranged my admission to Davidson College in North Carolina.

My two years at Davidson were truly an adventure in two-way pioneering and orientation. Davidson was a leading college of the Old South, founded by the Presbyterian Church and steeped in the English traditions of colonial Carolina. As a requirement for graduation, students were required to join one of the two debating societies and give an oration before the faculty and the college community. Although the college had sent missionaries to China, it had not seen a Chinese before. The administration must have given thought to my coming and made advance preparations. It thought dormitory life might be too rough and created a special room for me in the infirmary, because the nurse in charge, Mrs. Robson, was a motherly widow who knew how to cook rice well and how to take care of homesick boys. It also alerted a family, whose residence was close to the campus, to befriend me and offer some of the warmth and amenities of home life.

In more than one way I believe I surprised the college community. My English was understandable, I played pretty good tennis, and above all I spoke boldly and frankly about political and social matters, like the revolutionary and radical I considered myself to be. In my first speech before the student body I told about the May Fourth demonstrations and bitterly denounced Woodrow Wilson for his betrayal of China at the Paris Peace Conference. My attack on the American president sent a shock wave through the audience because Wilson was Davidson's most distinguished alumnus—he spent one year there before transferring to Princeton—and southern Presbyterians revered him as their greatest political and spiritual leader since the Civil War. The subject of my junior oration was "The Korean Revolution." In fact, no revolution had yet been achieved, but resistance to the annexation by Japan in 1910 and to its subsequent suppression of Korean patriots was fervent and continuing. In 1919, shortly before I spoke, a provisional government in exile was established by Korean refugees in Shanghai with Syngman Rhee as president. The cause was close to my heart because of my family connections with Manchuria; on visits there as a youth I had made friends with several Koreans, including Younghill Kang, later a writer and teacher at NYU. When I first met Rhee, at Mukden in 1918, he had just been released by the Japanese under an amnesty. He was worn out by years of imprisonment, for leading an anti-Japanese demonstration in 1897, and could hardly speak without stammering. I soon learned that he had a will of iron. Twenty-nine years later he would become the first president of an independent Korean republic.

My home away from home at Davidson turned out to be that of Mr. and Mrs. Thomas H. Hamilton. He was a farmer, an elder of the Presbyterian church, a devoted husband and father of five children. They were a wonderful family. I loved every one of them. The Hamiltons' life resembled that of my family in that all members knew their proper places, their duties, and their relationships among themselves and with God.

My Americanization started at Davidson. My many Davidson friends, I dare to think, were a little bit Sinofied in return from me, their Chinese specimen Number One. Years later, upon visiting Davidson, a special convocation was called to hear me. Among other things, I said that the Orient and Occident were turning around in a two-way cultural traffic; hence, we should reset our relative concepts and perspectives, so that for Americans it would be Orientation and for the Chinese "Occidentation."

In the Shenandoah Valley of Virginia, where I worked on a farm one summer, I found the people thrifty, hard-working, home-centered, and God-fearing. There were basic similarities between these rural Virginian communities and those of Shantung province. In common were the high degree of ethnic homogeneity, local and family pride and loyalty, and firmly established moral attitudes and behavior. With hardly any exceptions, women, young and old, did not smoke, drink, flirt, or use vile language; the men behaved more or less the same way and fully confirmed the tradition of southern chivalry. Universally observed were the obligations of hospitality and respect for elders. What made me envious, however, was the more enlightened and profound religious life of the Virginians. In Shantung the farmers certainly were religious, and every community had its own temples with monks and nuns. But our professional religious leaders were not highly educated, and our religious rituals and exercises had not kept pace with the aesthetic development and spiritual needs of the community. Here the church was the social center. Saturday evening the grownups saw to it that they and the children took their weekly baths, had their Sunday-best apparel ready and their Sunday school lessons studied. On Sunday morning the whole family went to church, where the minister was their respected leader. After the worship service the congregation stayed on for an hour or two to visit. Most vital, Americans learned to pray, to sing hymns, and to deliberate on important issues of life *together.* Although American Christians were divided into denominations, their sense of fellowship was much greater than ours, extending even beyond national barriers. I noted the segregation between whites and blacks, but both seemed to me to have accepted the status quo. I loved the people of North Carolina and Virginia. The way of life exemplified for me a simple, natural, and full enjoyment of the resources of heaven, earth, and man.

My transfer to New York City to pursue graduate study at Columbia thrust me into a new and different America. New York was filled with wonders and excitements. Practically all Chinese students came here sooner or later, and it was an excellent place for keeping in touch. Immediately I discovered, and got involved in, Chinese and American student activities and organizations.

In the 1920s, American students were very conscious of their worldwide responsibilities and were eager to do something to improve not only their own country, but other countries as well. They wanted to unite the students of all nations to achieve this goal. This powerful current originated with the American Student Volunteer Movement, which was inspired with fresh strength by the dynamic personality and superb ability of leaders like John R. Mott, the general secretary of the YMCA, and Sherwood Eddy and Norman Thomas.

The student YMCA and YWCA organizations were also at their peak influence, and American students were enthusiastically tackling vital issues of their day: war, labor unionism, racism, socialism.

Often I found that I was neglecting my studies to spend time attending meetings at the Fellowship of Reconciliation, or the League for Industrial Democracy, both of which used me as a speaker representing the Chinese student government. The Fellowship of Reconciliation arranged trips for students to visit places of racial and class conflict, such as black Harlem and mining parts of Pennsylvania. The Social Service Group of the Y enlisted volunteers to do part time work among deprived children on the Lower East Side. Hence, my weekends and vacations were busily occupied. I thought of my fellow students at home and how beneficial to them it would be if they were provided similar opportunities to know and help solve social problems in China. I also kept in touch with other foreign students, particularly Asians, who frequently met to air mutual grievances, not least of which was the difficulty of finding suitable rooms and of getting personal attention from American professors.

Among the sympathetic student secretaries at Columbia were Herbert Evans and Harry Edmonds, who hoped one day to establish an international student center. One Christmas morning, according to legend, Edmonds and John D. Rockefeller, Jr., were walking down the steps of Seth Low Library and ran into a Hindu student. They greeted him with a cheerful, "Merry Christmas!" and shook hands with him. The Hindu responded but broke into tears. He had been at Columbia for almost a semester and these were the first personal greetings and handshakes he had received. The episode may have strengthened Edmonds' hand in securing Rockefeller funds for the establishment of International House.

Negro students and intellectuals—the term "black" was not current then—were well received in the radical student organizations in which I made quite a few friends. But W. E. B. DuBois, the Harvard-educated historian, sociologist, and author, thought my impressions of the United States were too rosy. As an ardent advocate of Negro equality and an official of the National Association for the Advancement of Colored People, he suggested that I should become better acquainted with the plight of the Negroes. He made arrangements for me to visit some of the Negro colleges of the "Black Belt." After I returned, he asked me to report my experiences to him and a few friends. Among other things, I said at this intimate gathering, "It is true that the treatment of Negroes in the South is both insulting and unjust. But I also found that most Negroes, including Negro students, looked down on me worse than the whites; their prejudices and misinformation on China are just as bad." Dr. DuBois was surprised and not a little shocked. He and I put our heads together and eventually succeeded in introducing Chinese faculty members and students to such Negro colleges as Fisk, Tuskegee, Howard, and Hampton Institute for the purpose of promoting mutual understanding.

Chinese students in the United States were well organized. The small group brought to the United States at the beginning of the century had come at an early and impressionistic age and were soon throughly Americanized.

At their beginning, around 1905, Chinese student movements were intensely patriotic and religious. Sun Yat-sen and his sympathizers organized secret societies among the Chinese in Hawaii and the United States. The oldest included fraternities such as David and Jonathan, Cross and Sword, Rho Poi, Phi Lambda, and Awakening Lions. Virtually all the organizers of these fraternities were also active in establishing public societies, which eventually grouped into regional and national associations, and they went on to prominence in the revolution and the successive governments of the Republic of China. Leaders like V. K. Wellington Koo, Sao-ke Alfred Sze, and Wang Cheng-ting (C. T. Wang), all of whom served in diplomatic posts of the highest importance, had their apprenticeship here in the modernization of China, American-style, which also embraced equal rights for women.

By 1921 there were two cooperating groups, the Chinese

Students' Alliance (CSA) and the Chinese Students' Christian Association (CSCA) of North America. They held annual conferences, published monthly magazines and news bulletins, directories and year books. At the Alliance Conference held at Hotchkiss School, in Lakeville, Connecticut, that year I was happy to see a number of old friends and schoolmates and to meet many new students, including women, from all kinds of colleges and universities. We had serious discussions, games and sports, and some of us even ventured into the great American cultural movements of ballroom dancing and dating.

The conference queen was Hilda Yen. Her grandfather was among the earliest Christian converts of American missionaries. Her father was F. C. Yen, a Yale M.D. and younger brother of the notable W. W., who would soon be China's prime minister and later her minister to the United States and the Soviet Union. Her background and Smith College education combined to create in her a lively American girl's personality with beautiful Shanghai features. P. T. Chen from Princeton and T. H. Chang from West Point vied for Hilda's favor. Chang even challenged his rival to a duel. Several of us decided that things had gone too far and undertook to settle the dispute. To everyone's satisfaction, we, the self-appointed jury, announced that, while Chang had in his possession a pistol, we had failed to find a similar gun for Chen, and therefore the duel must be canceled.

Perhaps not quite so beautiful as Hilda, but equally popular was Nora Hsiung, daughter of Hsiung Hsi-ling, reformer, cabinet minister, millionaire, and philanthropist. She was charming and feminine, yet stood out as the most extreme radical in the cause of women's equality. She announced that she intended to organize a woman's movement for social and political reforms, that she would choose her own husband, and that she would bear six children—no more, no less.

There was a somber undertone to all this, created by the impending Nine-Power Conference in Washington. Although principally concerned with the balance of naval strength among Great Britain, the United States, and Japan, its agenda also included a number of unsettled Far Eastern questions of burning importance to China. The memory of China's dashed hopes and expectations at Paris after World War I was still fresh. Thus, it was the unanimous resolution of the conference that our Government permit representatives of the CSA to take part in the deliberations of the Chinese delegation. The Government acceded to this request. Five student delegates not only participated, but contributed significantly. Among them, showing his potential as a future diplomat, was Chiang T'ing-fu (T. F. Tsiang), who eventually became China's ambassador to the Soviet Union and permanent representative at the United Nations.

The Nine-Power Conference found it easier to adjust the naval ratios among its various members than to deal generously—or realistically—with the problems of the Far East. For one thing, it excluded Russia from the deliberations, despite its strategic position in Siberia. For another, it ignored China's strenuous demands to be relieved of the burden of the unequal treaties. The Powers made a pious declaration to respect China's territorial integrity, but no provision for backing it with force. Japan could expect to proceed in China without impediment.

Largely through American pressure, Japan agreed to return Shantung to China, although this was arranged in separate one-on-one negotiations, with the United States and Britain as occasional mediators, because Japan would not concede it as an issue for international settlement. On nothing else would Tokyo give an inch. Beguiled by Nine-Power rhetoric, the U.S. Congress ratified the essentially hollow treaties, then went on to vote a Japanese exclusion act which hardened the determination of the Tokyo militarists to pursue their extremist course.

In China, Sun Yat-sen and other adversaries of the irresolute Peking regime began to voice disappointment with their former western Allies and, at the same time, to express appreciation for the Soviet Union's sympathy and action on behalf of the oppressed peoples of the world. In the United States, a few expert observers including some YMCA secretaries, sensing that the winds of public opinion were changing in China, prepared and organized a Baltimore Conference on

Chinese-American Relations in 1924. It was attended by several hundred Americans and Chinese, including Government officials, professors, and students. One result was the establishment of the Institute of Pacific Relations (IPR), which soon became an important organ for research and the discussion of problems between East Asian nations and the western powers.

I was quite vocal at the Baltimore conference, both at open sessions and in private conversations. It was here that I got to know a number of Chinese and American leaders. Sao-ke Alfred Sze, then Chinese minister to Washington, and Dr. P. W. Kuo (Columbia 1914), founder and first president of Southeastern University, at Nanking, thought well of my ideas and asked me to write a paper which was published by *Asia* magazine. W. W. Willoughby, a professor at Johns Hopkins and an adviser to Sze, suggested that I pursue graduate research with him at his university. J. Merle Davis of the YMCA and a prime organizer of the conference, invited me to join him at IPR.

In New York City I made many other connections. Hu Shih and P. C. Chang both studied at Columbia; they gave me introductions to their friends, some of whom became my friends and involved with my work and career for years to come. American friends in Peking also gave me entrée at the YMCA, especially among the people in the Student Department and the Committee on Friendly Relations among Foreign Students.

Most Chinese students had American friends who were missionaries or whose orientation was through the Christian Church or the YM or YWCA's. One resulting phenomenon had been our general adoption of Christian or Anglicized names. When a nationalistic spirit with an anti-Christian undertone set in, many of us began to drop our Christian names, but the personal ties remained strong, whatever the vicissitudes of politics or ideologies. Two outstanding examples of American Christian involvement with Chinese came into my experience at this time. Dick Ritter introduced his Chinese friends to his parents, Mr. and Mrs. Phillip Ritter, who lived in Brooklyn. The

Ritter home was a center of hospitality for generations of Chinese students, to whom their hosts were affectionately known as Uncle Phil and Aunt Dora.

When I first visited the Chinese Presbyterian Church at 223 East 31st Street, the Reverend Huie Kin and his wife, Louise Van Arnam, were already well known among Chinese students in the United States and China. Theirs was an early case of successful intermarriage; three sons and six daughters made up the happy family, and their church and home had helped and entertained many Chinese students and leaders, including Sun Yat-sen.

In the summer of 1921, I was fortunate to get a job as a translator. A poet, Mabel Lorenz Ives of Upper Montclair, New Jersey, was interested in Chinese poetry, but she was not satisfied with reading it in English. She asked the Chinese Department of Columbia University to recommend an interpreter. My friend, Chi-chen Wang, who was on the faculty, introduced me to her. I was invited to stay in her home that summer, reading to her in Chinese and then interpreting in English. As a result of these studies, she published a volume entitled *Chinese Love Poems*. She ferreted out love poems in particular, because western translators had created the impression that China discouraged romance and that its poets rarely wrote of romantic love.

Mrs. Ives and her husband, Herbert, were a perfect match of opposites. She personified all the feminine qualities of Yin. She was small and slender and always spoke in a subdued voice. Her low-grade asthma somehow enhanced her modesty and induced people to listen to her carefully chosen and well-enunciated words. Dr. Ives was a large and husky Yang whose movements were strong and decisive. He seldom talked or did anything except with precision and concentration. He was the son of a successful inventor who had pioneered in photoengraving and color photography, and was himself a well-known research physicist at the Bell Telephone Laboratories. He was instrumental in the development of the vacuum tube and the transmission of photographs by telephone wire. At the dinner table he ate very fast and seldom joined in conversation. More often than not, he thought of some problem, took a slide rule from his pocket, and began making notes, oblivious to the presence of his wife, his three children, and me. His occupation with his job was total. He took his exercises and other diversions in exact doses and by regular schedules. Occasionally, he would let Mrs. Ives take him to church or to a concert, and sometimes he accompanied his children to shows, but it was apparent that he regarded such sidetracks as necessary evils. It was his firm belief that the fine arts were products of lesser minds and he usually napped through concerts or his wife's poetry readings. Still, after he retired he became interested in art and eventually became a fine portrait painter! As a widow, Mrs. Ives continued to write and travel until she reached the age of ninety-four. She was the everlasting, even-keeled, gentle woman.

My excursion into Chinese poetry for Mrs. Ives necessitated long study hours at New York's Public Library at Fifth Avenue and Forty-second Street, and the Low Library at Columbia, both of which housed large collections of Chinese literature. On my many visits to those libraries I did not run into one Chinese reader. They were all westerners. Some of them spoke to me with enthusiasm and admiration about their findings. It soon dawned on me that my generation of Chinese students was so taken by western culture, especially science and technology, that it unconsciously regarded Chinese literature as irrelevant or obsolete. Furthermore, the wind of the literary revolution had swept most of us away from traditional things. In fact, hardly any Chinese students were engaged in Chinese studies or had prepared themselves to teach Chinese subjects in the United States. Chi-chen Wang at Columbia and H. C. Mui at Harvard were among a handful of exceptions. My own eyes were reopened to my heritage that summer by my American friends.

What should be my major subject in graduate school? The answer depended on my choice of career. Some of my close advisers, such as Hu Shih and Y. C. Mei, thought I should take engineering, which represented the best training America was offering in the application of science to technology. But they were in Peking, thousands of miles away; their advice seemed remote and unreal. On the other hand, certain personalities in New York were exciting admiration and inspiring emulation on my part almost daily. John R. Mott organized the World Students' Christian Federation and seemed to be making great strides toward using the Y as an instrument to realize world brotherhood. A church layman, Fred B. Smith, was attempting to arouse the churches through the World Alliance for International Friendship. John H. Holmes and Rabbi Stephen Wise did much to open the way for all great religions to cooperate in thought and action for their common faith in God and peace. The Community Church of Holmes and the Free Synagogue of Wise attracted large audiences, including Asian students. I was carried away by those dedicated people and what they championed. Moreover, Drs. Y. Y. Tsu and Henry W. Luce emphasized the fact that China needed indigenous social and religious leaders and expressed the hope that I might be one of them. I decided to major in sociology, aiming to work in China for the Y or the church.

My recollections of Columbia center around some of my professors. Professor Franklin Henry Giddings was an interesting lecturer and strict in his requirements. He wanted social studies to be scientific, precise, and specific. On the other hand, Dewey tended to take a broad approach and suggested that I audit a number of courses or professors before settling on any particular area of research. It was most enjoyable and illuminating to attend the classes of some of the greats like John Erskine (professor of English literature and violinist), John B. Watson (behaviorist psychology), Edwin R. A. Seligman (economics), John Bassett Moore (international law), James T. Shotwell (history and international relations), and Franz Boas (anthropology). Boas was regarded as a pioneer in cultural anthropology. He developed methods of study which related cultures or life styles to physical characteristics of heredity. His emphasis on investigating comparative cultures was of special interest to me because the Confucian school of thought had a similar theory asserting that "culture or education makes

113

a personality rather than race or physical differences." I got to know well two of his students, Ruth Benedict and Margaret Mead. The former was interested in Chinese culture and wanted to apply the Boas methodology to do research in the development of the Chinese people. Mead was critical of Chinese familyism and thought western individualism would have stimulated greater social progress among backward or primitive peoples.

My newly adopted Christian faith also underwent academic scrutiny. I audited some courses at the nearby Union Theological Seminary. Harry Emerson Fosdick was a convincing teacher and an inspiring preacher. He made the personalities, situations, and concepts of the Bible alive and applicable to modern life and living. Harry F. Ward, London-born professor of Christian ethics and longtime chairman of the American Civil Liberties Union, ably and forcefully separated Christianity as a religion from the institutional churches and sects, and especially from their involvement with politics and exploitation by governments and politicians. But most of the professors I encountered there were theological hairsplitters, highly orthodox in their methodology and interpretations. Students majoring in the Old Testament had to study classical Hebrew, and majors in the New Testament had to know classical Greek. It was quite a linguistic struggle for a novice to understand the relevance of distinguishing Jehovah from Yahwe and how Logos became God.

With increasing enthusiasm I devoted my spare time to participation in my favorite movements and to meeting kindred spirits among American and Asian students. In the Chinese Students' Christian Association I soon won nationwide recognition, because I contributed frequently to its publications and helped raise funds for its budget. In 1923 I was elected president; we had 2,471 members located at ninety-seven different student centers in the United States. We published news bulletins and yearbooks, held local and sectional meetings, and provided help and advice. We raised and spent an annual budget of about $4,700 from our membership and friends.

One of my most pleasant responsibilities was to persuade

Chinese students to attend YMCA and YWCA student conferences. These week-long meetings were highly regarded by the college administrations and by the students. They were held during summer or winter vacations at scenic spots with facilities for meetings, sports, and group living. The most notable conferences were held at Silver Bay in New York, Eaglesmere in Pennsylvania, Lake Geneva in Wisconsin, Black Mountain in North Carolina, and Asilamar in California. I went to conferences at all those places, but my first was at Silver Bay, on Lake George. For many reasons, Silver Bay has remained my Mecca, where I regularly renew my memories of Chinese-American friendship and my undying faith in the mutual benefit to be found in Chinese-American cooperation and cultural blending.

Nature has created Lake George to initiate us mortals into celestial and terrestrial beauty and poetry. Under the bright summer sun, the Adirondacks are a ragged green band between the azure sky above and the deep blue waters below. The full moon rises at night and transforms the mountains and lake with her silvery light; hence, the felicitous name Silver Bay. The conference campus was located on the west shore, about halfway between the towns of Lake George and Ticonderoga. Its main buildings nestled against Sunrise Peak. It looked east across a two-mile-wide rock-bottom lake framed by a sharp-rising mountain ridge, the Black Mountain and Sugar Loaf peaks to the south, Roger's Slide and Fort Ticonderoga to the north. The physical and spiritual aspects of the place remind me of Wo Fo Ssu in the Western Hills. Both Wo Fo Ssu and Silver Bay embody the magnificence of nature touched by men and history.

I was so enthralled by my first conference at Silver Bay that I could not think of leaving the place after such short acquaintance. Luckily for me, the Silver Bay Association employed college students and there was a vacancy on the kitchen staff. I applied for it and obtained the job of busboy. More than forty college boys and girls were employees, or "emps." We had our rooms on campus and we were organized into the Emps Association. Our elected officers arranged social, recreational, and religious gatherings. All summer long Silver

Bay was host to different groups and their respective leaders and speakers. Emps were privileged to attend all public meetings. I was thrilled to hear and meet prominent people like William Jennings Bryan, Clarence Darrow, William Lyon Phelps, and Roger Baldwin.

The very close daily contact with Americans of my own age soon overcame my feelings of strangeness toward them. I could converse better in English and even understand some slang and jokes. I got more used to wearing working clothes and eating hot dogs and other picnic foods. My long-standing prejudices or misunderstandings faded away, one after the other. I saw that American students, like their Chinese counterparts, were human, though they were more boisterous and more casual toward their elders. The hardest hurdle for me to negotiate was the social behavior between American boys and girls. I did not approve of their free and wild carryings-on. I could not be persuaded to dance.

It so happened that all my earliest American friends were blondes: Dick Ritter, Sam Shoemaker, and Norman Thomas. For the ten or more years of our friendship, I had felt they were close to me in everything but their light hair and blue eyes, which appeared unnatural, indeed inhuman. Now I not only reconciled myself to this physical strangeness, but even came to think that blondes could be good-looking. I was also learning popular songs and could sing "Smilin' Through" with feeling.

One of our emps, a waitress I will call Roberta Owen, held a special attraction for me. In a way, she resembled my favorite sister. She was slight and fair-skinned, and her hair was very dark. She was very shy but could be vivacious. In social gatherings she usually avoided noisy and unruly people. She was a freshman from Mount Holyoke and had decided to volunteer for missionary work in China. Naturally, she wanted me to tell her about my native land and we met frequently.

Roberta was from a rural part of Maine and a devotee of outdoor life. She excelled in swimming, canoeing, mountain climbing, and picnicking. She initiated me into all those activities and helped me to become an outdoor man. It was quite a miracle for me to become a swimmer. In China the fortune teller had told my mother that of the five basic elements of my earthly make-up, metal predominated. This meant that bodies of water were my earthly snare, for metal, of course, sinks in water. My mother had made me promise never to go swimming.

R. O. and I were enjoying each other's company more and more. We paddled and explored the islands of Lake George and hiked and scaled the mountains. Hence, by the appearances and customs of the time, we went steady. But what puzzled her was that I did not behave like her other boy friends. I did not walk or sit close to her, hold her arm when walking, or dance with her. Youthful petting and necking I regarded as immoral. In my cultural background there had been no dating or courting, or even social gatherings, between unmarried men and women for millennia!

One moonlit evening, R. O. and I were having one of our special hours tête-à-tête. We were alone, sitting on the floor of the boathouse balcony overlooking the lake. The scene, the stillness, and our unspoken communication created the feeling that we were the world and the world was ours and that time was standing still. Then the auditorium tower bell rang signaling "lights out" for employees. As we stood up to go, R. O. impulsively embraced me, held and pressed me hard, and kissed me. For days afterward the unique experience caused violent commotions in my inner self. It triggered new and powerful disturbances which raged alternatively like the ravishing cold and hot spells of malaria. From the mountaintop of ecstasy I would fall steeply into a deep valley of doubt and depression. The magic feminine touch electrified my whole being. But the fact that my mother and sisters had never embraced or kissed me raised questions about R. O. which troubled me deeply and would not go away. Nevertheless, we fell in love and thought of getting married. Alas, when she returned home after the summer, she found her family strongly opposed to racial intermarriage. A long period of soul-searching ensued for both of us. We finally agreed not to go against my misgivings and her family's opposition.

117

I have often wondered about the comparative merits of the American custom of dating and courting and the traditional Chinese way of parental matchmaking. The former puts the primary emphasis on romantic love between the individuals concerned, while the latter places highest priority on the welfare of the family. Perhaps a blend of the two practices would minimize impulsive and short-lived matches and bring about more judicious and lasting unions.

There are qualified observers on both sides of the Pacific, such as my friend Edward Lockwood, an American YMCA secretary in Canton, who would agree that when the aim is marriage romance can and should be enhanced by wisdom. On one of Lockwood's furloughs, he was assigned to the staff of the International YMCA's Committee on Friendly Relations among Foreign Students, while I was president of the CSCA. Working in the same office, we became colleagues. He confided to me that he was lonely since the death of his wife, and asked me to be on the lookout for desirable prospects for him in my travels. When I visited Chinese students at Northwestern University in May of 1925, I met Muriel Treman, a graduate student and widow of a missionary in China. After seeing her at Chinese students' meetings and discussing China with her, my intuition told me that I must arrange for her to meet Ed. I lost no time in appointing myself matchmaker, and briefed both parties on their "fortunes" and my intention. I persuaded Muriel to come to New York to continue her studies at Columbia. Within a year they married and lived happily ever after. Since then they have called me their "Kitchen God"—the guardian of domestic bliss!

Chinese Students in America and Europe

The spirit of the 1920's tended toward one world, and great efforts were made to organize activities for reconciling conflicting classes and peoples. I caught the spirit of the time and determined to know more about such organizations and their leaders. I went with Bishop Paul

Jones, an ardent pro-labor, antiwar Episcopalian, to the coal mines of northeastern Pennsylvania during a strike. Near Wilkes-Barre, we saw picketing miners beaten by company guards, while miserable-looking wives and children peered at us from their tumbledown shacks. I could not help thinking that conditions in the mines of Pennsylvania were not much better than those of North China.

Eugene Cerbaley, a black student leader, introduced me to a group which had banded together to stir up black pride and self-consciousness. Filipino *independentistas* in New York had a fiery leader in Juan Roderiquez. The antiwar pacifists were headed by the Friends' leaders, Clarence Pickett and Ed Schaal. Frank Buchman, whom I had known during his missionary days in China, had started the Oxford Group movement at the University in 1921. It concentrated on the personal and pietistic aspects of Christianity, emphasizing absolute honesty, purity, love, and direct communication with God. The Oxford Movement spread from Britain to Princeton and to many other institutions, and eventually to many social and political leaders of the United States and other countries when it changed its name to Moral Rearmament Association in 1939.

My personal involvement in all these movements, and with the leaders who befriended me, convinced me that the time was ripe for realizing the brotherhood of men. I felt that I had to enlist more co-workers to hasten its realization. An opportunity came through one of my friends and spiritual mentors, Y. Y. Tsu.

Dr. Y. Y. Tsu (Chu Yo-yu, Ph.D. Columbia, 1912), a professor at St. John's University in Shanghai, was on furlough in the United States and working as secretary for Chinese students on the staff of the Committee on Friendly Relations among Foreign Students of the International YMCA in New York. We worked closely together for a year. Returning to China to resume teaching at St. John's, Dr. Tsu recommended me as his successor. In June, 1924, I was appointed Chinese secretary on the staff of that committee and concurrently elected general secretary of the CSCA.

In my dual capacity, I had to keep in touch with Chinese

students in the United States and Canada, act as liaison among their organizations, raise funds for the CSCA, and render miscellaneous services to individual students in need. To carry out my assignments, I had to travel constantly, visiting Chinese student centers and exchanging information with foreign student advisers and YMCA or YWCA secretaries of colleges and universities. In the first four years, 1924–27 inclusive, I traveled some 92,000 miles to campuses in most of the United States. Between travels, I managed to edit a monthly bulletin of eight to twelve pages and a yearbook. I enjoyed my work immensely, especially the many opportunities for meeting new people and making new friends.

It was a new and fascinating experience to meet and get to know American women leaders in public life. Birth control would have had no meaning for me—a devotee of the prolific Chinese family—if Margaret Sanger, its leading exponent, had not taken the trouble to show me her clinic on the Lower East Side and explain her ideas. In the process of educating me, she made her statistics meaningful and convincing chiefly, I thought, because of her genuine qualities as a loving wife and mother.

Carrie Chapman Catt, a leader in gaining voting rights for American women, was elderly but still active when I met her. Like Norman Thomas, she was a pacifist and a wonderful speaker and crusader. She organized a National Conference on the Cause and Cure of War in Washington, D.C., and persuaded the Congress to hear some of the speakers. She selected me to represent Chinese students. I did not speak long and I was not the only one to be heard, but I believe the House of Representatives was somewhat surprised to be addressed by a Chinese student. In any event, it listened as attentively as it ever does to outside orators—particularly one who was so vehemently antiwar and pro-League of Nations.

For three years or so I had been speaking at international conferences and student conventions as a representative of the Chinese Student Movement. I had been elected president of the Tsing Hua and Nankai alumni associations and of the Chen Chih honorary fraternity. I had been published frequently in magazines and professional journals in the United States and China. My activities had attracted the attention of religious and educational leaders. John R. Mott, YMCA official and eventually a winner of the Nobel peace prize, recommended me to the national Y of China, whose head, David Z. T. Yui, a St. John's (Shanghai) and Harvard man, urged me to join his staff. Chang Po-ling of Nankai and Y. C. Mei of Tsing Hua wanted me to plan a joint institute of world affairs for them. Of course, my attachments there were very strong, and their project, which would involve seminars and summer sessions in world affairs, was a valuable one, certain to meet a need of students and faculty.

Finally, a search committee of the China Institute in America, to which the United States Congress had allocated a major part of the Boxer Indemnity funds, offered me the job of reorganizing it into an independent, self-supporting corporation. The proposal was made at a meeting with Dr. P. W. Kuo, the Institute's first director, and Dr. Stephen Duggan, founder and director of the Institute of International Education, who advised Dr. Kuo on many administrative matters. Dr. Kuo wanted me to be a channel of communication with Chinese students in the United States, and to help enlist Chinese and American volunteers to participate in China Institute's programs. Moreover, the grant from the China Foundation with which the Institute had been established as its American bureau was to terminate at the end of three years, and unless the bureau had become self-supporting by then it would have to close its doors. It was a challenging opportunity.

All three offers appealed to me in different ways. My first American connection had been with the Princeton student volunteers for Y work in Peking. Their friendship had meant a great deal to me and through them I had been able to know many Christian and world-oriented Americans and American organizations.

Fortunately, I was able to seek advice in person from both of my presidents and mentors of long standing, Chang and Mei, who happened to be in the United States. They pointed out that I had been

121

away from China for a long time and that it might be wise to return and reacquaint myself with conditions at home. Besides, they and Dr. Yui wanted someone to make a field survey of Chinese students in China and Europe, with reference to the problems of studying abroad. They thought I would be a good person to do it because of my familiarity with the problems of studying in America. After I had revisited China, they said, I would be in a better position to decide the direction of my career. They were pleased when I accepted this advice, and the International Y was good enough to defray my travel to China and Europe to visit Chinese student centers. The travel plan included a stop in Japan and visits to all important student centers in China and Europe from the autumn of 1927 to the spring of 1928.

During the stopover in Japan, I located Wang Mu-tien, a member of our May Fourth "dare-to-die" group, in Tokyo. He told me that the Japanese who favored friendly cooperation with China were losing influence and that the military clique which advocated conquering China by force was gaining the upper hand. The Japanese secret police had learned the names of the students responsible for exposing the Twenty-one Demands and engineering the May Fourth demonstrations, and succeeded in liquidating most of them. Wang knew personally how they had murdered some students during the recent earthquake in Yokohama.

In China I went first to Canton. A number of my old friends and schoolmates were in positions of importance there. K. P. Pao (MIT) was head of the electric power plant, K. C. Liu (NYU) managed the Bank of Canton, S. C. Chen (VMI) headed the Chemical Warfare Department of Whampoa Military Academy, Y. Y. Wong (MIT) was a leading architect who had designed the new municipal hospital and the Tung Shan housing development. Y. C. Koo (Harvard) was Commissioner of Finance. At Lingnam and Chung Shan universities, the several middle schools, and other institutions, more than eighty percent of the faculties, or administration, were American-educated students.

American Presbyterians and Baptists had made the first and most substantial contributions to modern educational and religious institutions, which, once established, they had turned over to Chinese leaders. L. Y. Li (Columbia) was president of Lingnam University. Y. P. Yao (Baptist Seminary, Louisville, Kentucky) and Miss Y. F. Liang (Richmond) were principals, respectively of Pui Cheng and Pui Tao academies. Secretary of the YMCA was H. W. Hsu (Chicago), of the YW was Y. T. Lao (California). And head of the time-honored Todd Hospital was Lois Todd, a Chinese orphan whom Dr. Todd had adopted and helped to graduate from Mount Holyoke College and Johns Hopkins medical school.

I found that some of my American friends had become old hands. They spoke the Canton dialect fluently, were "savvy" in their knowledge of Chinese politics, and talked freely about the ongoing struggle between the left and right wings of the Kuomintang for control of the party.

In November, 1927, the political atmosphere of Canton was cloudy. Sun Yat-sen, father of the Republic and Canton's cherished son, had died two years earlier, and while his significance as a symbol of China's aspirations was destined to grow, his immediate legacy appeared to be confusion in politics and contradiction in personal life. He had been disappointed by the failure of foreign governments, particularly the United States, to answer his plea for funds to underwrite his revolution, although in the post-World War I years most outsiders thought China too chaotic to be capable of self-government under any leadership.

Accordingly, he turned to Russia, welcoming its advisers and its military supplies. It was a quixotic move, for Russia's interests in Outer Mongolia and Manchuria were as imperialistic as those of any western power. But, like China, it was developing a revolutionary society in the face of international hostility and it did offer China concessions, sympathy, and support such as it had never received before.

Communism had a strong appeal for China's intellectuals, despairing at the disintegration of the country, as well as for the working classes, for whom it held out the hope of a better life. With advisers constantly at Sun's elbow, the KMT was reorganized into a highly centralized party, rather on the Russian model, and at the first national party congress in 1924 it admitted individual Communists as members. Communist cells soon were implanted in Sun's armed forces and government.

On my visit three years later it was evident everywhere how the efforts of the KMT-Communist coalition to organize workers and farmers had been influenced—and advanced—by the Russian advisers. Arriving late at night, I booked into the Y in the center of Canton and was awakened early next morning by loud shouting in the street. From my window I saw squads of people drilling in formations of ten. I went out to watch. The squads were shouting slogans as they marched about: "Down with the Powers"—meaning Europe—or, "Down with the warlords," meaning the local satraps who were filling power vacuums in the provinces with bandit governments of their own. "Let all the workers unite," cried others, singing to the tune of "Are You Sleeping, Brother John?"

I learned that the marchers all were workers, and the morning drill was one of many techniques for keeping morale high and communications open.

The city was reputed to have 276 labor unions, all very narrowly differentiated by craft. There were separate unions for peddlers of fresh or salted fish. Rickshaw men were divided into hard-wheel and rubber-tired unions, depending on the kind of vehicle they pulled. In each union, members were organized into ten-man cells, each with a number from one to ten. Rumor had it that the number ones of every ten cells formed a higher cell, and so on, so that unions were controlled pyramidally from top to bottom. Yet, in an emergency, each cell could go underground and function as a unit in itself.

By 1927, however, the rift between the KMT right and left was irreconcilably wide. Clashes had begun almost from the day of their joining, in 1924. Lines were drawn for what would become a twenty-five-year civil war—and men who were there at the beginning would see it end, among them Dr. Sun's two able aides, Chiang Kai-shek and Chou En-lai. Chiang, head of the Russian-inspired Whampoa

Military Academy, was instrumental in organizing and training the KMT army. Chou, a founder of the Communist party and, until the advent of Mao Tse-tung, its most important leader, had studied in France and Germany since our days in Nankai, and was particularly active in fomenting strikes.

While Sun lived, the antagonists maintained their uneasy alliance; his death removed the only restraint to their abiding conflict.

This was the moment of Chiang's ascendancy. At Sun's death he became generalissimo of the KMT's southern army. A year later he had achieved the crucial position of power within the KMT and begun to eliminate the left-wing opposition. With Canton and south China firmly in his grasp, he determined to bring the North and its squabbling warlords within the Nationalist fold. Hence, the Northern Expedition.

It was a great success. Province after province fell or rallied to his side. He established a Kuomintang Government at Wuchang. By 1927 China was very nearly one country.

But the internecine struggle continued. Chiang, with his armies in the field, was fearful that the Communists would take advantage of his victories to strengthen their position within the KMT, or take it over. In March his forces occupied Shanghai—all but the International Settlement—and, in a lightning stroke, launched a terrorist attack against the Communists. He sought to destroy them utterly and he nearly did. Chou En-lai, for one, escaped by a hair's breadth. The break between the former allies was complete and irreparable. Chiang, sweeping all before him, entered Peking and in 1928 became president of the Nationalist Government.

By then, incidentally, Chiang had taken one piece of Sun Yat-sen's advice. Sun, a Christian, had defied both church and tradition by marrying into the notable Soong family without divorcing his first wife. His bride was the second sister, Ching-ling. First Sister, Ai-ling, had married H. H. Kung, who, with Brother T. V. Soong, was banker and financial adviser to the Nationalist movement. A joke making the rounds had it that Dr. Sun's will called attention to the family's remaining sister and urged the comrades to compete "strenuously" for her hand. Chiang, also without divorcing his first wife, married Wellesley-educated Mayling, although only after pledging Mother Soong, a devout Methodist, to study the Bible and become a Christian. Mayling proved of inestimable value in gaining western support for her husband's Christian, pro-American, and anti-Communist regime.

My visit to Canton came in the aftermath of the Shanghai terror, but I witnessed two similarly violent incidents. A crowd of workers beat to death some Russian advisers for raising a hammer-and-sickle flag over the city and for issuing orders to Chinese comrades. Even more brutal and bloody was an attack by Nationalist soldiers on local Communists, many of whom were middle-school and college students.

Leaving Canton, I took a small coastal steamer to Amoy. Among the passengers were eleven overseas Chinese from Singapore who wore English suits. At Swatow, our first stop, we all went ashore to stretch our legs and stopped to watch a demonstration. The speaker was lambasting western imperialists and their Chinese "running dogs," who had been exploiting China for a hundred years. Noticing people in foreign clothes in the crowd, he pointed to them and snarled, "Look, we have some dogs right here." A threatening mob quickly surrounded us. Luckily, I was in Chinese clothes and was able to slip away. I cannot say for sure what happened to those eleven in English suits. Our boat sailed without them.

At Amoy I visited my friends at the university. T. H. Chen (Michigan) was dean of the Department of Business Administration; H. C. Chen (Tufts), professor of chemistry; C. Chiu (Teachers College, Columbia), professor of education, and C. S. Yu (Harvard), professor of meteorology. They showed me a unique product of East-West cultural mix. It was a Buddhist temple (*pu tu miao*) built and supported by overseas Chinese. It was located on a scenic mountain slope and built according to classical principles, except that modern reinforced concrete had been used. At the main hall we were greeted by ushers who showed us to seats among the worshipers. The abbot officiated.

The order of worship service followed closely that of a Protestant church. The congregation sang "Onward, Buddhist Soldiers" to the melody of the familiar western hymn.

At Foochow I expected to be met by my old Tsing Hua friend, David S. Hung, whom I had wired ten days earlier from Canton. David was not there, however, and I had a terrible time with the rickshaw men because I could not speak the Foochow dialect, China's most difficult. An American resident with—for me—the appropriate name of Mr. Christian came by and showed me the way to the YMCA, where I got in touch with David. My telegram came two days later. Foochow was also in the throes of political change, but American-trained returned students were in charge of nonpolitical matters. Hung (RPI) was commissioner of construction; W. Huang (Teachers College, Columbia), commissioner of education, and James Ding, president of Foochow College.

Sailing from Foochow to Shanghai I met four young men who could speak Foochow, Canton, and Peking dialects and who were well informed on current affairs. Two were Japanese, two Korean. They all had studied in the United States and were now visiting China. They told me that in Japan some students were for cooperation and equality among East Asian nations. They saw nothing but disaster for Japan if she should pursue her policy of conquest and colonialism toward Korea and China. The Government also embraced a liberal group which had some support from the intellectuals and the university people. But since the Washington Conference the military clique had determined on a policy of violence and had started to suppress dissension or opposition. My four acquaintances belonged to a Tokyo movement aimed at organizing students in China, Korea, and Japan to avert the looming disaster. They were pessimistic, and deeply discouraged by the climate in Japan and China. Many of their comrades in Japan had been liquidated or had had to go underground, and Japanese agents also were active in hunting down dissenters in China. They entertained hope that their movement would survive in the United States. They themselves felt threatened and would not reveal their identities to me.

They slipped away, still nameless, when the boat reached Shanghai.

Shanghai, at the end of 1927, manifested its peculiarity in more ways and to a higher degree than ever. It had become one of the world's busiest seaports, the largest city in China, and was divided into three parts governed by three separate authorities. It was policed and garrisoned by armed forces of fourteen foreign governments. Its most famous and conspicuous sections, the Bund, the International Settlement, and the French Concession, looked almost entirely European and were ruled by an international municipal council and the French consul general, respectively. The Chinese city remained a service part of the other two sections and a curiosity for tourists. Chinese nationalists pointed at Shanghai as a landmark of national humiliation because it was first conquered by Britain and subsequently had become the largest base for foreign economic exploitation and for foreign navies and armies. Ironically, the two foreign-controlled sections not only contained both foreign and Chinese big businesses, but also the headquarters of various conflicting political parties and revolutionary conspirators.

My friends told me of Shanghai's year of violent upheavals, including strikes, riots, and the blood purge of the Communists—the most famous account of which would be André Malraux's fictional *La Condition Humaine* (*Man's Fate*). Thanks to the Nationalists' agitation and intimidation, more and more representation was at last being given to Chinese in governing the International Settlement. My classmate at Tsing Hua, Dr. Chiao Wan-hsuan (Wisconsin), was chief justice of the Municipal Court, Cho Yen-ting (MIT) was commissioner of construction, and Chen Ho-chin was commissioner of education. Located in Shanghai were a number of well-known American-supported schools with famous alumni. Most of these schools, founded by Americans, were now headed by Chinese educators. William Sung (Chicago) was president of St. John's, Herman C. E. Liu (Teachers College, Columbia) president of Shanghai U., and Grace Yang (Mount Holyoke) was principal of McTyre School.

By rail I went from Shanghai as far north as Nanking, the

new capital, which still showed evidences of the recent fighting. My room at the Y had fourteen as yet unrepaired bullet holes. Many Government officials were working in makeshift and inadequately heated offices. But morale was high. Churches were crowded on Sundays. Students and teachers were optimistic about the future. People were surprised and favorably impressed by Chiang's soldiers, who did not plunder, but acted friendly and shouted patriotic slogans. Chiang declared that it would be the policy of the Nationalists to eliminate the warlords and, after a period of tutelage for the people, to establish a constitutional republic. He would shun the Soviet Union and cooperate with the United States and other western democracies.

Because there was fighting on land and along the railways, I again had to take a coastal boat to go north by way of Tsingtao, the former German naval base. It still looked very German in its public buildings and main thoroughfares. China had regained sovereignty over the area mainly through the good offices of the United States, but Japanese people and their vested interests were visible everywhere. The city, the railway, and the two schools were administered by some twenty-nine American-returned students, all of whom lived in fear that Japan would seize on any incident as a pretext to return.

When I got off the train at Tsinan, I had to walk between rows of soldiers with rifles and fixed bayonets. The city was under the control of a bad warlord, Chang Tsung-chang, who had imposed martial law. I went to stay with my friends at Chee Lu University (Presbyterian and Methodist), President Liu Shu-ming (Harvard) and Dean Cheng Chi-pao (Hamline and Columbia). The sympathy of the faculty, students, and populace was definitely with the Nationalists, which made General Chang doubly nervous.

It was homecoming to visit Tientsin and Nankai. My school had become a university with two campuses. The middle school at the original campus had grown and become coeducational since my time. The college and graduate school were located on a new campus at Pa Li Tai. President Chang Po-Ling remained the moving spirit and a close adviser to his students, who now numbered more than two thousand. The faculties consisted mostly of American-returned students. Among the members who later achieved distinction abroad were T. F. Tsiang, professor of history, and Franklin L. Ho, professor of economics. As a university, Nankai was making steady progress and its students continued to earn and uphold the reputation of being public-spirited and patriotic. But the general atmosphere in Tientsin was one of apprehension, because of the spread of civil war and the threatening posture of the Japanese. President Chang and the respected statesman W. W. Yen, recently prime minister, tried their best to evaluate and deal with the inroads made by communism and Communists among students and laborers.

I found Peking oppressive when I visited old friends and renewed my contacts at the different schools. Eight years earlier we students had been on the leading edge of progress. Now the Students' Alliance had been dissolved by the Government, and student demonstrations were being put down by force.

Whenever and wherever American-returned students met among themselves or with their American friends, however, there was gaiety and a breath of free air; also, more often than not, bridge and other card games and American refreshments. At the Y, and particularly at the American-returned student gatherings, there was spontaneous singing of college songs. (The Tsing Hua college song was composed by our American music teacher, Minta Stahl.)

Perhaps the most intimate center was the home of Mr. and Mrs. Y. C. James Yen, because he was an alumnus of Yale and Princeton and his wife was Alice Huie, one of the six popular Huie girls of New York. Jimmy Yen had been one of the Y secretaries working with Chinese laborers in France, and on returning to China after the war he founded the Mass Education Association. Its purpose was to enable the masses to read, so they could acquire enough basic knowledge in public health and civics to become better citizens of a democracy. A crash program was needed, because more than eighty percent of all adults were illiterate. While working in France, Jimmy Yen had found it feasible to educate his Chinese laborers in their free time, after work.

A similar situation, but greater problems, existed in China. The specialists on his staff were already evolving materials and tools for rapid and massive efforts, adaptable to rural areas first and then to urban areas. "One-thousand-character" basic Chinese was one of the results. With this efficient tool farmers could learn to read simple texts in a relatively short time. The staff was composed of people trained in the United States, such as C. H. Chuang (Teachers College, Columbia) in adult education, Paul C. Fugh (Cornell) in agriculture, C. J. Hsu (Iowa State) in animal husbandry, and Y. L. Mei (Chicago) in public health.

When several missionary medical schools decided to merge, the Rockefeller Foundation contributed funds for the new buildings and reorganization. Peking Union Medical College (PUMC) ranked high among medical schools in China and, indeed, in the world, because of its highly qualified faculty drawn from Harvard, Johns Hopkins, Columbia, and other well-known American medical schools, and also because of its up-to-date equipment and facilities. Harry Hussey, an American architect, had designed the buildings in Chinese classical style, but built them with modern reinforced concrete. It was really a medical center, thoroughly American in its administration and operation, consisting of schools of medicine and nursing and a full-fledged hospital. Roger S. Greene was the director. Dr. Y. Y. Tsu, formerly at St. John's (Shanghai), was the chaplain and also in charge of social work and service.

Like all other Government schools, Tsing Hua was under police surveillance. Faculty and students decided to confine themselves to academic work and to expand Tsing Hua into a superior institution, like MIT, for teaching science and technology. Almost next door to Tsing Hua was the newly built Yenching University, which became the largest American-funded school in China and had the most beautiful campus and buildings. The president, J. Leighton Stuart, personified an ideal bicultural person in religion, education, and politics. He started his career in China as a Christian preacher and theologian, yet his understanding of Chinese culture enabled him to achieve rapport with Chinese scholars like Wu Lei-chuan and Chao Tzu-chen. In education he consolidated the various Peking mission colleges into a great university. His familiarity with Chinese politics and officials served him well during political changes and with bureaucrats of different regimes. Much later, he was appointed ambassador to China, during the difficult Marshall mission which attempted, unsuccessfully, to mediate between the Communists and the Nationalists after World War II. He and his adopted Chinese son, Phillip Fu, exemplified our traditional filial relations.

I was happy to find at Yenching my old friend Dick Ritter and his wife Emma, Henry Chou, a professor of education, and his wife Ruth Huie, and William Hung—David's brother—who, more than any other Chinese, had helped Stuart to create a happy Chinese-American community at Yenching and a fruitful affiliation with Harvard. President Stuart and Vice-President Henry W. Luce were looking forward with optimism to turning over the administration to Chinese leaders and to promoting Chinese studies at Harvard. While there, I was particularly impressed by Hung's project of indexing Chinese history and classics, and T. C. Chao and Bliss Wiant's work on Chinese folk songs.

Field Marshal Feng Yu-hsiang, also known as "the Christian general," had been a friend of Teng Chieh-min, a Nankai schoolmate of mine. An excellent soldier and administrator, Feng had recently married Miss Li Te-chuan, a YWCA secretary and a friend of Mrs. Y. C. Mei. The Fengs had just returned from a visit to Soviet Russia, where they were favorably impressed with what they had observed. They stirred up heated discussions among their American friends and the American-returned students, who thought he and his wife should visit the United States before they decided on their future course of political action. In fact, Feng joined the Nationalist Government, although often opposed to Chiang, and served in a variety of posts.

Such controversies, taken together with the escalating strikes and public demonstrations of the Communists, awakened quite a number of Americans and pro-American Chinese in Peking to the need to know more about the Soviet system and its influence on Chinese students. As a result, I decided to visit the Soviet Union.

Because relations between Peking and Moscow were strained, it was not possible for me to plan my stay in Russia in advance. I was advised to book rail passage from Tientsin to Berlin with only a transit visa, and try to obtain the privilege of a stopover when I reached Moscow.

En route, I visited several educational centers in Manchuria, which remained an arena of imperialistic struggle between the Soviets and Japan. Manchuria consisted of the three eastern provinces of Fengtien, now Liaoning, Kirin, and Heilungchiang, which were brought into the Chinese empire in 1644, when the Manchus conquered China and established the Ch'ing dynasty. Since then the Manchus and the Chinese had blended through intermarriage and cultural assimilation. The acculturation process began with wide acceptance of the new dynasty and accelerated during the long reigns of the two great Ch'ing emperors, Kang Hsi (1662–1722) and Chien Lung (1735–1795), whose plaque hung over the entrance to my childhood home. These rulers were great scholars of the Chinese classics and patrons of Chinese art. They delighted in speaking and writing Chinese and they ranked high as calligraphers. Their example inspired their fellow Manchus, so much so that by 1928 there was no one in the Northeast who did not speak Chinese as his mother tongue. In fact, even the pure Manchus or half-Manchus I knew were proud to be Chinese citizens. Their sense of solidarity with the rest of China was greatly heightened by the aggressions of Russia and Japan.

I crossed the Great Wall and arrived at Feng Tien—later Mukden and today Shenyang—formerly the capital of Manchuria and now the home base of General Chang Tso-lin, already a legendary figure about whom Granduncle had told me a great deal. Originally the leader of a band of brigands, he nursed an ambition to become emperor of China. His bandits became famous for their false red beards and for their opposition to Russian encroachment on Chinese territory. The Red Beards sided with Japan in the Russo-Japanese War (1904–

5), but soon found the victors worse than the vanquished. Like most warlords, Chang found his interests sometimes coinciding with those of the national Government, but basically he was an autocrat who ruled Manchuria with a strong hand and defied Peking. His hostility to Japan was helpful to Chiang. Outwardly subservient, Chang covertly encouraged the Red Beards to raid any Japanese farmers who tried to settle in Manchuria. They were so effective that Japan was unable to colonize that thinly populated fertile land.

I traveled by the Peking-Mukden Railway, on which General Chang met his death, murdered by the Japanese, five months later. His inner circle of aides was already terribly apprehensive for his life. Japan knew that he had been frustrating its plans, but had so far temporized with him because of his power in the region. Japan decided to get rid of him when Chang joined hands with the Nationalists, whose avowed slogan was "Down with Japanese aggression and pro-Japanese traitors." I learned of these matters from two friends who were on Chang's staff, C. T. Tan (Nankai and Stevens), who was section chief, and C. J. Shih (Nankai and MIT), who was chief engineer of the China Eastern Railway. They took me to see Baron Gonsuke Hayashi, personal "high adviser" to General Chang. This elderly and experienced envoy was absolutely loyal to Chang and begged him not to make public the travel plan for his fatal trip from Peking to Mukden.

In Mukden and nearby cities I found my old friends C. K. Cheng (NYU), manager of the Bank of China, Y. J. Wang (NYU), secretary to Chang Hsueh-liang, Chang Tso-lin's son, later known as "the Young Marshal," and H. H. Pien (Brown), commissioner of Salt Gabelle, originally a French concession for collecting a salt tax, now an independent Government agency. Many American-returned students rallied around the newly established Northeast University because the region had become the land of promise for China's industrialization; it held our richest iron reserves, our most extensive virgin forests, and fertile soil for farming. The science and engineering departments had top priority and received sixty percent of the university budget. Paul Kwei (Chicago) was professor of physics and his wife, Helen Huie, taught mathematics. Y. P. Fang (Cornell) taught civil engineering, T. L. Yu (Columbia) chemistry, and T. M. Hsi (Colorado) mining.

Harbin was a frontier city on the Sungari, a tributary of the Amur River, at the heart of the ever-disputed border region. Russian influence was paramount, Japanese second, and American third, but barely visible. The two Y's here were the centers for students, and H. L. Hoag (Michigan) of the International Y and S. Y. Tung (Springfield) of the Chinese Y were very popular. A new department store, Ta-lo-tien, a crude but prosperous version of Macy's, had been established by H. Y. Chao (NYU).

At Man Chu Li, on the border between Heilungchiang and Soviet Siberia, there was a customs examination. A small group of assorted nationals was waiting. I met two Germans, who seemed to be frequent travelers of this route. They were giving advice to an attractive woman who looked Chinese to me. She had dark eyes and black hair and was wearing a fashionable Chinese gown. She spoke fluent Mukden dialect and English. The two seasoned travelers were suggesting that she should change to western garments because her passport was British, and that she should leave behind most of her books and papers. She changed into tweeds readily but discarded reluctantly only a small portion of her box of books and papers. When I passed through the border examination, the Russian official was still asking the young woman, a Miss White from London, to explain each document.

My German acquaintances explained that the Russians were still angry with the British and Americans because of their military intervention in Siberia in 1919, but had turned friendly toward the Germans, who were underdogs now, and also toward the Chinese, whom they wanted to win over to their side. Miss White had excited their suspicion because she looked Chinese but was not, and carried exotic books and papers. All very mysterious; she might be a spy!

The Germans knew Moscow well and helped me to get in touch with the Chinese secretary at Sun Yat-sen University. Unfortunately for me, he had been told by the authorities that I could not stop over, so he could only show me the Kremlin, the Museum of the Revolution, and the university, and those in a tearing hurry. The university had about three hundred Chinese students from the Northeast, of from fifteen to twenty years of age. They underwent a brief course of intensive study of the Communist revolution, were then divided into small groups and sent to different places to learn such skills as how to repair trains, run an electric plant, bomb a bridge, and so on. A few very able students were sent to a political institute to be trained in propaganda or to a military school to be trained as future officers.

In Europe, the International Y had given me introductions to Berlin, through the World Students' Christian Federation (WSCF), and the American Friends' Service Committee (AFSC). The Germans were most polite and hospitable. The nation seemed to pin its hope for recovery from the disaster of defeat on its students. A large number of student organizations had sprung up at the universities. Some of them befriended Chinese students. Dr. Reinhold Schairer, director of the *Wirtschaftshilfe der Deutschen Studentenschaft,* and H. C. Siao, chairman of *Deutsch-Chinesischer Kreis,* gave a joint reception in my honor, and I was surprised to see Herr Gustav Stresemann, who came early and stayed late in order to have a personal talk with me about students in China. Stresemann was then chancellor and foreign minister. He appeared at home with the students. In his private conversation with me he said he was very concerned that the students were hard up financially and were being torn apart by all kinds of political propaganda. With a smile, he asserted that he felt optimistic at seeing students of different nations fraternizing, and then drowned his worries in his favorite drink, Danziger Goldwasser. He went to the refreshment table and brought two glasses of that white liquor with sparkling gold specks. Offering a toast to the Chinese student movement, he asked me to bottoms-up with him. That was the first and last time I drank Goldwasser.

In Germany there were at least three hundred Chinese students at fifteen universities, two-thirds of whom were at Berlin. Chinese students in Germany kept in touch more or less, but there was no closely knit overall organization. The *Chinesischer Christlicher Studenten Verein* had a small membership, but its members had more frequent and wider contacts with students of other nations. Similar to American fraternities were the *Burgschaften, Landsmannschaften, Turnerschaften,* and *Gildes,* which did not admit Chinese students. The *Studentenhaus* and *Akademische Auslandstelle* resembled somewhat the International Houses in the United States. At the Munich Studentenhaus, Director Fritz Beck was very much liked by foreign students. He was an ardent advocate of One Europe and of internationalism, and he was among the first to be liquidated by Hitler's Storm Troopers.

In Belgium there were about a hundred and in Holland about a hundred and fifty Chinese students. In both countries the Government oversaw more strictly the admission and behavior of Chinese students. As a result, they were quite isolated from one another and from other Chinese student centers on the continent.

In Holland, I visited my friend, Professor J. J. L. Duyvendak, an authority on Chinese history, at Leiden University. While we were having lunch at the university commons, a young woman student with pigtails and carrying a dark green cloth bag of books stopped to greet the professor. He introduced me to her: She was Princess Juliana.

In the United Kingdom there were about four hundred and fifty Chinese students in London, forty-five in Edinburgh, fourteen in Oxford, eight in Cambridge, and five in Glasgow. About half of them were from British colonies and were Christians. They were a quite homogeneous group who had organized themselves into the Chinese Student Central Union of Great Britain and the Chinese Student Christian Union of Great Britain and Ireland. The former was larger, with many non-Christian students from China proper, and practically all members of the Christian Union were also members of the Central Union. They worked together in holding meetings and each issued a monthly publication, the Central Union putting out a forty- to eighty-page journal called "The Chinese Student," and the Christian Union a four-page news bulletin called "Chuan Pao." There were plenty of opportunities for Chinese students to know British people and culture, provided by organizations such as the British Council, the Sino-Scottish Society, and the International Clubs. At Oxford, Cambridge, and London Universities there were collaborations of long standing between British and Chinese scholars in Chinese studies and research.

In France there were about fifteen hundred Chinese students, half of them concentrated in Paris and a third in Lyon, the rest in twelve universities and technical schools. The French university system permitted open lectures and there were comparatively few scholarships available to Chinese students. Consequently, about half of them did not register and avoided paying fees.

In Paris there were at least six political organizations reflecting closely political divisions in China: the Kuomintang, Communist, Social Democratic, Young Nationalist, Anarchist, and Feng Tien (Mukden) clubs. The important binational organizations were L'Association Amicale et Patronage Franco-Chinoise d'Education, and in Lyon the Institut Franco-Chinois financed by the French Boxer Indemnity Fund. It administered scholarships for Chinese students, conducted courses in French language and civilization, and maintained a Chinese library.

There was no central social or religious organization for Chinese students in France. They gravitated to Paris from all parts and met at five Chinese restaurants in the Latin Quarter, two cafés on the Boulevard St. Michel, and two on the Boulevard Montparnasse. By the particular restaurant or café one could usually tell their politics. Occasionally, however, one faction would invade another's café to quarrel and fight.

The presence and the problems of the Chinese laborers in France during World War I did change the life of at least one Chinese student. The laborers and the student, in turn, ultimately changed China.

According to my old friends, Li Yu-ying and Loo Chin-tsai, who lived through World War I and the postwar years in France, the Chinese laborers discovered in France that labor could organize and make collective demands. The student, Chou En-lai, was being hunted by the police in Tientsin for his radical agitation and open defiance of the authorities. Under a pseudonym, he enlisted with the *Société des Étudiants-Ouvriers Chinois* and escaped to Paris. He worked in factories while learning French. During the next four years, he became well acquainted with the Chinese laborers and the French labor unions. His first-hand experience with their life and needs developed his remarkable ability to communicate with them and arouse them to action when he returned to China in 1923.

Back in the United States, I reported my observations to my advisers and undertook to decide which of my three job offers to accept. In a number of meetings and personal consultations, a consensus was reached that conditions both in China and the United States were very difficult for the launching of new projects. The projects in China that I had been asked to participate in were sponsored by well-established institutions, the YMCA and the two well-known universities. The troubles were political: domestic strife and foreign aggression. In the United States the idea of an independent China Institute seemed to have wide and enthusiastic approval and at least moral support. Finally, I made up my mind to cast my lot with China Institute, chiefly because I was already deeply involved in Chinese-American relations, and because by nature I abhor politics and war. I went to see Y. C. Mei to sound him out on my decision. He was somewhat disappointed at my declining his offer, but he pointed out that all three jobs were gambles under the circumstances. "Some young men start out seeing their careers only as stepping stones, without any dedication," he said. "I rather like to see you choose wisely some work you believe in and stick to it."

Part 4

An Experiment in Chinese-American Partnership

Thirty-seven Years of China Institute

Reflections

Thirty-seven Years of China Institute

China Institute owed its inception to John Dewey and Paul Monroe. At Columbia Dewey had a number of devoted Chinese students, among them Hu Shih, who so admired his teacher and friend that he named one of his sons Ssu-tu, meaning "Thinking of"—or, in memory of—"Dewey." In 1919 Hu invited Dewey to lecture at Peking University. Dewey accepted and was surprised to discover that a large number of faculty members and students had ample background information about America and could understand his lectures without interpretation. Hardly any faculty members or students at Columbia, with the exception of a few members of the Chinese Department, could understand lectures given in the Chinese language. Dewey was troubled by this absence in the Columbia community of a reciprocal understanding of China, and upon his return he discussed the problem with Paul Monroe, a professor of comparative education who was his colleague at Teachers' College and also interested in China. Monroe had been similarly concerned by the general absence in American school libraries of good books about China. Together they urged that something be done to disseminate authentic, basic, up-to-date information on China among university communities in the United States. Of course, funds would be needed for such a project. And funds became available when both of them were elected trustees of the China Foundation.

The second remission of the American Boxer Indemnity in 1924 endowed the China Foundation for the Promotion of Education and Culture. The first remission had reaped fruitful results beyond the expectations of its sponsors. Tsing Hua scholarships had aided a number of students who achieved excellent records and had begun to make significant contributions to the modernization of China and to China's relations with the United States. Some of them, like Y. C. Mei, Y. R. Chao, and Hu Shih, had already obtained world-wide recognition. Hence, it was comparatively easy for friends of China to obtain congressional approval for remitting the unclaimed balance of the indemnity, accumulated between 1908 and 1924, in order to establish a foundation for the promotion of education in China.

The Chinese and American Governments agreed to appoint a board of trustees (ten Chinese and five Americans) which would be self-perpetuating. Monroe and Dewey were among the first Americans. Although the funds of the Foundation were intended for use in China, the persuasive pair got the trustees to make an initial appropriation of $25,000 a year for three years, starting in 1926, to establish a bureau in New York City to see what could be done in the United States to accomplish the same objectives. The bureau was named China Institute in America, and its purpose was fourfold: to disseminate information concerning Chinese and American education; to promote a closer relationship between Chinese and American educational institutions through the exchange of professors and students; to assist Chinese students in America in their educational pursuits, and to help American students interested in the study of things Chinese; and to stimulate general interest in America in the study of Chinese culture. The first director appointed by the Foundation was one of its trustees, Dr. P. W. Kuo, president of Southeastern University.

On May 25, 1926, China Institute commenced operations under his leadership and met with an enthusiastic response in both countries. Soon the demands in the United States exceeded the capacity of its staff of four and its extremely limited resources. In China the supply-and-demand situation was even more disproportionate. Chinese colleges and universities were in dire need of more faculty and more laboratory and library supplies. The nation and Government were impoverished by constant warfare and not in a position to meet the growing needs of educational institutions. Public criticism arose over the sending of funds by the Foundation to America, which was accustomed and able to support its own educational and charitable institutions. The Foundation accordingly informed Dr. Kuo in 1927 that it could not provide funds beyond 1929, and requested him to consider reorganizing the Institute into an American corporation, so as to be financially independent.

Neither Dr. Kuo nor any member of his staff was ready to

undertake the work of reorganization and the necessary fund-raising, so he formed the search committee with which I was in touch prior to my visit to China in 1927. For over a year John Dewey, Paul Monroe, and Stephen Duggan interviewed prospects. Having failed to secure someone of standing comparable to that of Dr. Kuo, they decided to select someone from among the Chinese student leaders in America and finally offered the job to me.

On September 11, 1928, I began working as honorary secretary for reorganization. It was our intention that the new corporation should not be a local New York affair, but should have men and women members from all parts of the United States and China; and from all walks of life. While maintaining good relations with both Governments, we would not be beholden to either, nor would we involve the Institute in politics.

Our first task was to enlist a number of sponsors to assume responsibility for creating the corporation. Secondly, we needed a number of advisers to help develop the program of activities. Dewey, Monroe, and Duggan were well known in educational circles. Dr. Kuo, Dr. Sao-ke Alfred Sze, K. C. Li, president of Wah Chang Corporation, and C. F. Yau, president of Ton-ying Company, had the respect of Chinese communities in the United States. Under their guidance and with their introductions, I was able to interview many prominent American and Chinese leaders who were potential sponsors or advisers.

My most stimulating experiences were my meetings with outstanding people in the academic world. In Cambridge I was cordially received by Ada L. Comstock, president of Radcliffe College. I expected to find a businesslike administrator and a feminist, but was surprised to meet a beautiful woman who gave me the feeling that she had unlimited time to talk to me. George H. Chase, dean of Harvard Graduate School, went out of his way to be helpful. He introduced me to Professor Irving Babbitt, the well-known humanist who was interested in Chinese classics. Hearing that I was a descendant of Mencius, Professor Babbitt invited me to talk to his students about my ancestor's teachings. During the course of discussion, he warned that China should be wary of the differences between Confucianism and pragmatism, and he characterized John Dewey as "the greatest catastrophe in western thought since Rousseau." At tea after class, Professor Babbitt asked me to settle an argument between him and a Chinese student. He had commented in one of his lectures on the Chinese fondness for symmetry in patterns, symbols, and styles, noting that even shoes were exactly the same for both feet. The student had contradicted him; he had never known or seen any Chinese who wore identical shoes, and furthermore a university professor should not dispense such misinformation. I discovered that my countryman was from Shanghai and had never been outside that modern port city until he came to the United States. To his surprise, I told him that I had worn identical shoes until I was nineteen and that, in the rural districts of North China, people still made, bought, and wore shoes not shaped right or left.

Edwin R. A. Seligman, professor of political economy at Columbia, told me he had had the distinction of teaching a Chinese *chiu shih,* that is, a holder of a Chinese traditional degree comparable to the western Ph.D. Ch'en Huan-chang, who matriculated at Columbia in 1906, had become a *chiu shih* the previous year. He obtained his Columbia Ph.D. in 1911 with a two-volume dissertation on *The Economic Principles of Confucius and His School.*

In his first class with Seligman, Ch'en, according to Chinese custom, presented a written petition saying, "Your student wants to express his deep gratitude to you for accepting him in your class. He has traveled ten thousand *li* to sit at your feet in order to learn from you how high is Heaven and how thick is Earth."

"Heaven and Earth" is a Chinese expression signifying wisdom and erudition, but, of course, unfamiliar to Seligman, who responded with a chuckle, "Heck, I don't know about them myself."

I enjoyed Seligman's story, but had to say that he and Columbia did not win Ch'en to the American way of life. Returning to China, Dr. Ch'en advocated constitutional monarchy and the adoption of Confucianism as China's state religion.

144   Our search went into fields beyond academia, of course,

and in time we assembled people of quality whose dedication was everything we could wish.

One was Roger S. Greene, acting director of Peking Union Medical College, who was home on furlough. He had endeared himself to the Chinese people by recognizing the Republic of China when he represented the United States as consul general at Wuhan in 1911. At a small dinner I attended, a discussion arose about the folk virtues of the two nations. Hu Shih quoted an old Chinese proverb: "To embroider more blossoms on a brocade cannot be compared with giving charcoal to someone in a snow storm." "In New England," Greene said, "one regards a voluntary undertaking as more sacred than his bread-and-butter occupation." Greene exemplified this virtue and worked conscientiously for China Institute as adviser and trustee even after he contracted emphysema.

Another was Dr. Edward H. Hume, who originally had prepared to be a missionary in India. Yale student volunteers had adopted Changsha, in Hunan, as a base and pressed him into starting there instead for the purpose of organizing China's first modern hospital and medical school, later known as Hsiang Ya, or Yale-in-China. Hume soon mastered Chinese as his third language, after English and Hindi, and found time to study Chinese medicine, which he regarded as having a psychosomatic approach and as having discovered the circulation of blood much earlier than the West. Like Greene, he remained an active trustee of China Institute until the day he died.

The initial board of advisers had a broad representation of areas, professions, private organizations and public agencies, so that the Institute could function as a truly binational organization:

Julean Arnold, commercial attaché, American legation in China
George H. Blakeslee, professor of history and international relations, Clark University
Arthur E. Bostwick, librarian, St. Louis Public Library
Fletcher S. Brockman, secretary, Committee on the Promotion of Friendship between America and the Far East
Mrs. William H. Bush, a founder, American Friends of China

Chang Kia-ngau, governor, Bank of China
Chang Po-ling, president, Nankai University
K. P. Chen, managing director, Shanghai Commercial and
Savings Bank
Chiang Monlin, Minister of Education
John Dewey, professor of philosophy, Columbia University
Mrs. Julia Ellsworth Ford, author; director of China Society
Sidney D. Gamble, sociologist and author
Jerome D. Greene, chairman, Pacific Council, Institute of
Pacific Relations
Roger S. Greene, acting director, Peking Union Medical College
Raphael Herman, founder, Herman-Jordan Peace Plan
Hu Shih, professor, National Peking University
William Hung, professor, Yenching University
H. H. Kung, Minister of Industry, Commerce and Labor
Kenneth S. Latourette, professor of Oriental History, Yale
Frank W. Lee, Vice-Minister of Foreign Affairs
Herman C. E. Liu, president, Shanghai College
Y. C. Mei, director, Chinese Educational Mission in Washington
John R. Mott, president, World Alliance of Young Men's
Christian Associations
Frederick Peterson, physician and author
T. V. Soong, Minister of Finance
J. Leighton Stuart, president, Yenching University
Sun Fo, Minister of Railways
R. B. Von Kleinsmid, president, University of Southern California
C. C. Wang, director, Educational Mission in United States,
Ministry of Railways
C. T. Wang, Minister of Foreign Affairs
A. L. Warnshius, secretary, International Missionary Council
Ray Lyman Wilbur, Secretary of the Interior
Mary E. Woolley, president, Mount Holyoke College
W. W. Yen, former premier of China
Y. C. James Yen, director, National Association of the Mass
Education Movement, China
Samuel S. Young, Chinese consul general, New York
David Z. T. Yui, general secretary, Chinese National YMCA
H. C. Zen, director, China Foundation for the Promotion of
146   Education and Culture

September, 1928, to December, 1929, was a period of initiation for me, a transition from the idealistic student world into the world of cold realities. The advisers gave me introductions to prospective contributors and to people who could assist us in securing funds. I soon discovered, however, that the richer a person is the harder he is to see. An American millionaire usually protects himself; he has a staff or committee to screen letters of introduction and to interview callers; he takes a long time to decide whether his name can be used to sponsor anything. It took time for me to acquire in the American way a thick skin with which to turn aside the snubs I bore for our good cause.

But most of the time I was lifted up and cheered by people who sincerely loved the Chinese people and were willing to listen to what I had to say, no matter how busy or occupied they were. Finally, in January, 1930, we completed the reorganization and became a membership corporation with the following board of trustees:

Paul Monroe, director, International Institute, Teachers College,
Columbia, *president*
Mrs. W. Murray Crane, civic leader, *vice president*
C. F. Yau, managing director, Ton-ying Company, *vice president*
Ernest K. Moy, president, Association of Foreign Press
Correspondents, *secretary*
Edward H. Hume, executive vice president, New York Post-Graduate
Medical School and Hospital, *secretary pro tem*
D. E. Douty, vice president and general manager, United States
Testing Company, *treasurer*
Edward C. Carter, honorary secretary, Institute of Pacific Relations
Grover Clark, consultant on Far Eastern affairs
Stephen P. Duggan, director, Institute of International Education
Walter H. Mallory, executive director, Council on Foreign Relations
Henry Killam Murphy, architectural adviser to the Chinese
Government
Edwin R. A. Seligman, professor of political economy, Columbia
University
Mrs. F. Louis Slade, civic leader
J. A. L. Waddell, consulting engineer and adviser to the Chinese
Government

Below: Staunch friends of China Institute
enjoy a social cup of tea in 1954.
From left: Hu Shih, Elisabeth Luce Moore,
Mrs. W. Murray Crane, and K. C. Li.
Bottom: C. T. Loo, founder of the
educational fund bearing his name,
with author at China House in 1944.

Our treasurer, Dan Douty, was an expert on sericulture as well as a successful businessman. In financial matters he was strict and impersonal, but patient and fatherly in advising me, which was fortunate as I knew nothing about office management. At the first executive committee meeting, he reported a bank balance left by the parent bureau of $137.27, plus $39.46 in petty cash, with accounts payable of $150 in rent and $520 in salaries. He patted me on the back and remarked half facetiously and half admiringly, "Meng, only an amateur like you takes on such a job!"

Of course, Douty and I shared the prior knowledge and assurance that we had two generous underwriters, Mrs. W. Murray Crane and Mr. C. F. Yau. It was Dr. Sao-ke Alfred Sze who introduced me to Mrs. Crane, widow of Senator Crane from Massachusetts. When Theodore Roosevelt was in the White House, Senator Crane of the Crane paper fortune was a member of "Teddy's tennis cabinet." The Chinese legation was in financial difficulties and President Roosevelt asked Mr. Crane to bail it out. The Crane and Sze families became friends. Mrs. Crane was Josephine Boardman, a wealthy woman and civic leader in her own right. She was a collector of Chinese art and maintained a spacious apartment in New York. Mr. Yau, though descended from Hangchow ancestors, was born in Tsinan, Shantung. With his friend C. T. Loo and his brother-in-law Chang Ching-chiang he had participated in the revolutionary activities of Sun Yat-sen. Eventually, the three of them fled to France as political refugees. They introduced soybeans from the great cuisine of China to the great cuisine of France and, incidentally, sold Chinese antiques, acquired from French collectors, in Lyon and Paris.

Their soybean products flourished, and they each made a fortune from which they contributed generously to the republican revolution in China. Yau established the Tong-ying Company in Paris, London, and New York. It was my good luck that he also learned of my family's Shantung connection and came forward as a fellow provincial to befriend me when I first enrolled at Columbia. He and Mrs. Crane thus became staunch friends of the struggling China Institute

149

and pledged to defray the overhead of the new corporation until it found its financial feet.

How easy was it to launch a new organization and to raise funds for its support? In 1929 and 1930, not very. Shock waves from the New York stock market crash were traveling, with stunning effect, to all parts of the country. Bank failures and business bankruptcies caused massive unemployment. Long lines were already forming at soup kitchens, and sidewalk apple vendors, perhaps the best-known symbol of unemployment, could be seen on the streets of New York. Well-established charities were experiencing financial difficulties. Open-handed donors of the past found themselves pressed for funds and unable to give. Some charities closed their doors.

Americans in the 1930's had more good will than respect for Chinese. Most of them felt sorry for the foreign-exploited nation of underdogs and most church members would contribute money to save the souls of the "heathen Chinese." But when it came to talking about Chinese culture: "What is it? Why should we bother? If Chinese culture is any good, how come the Chinese nation is in such a terrible fix?" I got such responses even from some of my own people. In New York City, Chinese were known for their hand laundries and chop-suey restaurants. Adventurous tourists who explored Chinatown tended to spread sensational tales about opium and gambling dens. Chop suey and chow mein were all most Americans had tasted of Chinese cooking, and what little was known of Chinese theater and music was an opportunity for jokes at the expense of the inscrutable Chinese for enjoying noisy performances of dissonant percussions and screechy falsetto voices. Such cliché attitudes were what we hoped to change through a vigorous educational program at the Institute.

Broadway had never heard of Mei Lan-fang; neither had Mei Lan-fang known Broadway. But P. C. Chang knew both. He had studied under John Dewey and received his Ph.D. from Columbia, like Hu Shih. But Chang did not accept Dewey's pragmatism in toto and believed that while Chinese and western cultures had developed along different tracks, the two could be supplementary. Although his mind was in educational philosophy, his heart was in Peking opera.

The greatest authority on the Chinese theater in 1930 was Chi Ju-shan and the reigning superstar was Mei Lan-fang, a male artist who played female roles. Chi and Mei had collaborated in restoring classical stage properties and in reviving historical drama, and Mei's superb performances were greatly enhanced by Chi's erudition and direction. While studying at Columbia, Chang became familiar with Broadway, and he believed that American audiences could enjoy authentic Peking opera. He suggested to Mei and Chi an American tour sponsored by China Institute. Mei had long wished to visit America and was immediately agreeable.

Not unexpectedly, he scored a triumphant artistic success, being received enthusiastically in New York, Chicago, San Francisco, and Los Angeles.

The tour could also have been a great commercial success and have gained far more publicity for the Institute if Chinese customs had not prevailed over American business practices. Talks about the tour began in January, 1928, when I visited Chang, Mei, and Chi in Peking. Small talk began to get serious in August, 1929, when I received a letter from Chang and Mei that they wanted to open the engagement in New York at the auspicious beginning of the New Year of the Horse—that is, February, 1930. I consulted a number of Broadway experts and agents, and their unanimous opinion was that we should look ahead to the September-May season of 1930-31, because all important theaters already were booked for the upcoming season.

Messages went back and forth for the next three months, with Peking insisting, "Why not February? Do your best." Finally, we got a long letter from Chang explaining that Mei could not understand our inability to find a theater to suit his convenience. In China he could command any theater in any city at any time, and he had offers of $50,000 a month for tours of Japan. Furthermore, farewell parties had been given for him in Peking and Shanghai, and his fortune-teller had recommended February, 1930, as the most propitious month for him.

Fortunately, Chang assured me that Mei and his supporters were in a position to defray all expenses, including that of the agent, so that it was not necessary to guarantee a profit on the tour.

So it was that in February, 1930, Mei opened at the National Theater and took Broadway by storm.

"One of the strangest and most exciting evenings I have ever spent in a theater," wrote Robert Littell of the *World*. "Mei Lan-fang is one of the most extraordinary actors you have ever seen. An actor, singer and dancer combined, and combined so that you never see the boundary between these three arts.

"When you see him on the stage you . . . find yourself in some timeless region as lovely and harmonious as an old fairy tale. You forget that he is a man playing women's parts, in a curious but irresistible falsetto voice. You forget everything but the pictures he is making, as strong and delicate in every eloquent gesture as an old Chinese painting, very beautiful to look at for the costumes and poses alone, but also full of an immensely subtle dignity and repose.

"Nothing like this has ever been seen in New York."

"It is beautiful as an old Chinese vase or tapestry," wrote J. Brooks Atkinson of the *Times*. "You can appreciate something of exquisite loveliness in pantomime and costume, and you may feel yourself vaguely in contact, not with the sensation of the moment, but with the strange ripeness of centuries. Perhaps you may even have a few bitter moments of reflection that although our own theatrical form is enormously vivid it is rigid, and never lives so freely in terms of the imagination as this one does. The chief impression is one of grace and beauty, stateliness and sobriety, of unalloyed imagination."

"Lan-fang reaches across a barrier of language—and I have not seen anyone since Moissi* who reaches so far across," was the judgment of Richard Lockridge of *The Sun*. "What probably will strike you about the acting of China's greatest player will be its amazing universality. You will discover that, with glances and movements of the hands, with the undulating grace of his body and even with the inflections of his voice—he makes you understand most of what he

152

* Alexander Moissi was a prodigious European actor, contemporary with Mei, who appeared on the New York stage for several seasons although speaking only German. Famous for his performances in classical roles, he eventually mastered English sufficiently to play *Hamlet* on Broadway.

Mei Lan-fang, star of the Peking opera,
was a male actor who, in classic Chinese
tradition, played females. He is
shown here in the title role in Pa Wang
Pieh Chi—"The Tyrant's Concubine."
Horsehair whisk is one of many symbolic
stage props indicating personality,
mood, or action—in this case that the
character is riding a horse.

153

means, although you do not understand one of the sounds he utters."

For P. C. Chang, the tour definitely bolstered his ego and supported his theory that art of an entirely different culture could be appreciated intuitively.

China Institute did get some publicity and some new members in connection with Mei's tour. Among those who attended the performances were old friends of China who were glad to join us. I was moved by Mrs. John M. Gilbert, a widow and former student volunteer from Smith College, who contributed four gold coins which had been left her by her grandmother. Alvin S. Johnson, director of the New School for Social Research and formerly a student volunteer at St. John's in Shanghai, brought Henry Cowell, the prolific and controversial composer, who was a member of the New School faculty. Cowell was experimenting with arrhythmic tone clusters, mechanical sounds, and new techniques in piano playing, including banging on keys or strings with fists and elbows. Mei Lan-fang's performances directed his attention to Chinese music. He and Johnson requested me to organize a Chinese concert as a feature of the program being planned to celebrate the opening of their new auditorium. I told them that it would take too long and would be too costly to bring professional musicians from China for such a concert. So we agreed on a concert by amateurs living in the United States.

It took us almost a year to prepare. The performers all were college students. Their ancient and traditional instruments were *hu ch'in* (two-string violin), *pi pa* (lute), *yueh-chin* (moon guitar), *hsiao* (vertical flute), *ssu hu* (two double-string viola), *tung ssu ch'in* (bronze-string dulcimer), and *sheng* (mouth pipe organ). I played *san hsüan* (three string banjo), and a young woman from Barnard was our vocalist. The program consisted of ten items of instrumental solos and ensemble, two excerpts from Peking opera, and nine folk songs, all of which dated to the seventeenth century or earlier.

Henry Cowell informed the press that the concert was the first authentic Chinese music event in New York. It drew an audience that overflowed the New School auditorium on West Twelfth Street and received us enthusiastically. The critical response was kind and appreciative.

"There were solos upon plucked instruments of the banjo family," reported the *Times*, "upon bronze-stringed dulcimers, two-stringed violins, a primitive reed organ and flutes, as well as brief scenes from opera and folksongs. Inevitably, to the Western ear conditioned for counterpoint and harmony, the unison of the grouped instruments and their single melody lost much of the subtlety they hold for the Chinese, to whom the slight changes in modal scale must be more significant esthetically than they can be for us. But the tone quality, by its very strangeness, the crescendos of rhythm and the pronounced tonality of the pieces were interesting in themselves."

The *Times* also took notice of a little talk I gave to acquaint our audience with China's musical heritage. "Mr. Chih," it said, "spoke briefly of the great age of Chinese music . . . under the T'angs and its abrupt death as a scholarly art due to an edict forbidding its teaching. Since the seventh century it has existed only as an oral tradition among the people, and one can only guess what the imperial orchestra of the T'angs of more than four hundred pieces must have been."

Henry Cowell wrote me effusively: "I want to thank you for the magnificent occasion of Chinese music which required so much effort on your part. I was simply delighted with it, and the music moves me greatly, and stimulates me to joy and excitement. I was very pleased."

Leopold Stokowski was in the audience. Shortly after the concert he invited me to his home to talk about Chinese music. He lived in a splendid duplex on Park Avenue in the Eighties. The elegant drawing room had a formal concert grand piano as its centerpiece and lovely acoustics enhanced by a ceiling two floors high. We talked and I played my *san hsüan*—from eleven through lunch, until his wife reminded him that he must take a nap. Stokowski thought Chinese music could enrich western music and he wanted to lead a "music expedition" to China to do some firsthand investigating and collecting.

He had many questions about how to plan such an expedition. Later, Henry Cowell told me that the Maestro had obtained financial support for the venture from his friends, Mr. and Mrs. Gifford Pinchot. (Pinchot was first chief of the U.S. Forestry Service, a founder of Yale's School of Forestry, and recently had been governor of Pennsylvania.) The expedition had to be abandoned, however, because of the start of the long war between China and Japan in 1931.

These efforts to introduce Chinese theater and music to the American public were only a small part of China Institute's work, although our efforts were seriously hampered by the necessity of operating with minimal staff. I had a hard time even hiring that superb American invention, the woman secretary, because I could pay salaries only from week to week, without any assurance of job security. Eventually, however, my good friend Guy Harner, the personnel manager of the International YMCA, came to my rescue. He called to say he had found a suitable secretary for me. I went to his office at 347 Madison Avenue, where he introduced me to Virginia Runton, a secretary whom the Y had had to lay off because of a financial retrenchment. She struck me as a sincere young woman; I felt sure we would get along well. On the spot I offered her a job at $25 a week, subject to our having a sufficient balance in the bank! She accepted without hesitation and remained as my right hand from that day in 1930 until she retired in 1965.

She was a most impressive person from whom I learned that it was possible, and perhaps even natural, to be reliable, hardworking, and unfailingly good-natured, not only around the office clock, but also in off-hours, for thirty-five years. She took the work of China Institute to her heart. She never complained or, as far as I know, thought of finding a better job during even the most difficult years. As the Institute expanded, until it was dealing with thousands of students and required a large staff and many important men and women as trustees and associates, she acted as a most effective liaison, even though she had no China background and spoke no Chinese.

156 Another staff member who has stood by my side throughout

the years is K. Y. Ai. His principal job has been as registrar of the China Institute school, including the recruitment of our high-caliber faculty. Many of them already held distinguished university posts, but they never hesitated to add us to their heavy schedule and generously impart their wisdom to our students.

During China Institute's first two years, Dr. Kuo arranged a series of public lectures by well-known scholars. The celebrated Tai Hsü, a Buddhist monk, spoke on Buddhism; Henry K. Murphy, the designer of Yenching University, on Chinese architecture; P. C. Chang, entrepreneur of Mei Lan-fang's American tour, on Chinese philosophy, and my old friend Sidney Gamble, now a sociologist, on social conditions in Peking.

After I took over the work of China Institute, I found that members' interests centered on basic information and survey courses, rather than highly specialized subjects. Specialists on China were few, even in the teaching profession. It was necessary to cooperate with American school and college teachers to learn their needs as nonspecialists, and to design suitable courses and tools accordingly. Helen Parkhurst and Elizabeth Seeger of Dalton School and Elmina Lucke and Rachel Davis of Horace Mann were among the first teachers to help collect data on how much and what kind of background information American public school teachers had, and what books and other materials were available in school libraries. We finally designed two basic survey courses in Chinese history and culture which were open to teachers at a registration fee of $5 per semester. Our enrollment averaged eight to twelve per class, chiefly because the New York City Board of Education would not grant in-service credits for the courses. Even the prestige of John Dewey, as one of our sponsors, could not move City Hall in this matter.

My opportunity came when Fiorello H. LaGuardia was campaigning for mayor of New York in 1933. One of his campaigners was Irving Huie, son of the Reverend and Mrs. Huie, whom I have mentioned earlier. Irving had flown with Captain LaGuardia in a U.S.

Exquisite calligraphy celebrates
Sino-American friendship. Reading (from
right) Mei chu hua yung, it says,
in effect, that China melts with America
to forge a new alloy. Executed by Tai
Hsü, abbot of Pu Tu monastery in Amoy and
founder of Chinese Buddhist Society,
it was a gift to China Institute.

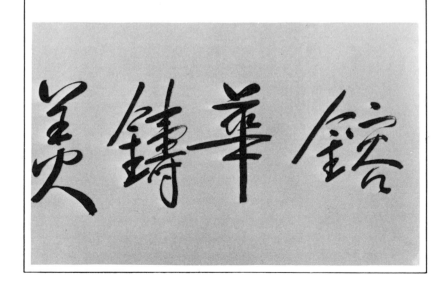

Air Service unit on the Italian-Austrian front in World War I. He had saved his captain's life in combat and the two became close friends. I presented my problem of teachers' credits to Irving who, in turn, introduced me to LaGuardia. Shortly after he was elected mayor of New York City I made an appointment to see him at City Hall. To my surprise, he remembered me and even my problem. He picked up the telephone and said to the superintendent of schools, "Dr. Wade, I want you to see Mr. Meng as soon as you can. He has a proposition which has my hearty approval." Then he put his feet on the desk and began to reminisce about Irving—"what a wonderful Irish-Chink he was"—and the war. (Irving's father was Chinese; his mother of Dutch ancestry. Holland predominated: Irving had brown hair, blue eyes, a husky build and a voice like a New York City Irishman's.) I winced at the ethnic pejorative, but LaGuardia was one of those rare individuals truly without prejudice. He emanated instant sincerity and conviction, and I was impressed by his willingness to talk to a young nobody as a friend.

Shortly thereafter, Dr. John E. Wade granted China Institute the privilege of offering in-service credit courses for teachers, and we were soon recognized as the nation's first and largest school of Chinese studies for nonspecialist teachers.

China Institute was now a membership corporation. As its executive director, it was imperative for me to launch a membership campaign and, at the same time, to begin organizing other educational programs. I was deeply concerned with the problems of Chinese students in America, many of whom were in need, while their local and national organizations were demoralized by factional strife.

What had awakened the Chinese in the United States and their American friends was Japan's attack on China, which brought the Institute new problems, but also brought instant and enthusiastic support for its programs. China and the Far East became front-page news when the Kwantung Army—Japan's permanent military force in Manchuria—manufactured an incident on September 18, 1931, which served as an excuse to occupy Mukden and eventually the entire region.

China's Manchurian troops were no match for the highly trained and disciplined Japanese. Chiang Kai-shek's Nanking Government made no move to aid them. Within a few months Manchuria was declared independent of China, renamed Manchukuo, recognized by Japan, and nominally ruled by Henry Pu-yi, deposed Manchu emperor of China now, by persuasion or coercion, Japan's puppet.

Chiang also stood by when the Japanese, irked by the effectiveness of a Chinese people's protest boycott emanating from Shanghai, sent naval forces into the harbor to bomb and shell the densely populated Chapei district. Local Chinese troops offered stiff resistance, but Japan landed an invasion force that took the city. Although western mediators achieved a withdrawal, Japan's aim was clear: conquest of China.

The Tokyo Government sent speakers and writers to the United States to explain and justify its actions. They flooded the lecture platforms and the press, trying to create the impression that the Chinese did not know how to govern themselves and needed Japan to maintain peace and order for the benefit of all concerned nations, including the United States.

Oddly, even Pearl Buck's fictional best-seller, *The Good Earth,* a book sympathetic to China if there ever was one, became grist for the pro-Japan mill. Published in 1931 by the John Day Company, the book contained vivid descriptions of the chaotic life of China: civil strife, famine, floods, the ravages of opium addiction, and so forth. It was an immediate hit, won a Pulitzer prize for the author, and tided the publisher financially over an otherwise unsatisfactory Depression year. But because Mrs. Buck had lived in China as the wife of Professor John Lossing Buck of Nanking University, *The Good Earth* was offered by pro-Japanese speakers and writers as authoritative evidence of China's disintegration! At a Waldorf-Astoria meeting honoring Mrs. Buck in 1932, I told the guests that the book was a moving story, beautifully written, but that it should be understood as fiction, not history. Even so, for many years, a number of people continued to feel that Pearl Buck had done China a disservice with her book.

When the Chinese community saw the need to counter such misinformation, it asked the Chinese Chamber of Commerce to take action. Honorary president of the Chamber was our China Institute trustee, K. C. Li. He was from Hunan province, had studied mining at the London Royal School of Mines, came to New York to work for Wah Chang Trading Corporation, and in twelve years had risen to the presidency. Wah Chang controlled much of the world's supply of tungsten and antimony. Li and I raised funds to enable a few Chinese speakers and writers to counter the Japanese.

We did not have enough money to employ professionals or bring speakers from China. I had to appeal to the few Chinese scholars and students who were qualified and willing to help. Two things did work in our favor. One was the usual generous American sympathy for the underdog, which in this situation China certainly was. The other was the inability of many of the Japanese to express themselves fluently in English. Coupled with a stiff, humorless platform manner, this often meant a lack of rapport with audiences. I remember an instance in Cleveland when I debated one of Japan's speaking team at a meeting sponsored by the Adult Education Association. The chairman was Newton D. Baker, a former Cleveland mayor and Secretary of War in Woodrow Wilson's Cabinet. My train from New York was late. The meeting was already in progress in the grand ballroom of the Hotel Cleveland, which was connected to the railroad station, when I arrived. The shortest route to the dais was through the pantry, but when I dashed through the door the headwaiter, thinking I was one of his crew, shushed me and held me back until I was rescued by the chairman. When it was my turn to speak, I mentioned that I had almost lost an argument with the headwaiter. The audience roared with laughter and seemed to warm up to my side.

Shortly thereafter, George P. Brett, Jr., president of the Macmillan Company, invited me to write a book presenting China's side of this important international issue. Macmillan was planning to publish *Japan Speaks* in April and we agreed that it would be in China's interest to

161

have *China Speaks* come out at the same time. *Japan Speaks* had been written by K. K. Kawakami, a veteran Japanese news correspondent in Washington, and would have an introduction by the Japanese prime minister, Ki Tsuyoshi Inukai. Brett had read articles on the Sino-Japanese situation I had written for the New York *Evening Post* and had attended one of my public debates, as well as what was really more of a discussion with Baroness Keichi Ishimoto, the Japanese feminist, who felt that birth control was a better answer to Japan's population pressures than conquering Manchuria. (My affection for large Confucian families notwithstanding, I heartily agreed with the Baroness!) Brett seemed confident that I could do the job. In any event, it was already February and I would be unable to find anyone better known and more able in the time remaining. With foolhardy optimism, I signed a contract on March 3, agreeing to deliver the finished manuscript April 1. During those twenty-seven days I had to attend to the office and prior appointments, so my fond recollections of writing *China Speaks* are two: twenty-seven sleepless nights drinking potsful of black coffee, and meeting James Michener, then George Brett's assistant, who copy-read my manuscript.

I met my deadline with a text that ran 221 printed pages, or some 50,000 words. Produced as it was in such a tearing hurry, it was perhaps not the best writing I have ever done, but I felt strongly that the tidal wave of Japanese propaganda had to be refuted wherever possible, and I was determined that *Japan Speaks* should not have the field to itself. *China Speaks* appeared simultaneously, as planned, in April—priced, as books then were, at $1.50!—with a sound and helpful introduction by W. W. Yen, China's minister to the United States and chief delegate to the League of Nations.

Both were reviewed by George E. Sokolsky in the New York *Times* Sunday book section on May 1. In those days, before his evolution into a vehemently right-wing columnist and scourge of communism for the Hearst papers, Sokolsky was a sympathetic student of Far Eastern affairs and, in fact, married to a Chinese wife.

He did not find much to choose between our arguments,

and, indeed, what observers of the day liked to think was hardheaded practicality and judicious realism dominated most judgments of the fateful but little-understood struggle developing in Asia. In those Depression-ridden years no western nations were eager to become embroiled in regional squabbles that could lead to war.

Of Kawakami and me, Sokolsky said: "Both represent specific attitudes of important groups in their own countries: Mr. Kawakami of the liberal nationalistic Japanese, Mr. Meng of the intensely nationalistic student element in China. Both men are able students of Oriental politics and both are frankly propagandistic in their mission. The books then reflect quite accurately the difficulty of finding a solution for Sino-Japanese controversies, for all the facts are in conflict, all the purposes are in opposition."

The introduction by Premier Inukai in support of a bellicose position was a subtle stroke, for he had been a friend of Sun Yat-sen and Chinese nationalism for some thirty years, and an advocate of peaceful relations with China. "When Sun Yat-sen and his associates were exiles among us," he wrote, "hounded by Chinese emissaries and threatened with deportation by our government, I shielded them. . . . For a time Sun Yat-sen lived with me. My house was a secret meeting place for the revolutionists. Often they shared my food and clothes and even my meager income. None could have been more jubilant than I when the new republic sounded the knell of the Manchu dynasty."

All true. The irony and the tragedy was that even as these words were circulating in Kawakami's book, China's good friend Inukai was assassinated by Japanese extremists. The deed overturned parliamentary government in Japan. The army seized power and plunged onward to World War II.

China Speaks was given widespread attention in the United States, China, and Europe. As a result, my invitations to lecture soon doubled. In all of my talks on behalf of China, I think perhaps my most prescient remark was made at an antiwar demonstration at the Brooklyn Academy of Music, under the auspices of the Socialist Party of Greater New York, shortly after the assault on Shanghai. A Japanese graduate of Cornell, then working as a chemical engineer in the United States, had just pleaded—rather fatuously, I thought—that Japan was no more imperialistic than anyone else. On the contrary, I said. The Japanese people have been told for twenty years that they would become world leaders through economic supremacy. "To achieve this leadership," I cried, "the people were told it would be necessary to seize Manchuria. Now it is Shanghai. *Later it will be the Philippine Islands, then the Hawaiian Islands,* and finally the Japanese people will be told that they have the right to migrate to California."

They never made it to the States, but for a ten-year forecast I was more accurate than I dreamed!

After I spoke to a special convocation at John B. Stetson University in DeLand, Florida, the Chamber of Commerce invited me to visit the home of my countryman, the late Lue Gim Gong, the legendary "Chinese Plant Wizard." Lue had come to live and die here during a peculiar period and amid unusual circumstances in the history of Chinese-American relations. His story is worth a digression.

The aggressive western imperialism that opened China to commercial exploitation in the 1840's and fifties also gave impoverished Chinese a tempting view of the outside world. Thousands of Cantonese, in particular, began to emigrate to the gold fields and railroad camps of California. "Old Gold Mountain" (Chiu Chin Shan) as San Fransisco, their port of entry, was called, was not the promised land, although many stayed and some thrived. Chinese contract laborers were paid far less than their white counterparts, which, ironically, became an advantage when Civil War veterans and European immigrants found themselves unable to compete for the jobs. Anti-Chinese feeling ran high, however, and there were political agitation and labor riots to limit the influx of Orientals.

Lue Gim Gong arrived in San Francisco, a twelve-year-old, in 1870. Encountering hostility in California, he continued East and found a job as a strikebreaker at the Model Shoe Factory in North Adams, Massachusetts. Frances Burlingame—"Miss Fanny"—a spinster school teacher and daughter of a prosperous merchant, saw him one day on the street, shivering with cold. She learned that he had been discharged from the factory without food or lodging, and also that he had tuberculosis. She took a friendly interest in him because her cousin, Anson Burlingame, had served as President Lincoln's special envoy to China, and so earned the regard of his hosts that he was appointed chief of a Chinese Government delegation to visit western nations and conclude treaties. Miss Fanny took Lue home, nursed him, and coached him in secondary-school subjects. He passed the entrance examination for Harvard College, but could not attend because his health worsened; he returned to Canton, where the climate was milder. By now, however, Lue was so Americanized that he and his family could not stand each other. In a letter to his adopted mother Fanny, he reported that he had been severely punished for daring to tell his grandfather not to spit freely because it spread TB germs. When Miss Fanny inherited a farm in DeLand, and decided to retire there in 1886, she brought Lue back to live with her.

He soon became the talk of DeLand. Townspeople noticed that in front of the farmhouse there grew pillar roses from one trunk with red blossoms on one branch, yellow on another, and white on a third. A fruit tree bore three kinds of fruit: oranges, lemons, and grapefruit. Miss Fanny died in 1903, bequeathing the farm to Lue, who concentrated his efforts on improving the citrus trees of Florida. He came from the orange-growing section of China and had learned from his parents the technique of grafting and cross-pollination. At the time, California oranges were driving Florida's off the market because the latter rotted quickly after ripening. Lue evolved a variety which would retain its juiciness for as long as three months after ripening. He refused to patent his invention and permitted it to be propagated freely by all the commercial nurseries of the state. The American Pomological Society named the variety the Lue Gim Gong Mediterranean Valencia Orange, and awarded him the Wilder Medal for scientific achievement benefiting the American people.

Lue died in 1925. When I visited the farm there were only

two survivors: an old gray horse named Fanny, and a Negro caretaker, Johnson. Johnson gave me a snapshot of Lue and told me a great deal about him. Lue could also handle animals. He had trained two horses and a rooster to say grace with him before each meal. He called his oranges Christian-Confucian Golden Rule Oranges and permitted anyone who wished to pick freely all he could carry. He always told visitors how much he owed to Christ and Confucius, and to the generosity of Mother Burlingame.

China appealed to the League of Nations, accusing Japan of duplicity in creating Manchukuo, and scorning Pu-yi as a puppet of the Japanese army. The League appointed the Lytton Commission to investigate on the spot. Its findings fully substantiated China's charges that Japan was engaging in unlawful conquest, and urged that Manchuria be returned to Chinese sovereignty. Japan replied by invading Inner Mongolia, penetrating China south of the Great Wall, and quitting the League.

The world was confronted with a crisis of choice between forceful and peaceful means in resolving international disputes. It did not really resolve the crisis, but at least one international figure emerged from the confrontation with honor: Henry L. Stimson, then President Hoover's Secretary of State.

Stimson (Yale 1888) had already achieved distinction as a statesman, having served as Taft's Secretary of War and as governor general of the Philippines during the Coolidge Adminstration. As Secretary of State, he enunciated what came to be called the Stimson Doctrine, the principle of nonrecognition of territories and agreements achieved by aggression, shortly after Japan's initial plunge into Manchuria.

Stimson retired from politics after the Democratic election victory of 1932 and resumed the practice of law in New York. I went to see him several times, eventually persuading him to become a trustee of China Institute, and always had interesting conversations with him. Among the matters we talked about was the rise and decline of Woodrow Wilson, with particular reference to Wilson's ideals and how they became compromised at the Versailles Conference.

When W. W. Yen passed through New York, I was instrumental in bringing these two elder statesmen together for two long interviews in Stimson's apartment in the Hotel Pierre. Stimson believed that Japan was bent on aggression but he did not see any way for the United States to aid China directly. The American people, however, should be made to see, he thought, that it was morally wrong for America to sell war supplies to Japan, which enabled her to wage total war on China, including the bombing of a defenseless civilian population. Soon afterward, Stimson headed just such a campaign as chairman of the American Committee for Non-participation in Japanese Aggression.

While teaching at the summer session of the University of Virginia in 1933, I received a letter from Senator Elbert D. Thomas, of Utah, inviting me to call on him when I passed through Washington. Senator Thomas had made a study of state control agriculture in Chinese history when he was a Mormon missionary in Japan. He traced its development from Mencius' advocacy of state control of forests and fishing to the state socialism of Wang An-shih, during the reign of Shen Tsung (A.D. 1068–1085) in the Sung dynasty, when the government imposed income taxes, aided farmers with loan and storage facilities, and nationalized interprovincial commerce. When I finally met the Senator, he introduced me to Secretary of Agriculture Henry Wallace, with whom he evidently was working closely in planning agricultural programs for the New Deal. Wallace also knew a great deal about Chinese grain and vegetable crops, including the soybean and t'ung oil, and the research efforts of F. H. King of Wisconsin in Oriental soil management, and the botanical findings of E. H. "Chinese" Wilson of Harvard.

In spite of Japan's attacks and occupation of the Northeast, Chiang Kai-shek steadily consolidated his Nationalist Government at Nanking and, with armed force or political deals, eliminated or won over all the military governors and warlords. Chiang proclaimed himself Sun Yat-sen's successor and pledged the nation to take three basic steps to realize the goal of the Republican revolution: to eliminate all independent warlords (the *tu chün*), provide political tutelage for the people under the Kuomintang, and to implement constitutional democracy. American-trained men were put in positions of importance, but there were not enough American-returned students to meet the demand. The problem of training more students in the United States became a question of national urgency.

Until 1930, there was no coordinated policy for sending Chinese students abroad. Some students traveled on their own resources, some were sent by Christian mission boards, some won scholarships through their academic achievements. Now heated discussions arose in governmental and educational circles whether or not particular needs or projects in China should determine students' subjects of study. Some argued for limiting subjects to science and technology, and for sending abroad only graduate students. Some favored freedom of choice and opposed any form of governmental control.

An important figure in these debates was Y. C. Mei, the president of my alma mater, Tsing Hua, which by now had expanded into a university. In his student years Mei achieved highest honors when he graduated from Nankai Middle School and was Number One in the first competitive examination for a Tsing Hua scholarship. He studied electrical engineering and graduated with honors from Worcester Polytechnic Institute, in Massachusetts. He caught the spirit of the American Student Volunteer Movement, was treasurer of the Chinese Student Christian Association in America, and pledged to give one year of service to the YMCA of his native city, Tientsin. In 1915 he went to Tsing Hua to teach mathematics and physics. As a student I elected his classes in both subjects for three years.

Mei was of medium height, had a medium low voice, medium handsome looks, and a neat appearance. In class his movements were deliberate. He lectured slowly, making sure that the dullest student understood a difficult point, and was always willing to see his students after class to visit and talk shop. He lived his private life in the same methodical way. Even in playing tennis, he covered the court with medium speed and returned shots with medium force. In a personal or public controversy, he pleasantly considered the conflicting points of view and attempted to minimize emotional outbursts. His most famous saying was, "Perhaps. Possibly. It may be so. But, nevertheless, it could turn out to be otherwise."

Mei married the first of the three Han sisters, who were all brilliant and beautiful. He was himself the eldest of three brothers, all of whom attended Nankai and Tsing Hua. Y. L. Mei (M.D., Rush) was an athlete and physician. Y. P. Mei (Ph.D., Chicago) was president of Yenching and then professor of Chinese philosophy at the University of Iowa.

In 1933 President Mei appointed me honorary director of the Chinese Educational Mission in the United States to look after Tsing Hua scholarship students, to study the problems of all Chinese students in the United States, and to make recommendations. During the next three years I visited 288 colleges and universities in forty-six states and met with some seventeen hundred Chinese students.

As individuals, Chinese students were comparatively more serious than Americans in their social contacts and studies. Most of their troubles were financial, stemming from delayed or inadequate remittances from home; there also were isolated cases of intermarriage which caused painful difficulties for the partners. At the University of Cincinnati Medical School a Chinese woman married an American classmate. Her two brothers threatened to disrupt the wedding. A Chinese honor student at the University of California at Berkeley, barred by state law from marrying an American, brought his sweetheart east, to a less restrictive state, for the ceremony. A Chinese student in Tennessee married a Negro girl, and both they and their children were required to live in the Negro section of town and sit in the seats reserved for Negroes on trolley cars and trains.

What educators in China wanted to know was which schools were best for which subjects. They also were concerned whether—and how much—"Americanization" would "denationalize"

Chinese students and diminish their usefulness on returning home. I never felt that an American education would denationalize Chinese students. As a matter of fact, I felt that it would be beneficial for China to send some of its youth abroad to be educated not only in science and technology, but in the American way of life. I urged this both in spoken and written reports.

In 1936 I was asked by Tsing Hua and the Ministry of Education to report and confer in person, and to make a survey of the effectiveness of American-trained men in China, just as I had in 1928.

En route from New York to San Francisco, I acted as honorary interpreter and aide to General and Madame Chiang Po-li. General Chiang was a high military adviser to his cousin, Chiang Kai-shek. He had studied military science in Germany and Japan, and he and his Japanese wife were visiting America for the first time. My old friend and schoolmate, the Chinese consul general in New York, James T. C. Yu, introduced me for the express purpose of inducing me to accompany them, since they could not speak a word of English. I enjoyed their company during the days on the train and was delighted at the opportunity to learn something about military affairs from the General. Incidentally, one popular Chinese impression was confirmed for me by what I saw of Madame Chiang. It is male wisdom that a French girl makes the best playmate, a Chinese the best mother, and a Japanese the best wife. Madame Chiang personified constant thoughtfulness and responsiveness to her husband's every wish, and outdid all the charms and virtues expounded in our *Book of Conduct for Women (Nü Chieh)*, which was written, appropriately enough, by a woman—Pan Chao (A.D. 50–112), who also completed her inprisoned brother's great history of the Western Han dynasty.

A shipping strike on the Pacific Coast delayed my sailing. A fellow victim of the delay was Hu Shih. We spent many of our waiting days together. We were invited by former President Herbert Hoover to his town apartment to listen to presidential election returns over the radio. He was an imposing man, tall and strong, with an air of self-confidence and solidity to match. He still seemed to smart from the general criticism of his Administration; he was sure that the American people would eventually view his efforts favorably, and he was satisfied that Franklin Roosevelt had proved to be better than he had expected. He strongly believed that war remained the most serious threat to civilization. He hoped that Stanford University—nodding to its president, and his former Interior Secretary, Ray Lyman Wilbur, who was also among the guests—would lead in the study of war and peace through the materials being assembled at the new Hoover Library.

Eventually we sailed from Victoria, British Columbia, on the *Empress of Japan,* stopping en route in Yokohama. There and in Tokyo, Hu Shih and I met a number of Japanese liberals, including the former ambassador to China, Yoshizawa, and Professors Abe and Akagi of the Imperial University. The liberals and their party had suffered catastrophes since the beginning of the Manchurian adventure. While the Japanese people had so strongly supported some liberal leaders that they became prime ministers and cabinet ministers, the ultraright militarists had dared to murder four of them and to destroy their party headquarters. There was no power in Japan to stay the military now.

Japanese students generally were for friendly relations with China. They joined the liberal leaders and a few liberal journalists on a good will tour of China that autumn, but found the Chinese people evermore fearful of Japan. Even the pro-Japan clique and the Japanese-educated Chinese were turning deaf ears to their pleading. In contrast, the American-educated Chinese formed a tremendous force for good will toward the United States. We and the Japanese discussed and compared our viewpoints frankly, but reluctantly concluded that it was so late that little could be done to avert the probability of war. One source of trouble was that the Japanese Government had been exploiting Chinese students for political ends for years. It had sanctioned unofficially open admission for Chinese students, who were awarded diplomas without fulfilling the standard requirements, providing they promised to support Japanese Government policy toward China. The

171

Japanese police closely watched Chinese students and acted promptly to deport or otherwise thwart those who were considered noncooperative or anti-Japan.

In China the Ministry of Education had planned that I should visit centers of reconstruction in fourteen provinces. The newest and most promising center was located in the Northwest, where irrigation projects to prevent Yellow River floods and afforestation to reclaim desert lands were in progress under the direction of American-trained engineers. I went to the railway office in Nanking in early December, 1936, to buy a ticket for Sian in the Northwest. I was told that no Sian tickets would be sold to civilians until martial law was lifted. I had already notified friends or correspondents and made appointments in Sian and many other centers, and it would have been complicated to make changes at the beginning of my tour. When the Ministry of Education gave up trying to obtain the desired ticket, I suddenly thought of General Chiang Po-li and went to see him. He seemed tense and preoccupied but listened patiently while I explained my problem. He said that martial law had to be strictly enforced, since an extreme alert was in force in the Northwest. There was no possibility of making an exception to help me. He pondered a long while without saying anything or looking at me. Then he went into his aide's office and came back wearing a more relaxed expression. "Now I can reciprocate for all you did for me in the United States," he said. "I am flying to Sian around the eighth and there will be room for one more man. I will appoint you as one of my personal staff and take you there."

Few in Nanking knew what made Chiang Po-li so tense. On the old German Junkers that flew us north, he told me that, against his advice, Generalissimo Chiang Kai-shek had gone to Sian to urge Chang Hsueh-liang, commander of the Army of the Northeast, to prosecute his campaign against the Chinese Communists with greater vigor. Chang—the "Young Marshal," as he was called—was the son of the Manchurian warlord Chang Tso-lin; Chiang Po-li felt him to be a man of doubtful loyalty and thought it unsafe for the Generalissimo, with only a small retinue, to visit him in his Sian headquarters. Chiang Po-li said he was going to try his best to persuade Chiang Kai-shek to return to Nanking.

The Communists obsessed the Generalissimo. He had driven them from their mountain stronghold in Kiangsi province, where they had regrouped after the Shanghai terror, by a resolute military effort in 1934. But after the famous Long March they had reestablished themselves at Yenan, in Shensi, where their growing military strength, their agrarian reforms and other benefits for the peasants, and their ardent efforts to oppose the Japanese invaders all were infuriating to Chiang Kai-shek. He was determined to extirpate them, and because of their location in the Northwest he had given the task to the Young Marshal. Although Chang had done little to stem the Japanese on-slaught, he was not eager to fight his own countrymen while a foreign enemy was within the gates. Chiang had arrived to see whether this was reticence or recalcitrance, and, in any event, to deal with it.

As our plane approached Sian from Cheng Chou, in Honan province, we flew over the central plain of the Yellow River valley, the cradle of civilization, and there arose in my mind many legends re-membered from my childhood regarding the Great Wall; Shih Huang-ti, the first Ch'in emperor who made Sian his capital; the famous T'ang poet Li Po, and the beautiful imperial concubine Yang Kwei-fei. It seemed that the Junkers had transformed itself into a bird of history and was flying me with a bird's-eye view on a winding course, following the serpentine Great Wall back to the early T'ang dynasty and still further back to Ch'in. In my mind's eye, I saw flashback scenes of thousands of drafted laborers carrying stones up the mountainsides, First Emperor Ch'in on a white horse directing the building of his hunting lodge and his favorite swimming pool, lined with white marble and encircled by carved white marble balustrades. I was humming to myself the folk song "Meng Chiang Nü" (Bride of Meng Chiang), mourning her husband's absence at the Great Wall, when shouted landing instructions awakened me and brought me into the twentieth century. My disengagement from history was efficiently completed by being boarded into an American-made Jeep, rushed into the city of Sian, and lodged in Hsi Ching Hostel, a modern hotel with wall-to-wall carpeting and private, white-tiled baths.

L. K. Chang (Tsing Hua and Cornell) was awaiting me, full of news and suggestions. The general situation was tense with uncertainty, but he felt we should do some sightseeing before going westward to see the development projects, both of them under the direction of old schoolmates. S. Hung (Tsing Hua and RPI) was supervising civil engineer for the irrigation work, S. C. Cheng (Tsing Hua and Iowa State) head of agriculture and forestry. "Here is your chance," L. K. proposed, "to see the historical monuments we heard so much about at school. You must visit the oldest public library the first thing tomorrow."

China's oldest public library opened about the third century B.C., a time when the Imperial Academy began to engrave on large stone slabs the full texts of the *Five Classics, Four Books,* and *Four Encyclopedias.* Each engraved slab *(pei)* was about nine feet tall, four wide, and one foot thick, and stood on a two-foot stone foundation. The hundreds of *pei* were planted in a park and arranged in such a pattern that the public could browse among them. People also were permitted to make facsimile copies of the texts by the technique known as "stone rubbing." Ink paste was rubbed on the selected slab. Silk or paper was placed on the inked surface and a cloth pad dabbed gently against it to transfer the text to the paper. The result was a "negative"— white characters on a black background—because ink did not fill the incised characters, only the uncarved surface. The library was called Pei Lin—the Forest of Tablets.

I was thrilled to find so many of the tablets still standing and their engravings even partially legible. Of particular interest to me was the Nestorian Tablet erected c. 745, which contains an account of the coming and spread of Christianity in China. The legend is that Nestorian Christians had come to preach the Christian gospel. They created a stir during the reign of T'ang Tai-tsung in the capital of Chang An (Eternal Peace, the ancient name of Sian, or Western Peace).

The emperor summoned them to court and asked for translations of excerpts from their scriptures. After due study, the court issued an edict in 638, which contained the following passage: "The meaning of the teaching has been carefully examined; it is mysterious, wonderful, calm; it fixes the essentials of life and perfection; it is the salvation of living being. It is right that it should spread through the empire."

The edict also encouraged the introduction and spread of other foreign religions such as Buddhism, Judaism, and Islam.

Further sightseeing and exploration was made impossible by the Sian coup détat. Just before dawn on December 12 sporadic firing was heard. It began in the southeast and spread to our part of the city. Shots were fired at our hostel, and soldiers rounded up General Chiang Po-li and his staff and took them away. L. K. Chang arrived with reports that the Young Marshal had captured the Generalissimo. The city was stunned and all normal business suspended. The best thing for me to do, Chang said, was to leave because the situation might worsen. He took me to the railway station and somehow managed to get me on a crowded train heading eastward to whatever point it could get through to. Eventually I reached Peking.

The Sian Incident was a bizarre event. The Young Marshal had, indeed, kidnaped his commander-in-chief, not, as it turned out, to do him harm, but to urge him to alter national policy and fight the Japanese instead of the Communists. The Generalissimo would not hear of it. Obdurately and imperiously, he refused even to discuss the matter with his subordinate, until, as the days passed, the Young Marshal lost whatever upper hand he may have thought he had and was reduced to the role of suppliant.

Nanking was of two minds. Some proposed bombing the rebels. Cooler heads counseled negotiation. T. V. Soong and Madame Chiang flew in to move matters along. Even Chou En-lai was reported to have met secretly with Chang and advocated moderation.

On Christmas day the Young Marshal released his captive. Chiang flew back to Nanking in triumph. He still was head of state.

And despite rumors that he had agreed to stiffen his resistance to Japan, his position, then and thereafter, was that he had promised nothing, conceded nothing. Most extraordinarily, he even had Chang Hsueh-liang along with him as a voluntary prisoner.

Throughout China there was relief and rejoicing. Even Chiang's severest critics applauded his courage and integrity. For me, the result was that, except for the projects near Sian, I was able to carry on my observation tour of the other thirteen provinces as planned.

In comparison with my previous tour, eight years earlier, there were notable changes and contrasts. Practically all of the country, except the Northeast, which was under Japanese control, was loyal to the central Government at Nanking. The means of travel, hotel accommodations, and banking facilities, all of them directed by American-trained men, were operating normally and reliably. University men—from MIT, RPI, Iowa, Ohio, and Michigan—ran the power plants, water works, telephone and telegraph systems, and airlines, and were constructing new highways, bridges, and factories. Almost everywhere there were alumni associations and American Returned-Student clubs. In large cities there also were subdivided groups, such as Harvard and Smith clubs.

My survey in China during 1936–7 involved about twenty-four hundred Chinese men and women who had earned one or more degrees from colleges and universities in the United States. They were exerting powerful influences in government, industry, commerce, and particularly in education. They had replaced the Russian advisers, who had been recalled or expelled. Good will toward the United States had been restored and reached a new high, so much so that America had become China's largest source of imports, outstripping Britain for the first time in a hundred years.

The number of these American-trained people, however, was too small to meet China's needs. One result was that although they occupied top positions in all fields, hardly any of them got to work at the grass roots. In education, for example, very few of them were in elementary or secondary schools; in industry they were found only in the highest echelons. The missing links were able elementary teachers and better elementary schools, as well as skilled workers, mechanics, and supervisors for industry. As for a crash program to improve the education of citizens, it would have taken too long to undertake step-by-step schooling for so many millions of illiterate adults. A planned shortcut, or at least an auxiliary way, was to use radio and documentary films.

I had myself only recently acquired new skills and equipment in the field of motion pictures and was able to utilize them to great advantage on my tour. The director of the Harmon Foundation, Mary Brady, had heard that I was interested in evolving audiovisual tools for the China Institute's teacher-training program in New York. She was among the pioneers in introducing educational films, and had created a film department and collected a number of documentary films on China. She convinced me that I should know something about filmmaking and do some filming. Through her staff, particularly Evelyn Brown, she gave me an intensive course of training and lent me the most up-to-date Ciné Special sixteen-millimeter camera and other supplies and equipment. Altogether, during my tour, I took more than 10,000 feet of film, some in Kodachrome. Through my old friend, T. L. Yuan, head of the Peking National Library and executive of the Palace Museum, I was the first to get permission to film the palaces of the Purple Forbidden City—exteriors almost entirely; unfortunately, I did not have proper lighting for interiors. I also photographed an airplane plant at Nanchang headed by Colonel Chien Chang-tsu (Tsing Hua and MIT) and the Yung-li chemical factory at Tientsin headed by Dr. T. P. Hou (Columbia).

Most interesting, in part because I did not have permission, was my photographic flight over the Yangtze River Gorges. At the time, the Gorges were a fortified zone and photographing them was strictly forbidden. I managed to do it because I was the only passenger in the back of a mail plane piloted by my old friend, Captain Hugh E. Chen, a graduate mechanical engineer from Stevens Institute, who had trained

Author's 16-mm film of Yangtze River
Gorges was shot from this single-engine
biplane. Captain Hugh Chen, old friend
who learned to fly with Curtiss-Wright, poses
in flying suit, helmet, and goggles.
Mailbag is one of a pile of several which
kept Pilot Chen from knowing his
passenger was breaking security by
photographing fortified, forbidden Gorges.

with Curtiss-Wright. Mail bags were piled high between us, so he could not possibly see me while we flew between Wuhan and Chungking. Years later, after Hugh's retirement, I showed him my shots of the Gorges. He scolded me, saying that my lark could have had him court-martialed and jailed.

I also took special pleasure in filming Nora Hsiung (Hsiung Chih, whom I first met at the CSA conference at Hotchkiss School in 1921), her family, her Planned Parenthood office, and her women's parades demonstrating for woman suffrage. She had fulfilled two of the three objectives she announced at that conference. She had organized a women's movement and chosen her own husband. As for the third— to beget six children—she had four, and I had no doubt the other two would follow.

As I traveled from the east coast to the south and west, I could not escape a feeling of unreality at what I saw. The scenes, the people, and their life styles were a grand juxtaposition of historical periods and an extraordinary mixture of Chinese and western objects, customs, and attitudes.

Thus, I went with K. H. Sung (Lehigh) to see the rural area along the Huang Sha River in Hunan. We traveled in two Jeeps with three trunks loaded with modern surveying instruments and excavating equipment. We passed through a village of Miaos, a minority ethnic group. They and their land were incorporated as part of China about a millennium ago. They still retained their own dress, speech, and, above all, their matriarchal social structure in which women were the heads of families, worked in the fields, and could marry more than one husband, who usually took care of the babies and did the cooking. We drove along roads often filled with farmers and their animals. Both regarded us as a nuisance and made way only after prolonged horn tooting.

Szechuan is the most fertile western province, famous for its three or four yearly harvests, as well as for its peppery cuisine, for being the locale of much of *The Romance of the Three Kingdoms,* and for the Yangtze Gorges. Among other historical spots, I visited the ancient tavern called Pu Tzui Wu Kwei Hsiao Chiu Chia, meaning, literally, "Not-Drunk-Don't-Leave-Small Tavern'; the pond where paper was first made, and the shrine of Chu-kuo Liang, who was Shu kingdom's prime minister, military genius, and legendary inventor of mechanical oxen and horses. I spotted people with marcel-wave hairdos and people chewing Wrigley's gum. I was driven in a Ford car to see the renowned Buddhist temple, Chao Chueh Ssu; the road was wide and clay-surfaced but we could proceed faster than walking only in short spurts because wheelbarrows had the right of way and because farmers would not allow culverts to be built over the main irrigation ditches. We carried two strong planks as a portable bridge with which to cross those ditches, which cut the road every three or four miles.

Szechuan was the chief source of t'ung oil, which the United States imported in large quantities for use in making paints and varnishes. It was the home of tangerines, a parent of a number of hybrid citrus fruits, such as tangelos and temple oranges. My guide, S. Y. Liu (Tsing Hua and Chicago), wanted me to film especially the suspension bridge at Kuan Hsien, which was built in 255–206 B.C. over a deep gorge. According to American civil engineers, the bridge embodied practically all modern principles of mechanics and the major features of steel suspension bridges. From a distance it resembled the Brooklyn Bridge. On close examination its tall towers could be seen to be constructed of sturdy wooden poles. The cables were hundreds of twisted strands of slivered bamboo. Planks laid crosswise on the cables made the passageway. It still was serving as a much-used transportation link. Twice every year, for more than two thousand years, volunteers gathered to keep it in good repair.

This prototype suspension bridge was the easiest thing for me to photograph. Far more difficult for an amateur was the monumental achievement of Li Ping, the engineer who in the third century B.C. built a statewide system of irrigation for Shu, the ancient name for Szechuan. Li had to dam and divide the four natural rivers into eight main and sixteen secondary irrigation streams, and then force the streams into myriad shallow ditches, quite a number of which were up on the mountainsides, thus creating the fabulous terraced farmlands. Li Ping could not complete the great project in his lifetime, but trained his son to carry out his plan and to realize his dream of a productive Shu. Since then Szechuan has been the most fertile agricultural area in China. Out of gratitude, the people erected a shrine near the bridge to remember father and son—the Two Li Shrine.

En route back from Kuan Hsien to Cheng-tu, the provincial capital, we passed a small experimental grove of Sunkist orange trees imported from Southern California, and Hua Hsi—West China University—which was founded by American Protestant missions.

The orange trees reminded me of Dr. Walter T. Swingle's research on citrus fruits, particularly oranges, for the United States Department of Agriculture. He discovered that the California orange had come from China, either directly or through Mexico, and that Florida's had been brought from Brazil. From Brazil he traced their origin to Portugal and from Portugal back to China, where, in the area of Macao, the Portuguese had succeeded in transplanting orange trees in 1516. In China Dr. Swingle found a vast literature on the cultivation of orange trees, including a monograph, *Chü Lu (Orange Record)*, about which he wrote, "It is a landmark in the history of civilization as it is the first scientific monograph on any fruit tree ever published in any country." Dr. Swingle first made known to western pomologists the contributions of Lue Gim Gong. In our several interviews, he told me that he was partly responsible for starting the Chinese collection at the Library of Congress. He had shown his friend Herbert Putnam, the Library's curator, his twenty-three hundred Chinese books and papers on the orange, and suggested that they be deposited in the Library. This led to the building of an extensive collection of Chinese literature, eventually the largest in any institution outside of China.

Should the Government limit the number of years a student can study abroad and/or should scholarships be awarded only to mature or graduate students? This was the question to which my recommendations had been directed, although events were soon to make it academic.

I wanted to consult my advisers before I submitted my report. I went to Tientsin to see Chang Po-ling and to Peking to see Hu Shih and Y. C. Mei. They and practically everyone else in the spring of 1937 were preoccupied with the imminent Japanese attack. The China Foundation meeting I attended in Peking included Chang, Hu, Mei, J. Leighton Stuart, and Roger Greene. They were extremely worried by reports of increased Japanese military concentrations and believed that Japan intended to conquer all of North China. They explored the advisability of moving universities to other parts of the country and transferring some funds to the United States for safekeeping. Greene was appointed chairman and I secretary to administer scholarships in the United States and, through the China Institute, to provide emergency relief for the Chinese students stranded there.

Soon after the meeting, Nankai University in Tientsin was destroyed by a punitive Japanese air attack, and on July 7 Japanese troops used a minor clash at the Marco Polo bridge as an excuse to seize Peking. The war had begun.

Japan expected China to collapse almost immediately. When it did not, the invaders launched a campaign of total warfare in which civilians and nonmilitary targets underwent indiscriminate bombing and destruction. The Nationalist Government was driven from Nanking to Chungking, in the west. The picturesque Yangtze Gorges now became the nearly impassable barrier behind which China regrouped and sought to preserve itself as a nation.

The immediate problem was one of supply. With the entire east coast of China sealed by a Japanese naval blockade, the only remaining route by which a war of resistance could be supported was overland from Burma. A certain amount could be airlifted, but the route was hazardous and air transport had not yet been developed to the point where the required tonnage could be handled. Cargo could be trucked from the port of Rangoon to Lashio, in the Shan States of eastern Burma. From there it would be necessary to build a road across the Himalayas to Kunming, in Yunnan province.

The building of the Burma Road was a prodigious engineering feat. The route ran for some four hundred and twenty-one miles through some of the world's most difficult and malaria-ridden terrain. Since there was neither equipment nor time to dig tunnels and erect bridges, the road was engineered to follow the contours of the land. It was carved out of hundreds of mountainsides, made hundreds of hairpin turns, rose to a peak altitude of 12,000 feet (3,658 m), and plunged to a depth of two hundred feet (61 m) below sea level. At about midpoint it went through mosquito-infested Man Shih, a town of some five thousand people which had been wiped out by malaria five times in the past two hundred years.

In spite of all obstacles, the Burma Road was completed and opened to traffic in less than two years. Credit must go to the American-trained Chinese surveyors and engineers, and the hundreds of thousands of laborers who cut the roadbed and broke rocks into pebbles by hand. Malaria control was carried out quickly by an American and Chinese medical team provided by the Rockefeller Institute in New York.

Traffic on the Burma Road was greatly hampered by washouts and by breakdowns of American-made trucks. The road needed a water-resistant surface and the trucks needed better maintenance. It was necessary to make use of available materials on the spot to bind the surface of the road and, at the same time, keep the trucks rolling. The situation highlighted the necessity of on-the-job training programs for skilled workers and mechanics. As the director of China Institute, I went about the United States asking for volunteers from among Chinese undergraduates and high school students. About eight hundred responded, and 474 were qualified and awarded trainee scholarships. Ford and Chrysler motor companies organized special, intensive courses on truck maintenance and loading. The United States Highway Adminstration extended its laboratory facilities to us for testing the road-binding qualities of materials of West China, such as t'ung oil, clay, and lime. With both technical-school and on-the-job training, we tried to give the trainees basic orientation to prepare them for war conditions in China. On the Burma Road and elsewhere these trainees performed invaluable service throughout the war.

As Japan's bombing of China heightened and its troops extended westward the territory under their control, governmental and private sources in China were no longer able to remit funds to students abroad. In the United States the number of Chinese students in need rose to more than two thousand. With the help of Roger Greene and Dr. Edward Hume, I was able to secure emergency relief from the Rockefeller Brothers' Fund, the Strong Foundation, and some mission boards. Because the needs were growing steadily beyond the funds available from private sources, I asked Dr. Duggan of IIE, who was a trustee of China Institute, to help me approach the American Government for aid. Secretary of State Cordell Hull listened to us cordially and referred our appeal to Assistant Secretary G. H. Shaw. After several interviews with Mr. Shaw, however, it became clear that there were no funds available for student relief. Just when there seemed to be no hope, a solution came from the helping hand of Eleanor Roosevelt.

Curiously, I met Mrs. Roosevelt because of my father's admiration for Theodore Roosevelt. Father read about Teddy's strenuous political life, while yet finding time to be a playmate of his children, and suggested that I should try to meet him when I got to America. He did not believe that such a great president could be an undignified father. Roosevelt died the year I came to the United States, but I longed to meet his family and to learn something about his personal life. I read with profound interest *Theodore Roosevelt's Letters to His Children* and *The White House Gang*.

Another Roosevelt, Franklin D., who was a distant cousin of Theodore, became president in 1933. I was attending a student conference at Rensselaerville, New York. The organizer of the conference was Mrs. Francis C. Huyck, a civic leader in nearby Albany, who brought foreign students together with American leaders at her summer home for their mutual interest and understanding. She was the one who enlightened me on the differences between the two Roosevelt clans. The Sagamore Hill Roosevelts, the descendants of Theodore, were Republicans, and the Hyde Park Delano Roosevelts were Democrats. Theodore's namesake followed his father's footsteps in politics. His other children were scattered about the country and not easy to see. But Mrs. Franklin Roosevelt, like Mrs. Huyck, was interested in foreign students.

I had no trouble in introducing myself to Eleanor Roosevelt because she came to New York frequently and had an apartment in Washington Square. I was pleasantly surprised to find the First Lady so modest and friendly. She gave the impression that she thought I must have something interesting to tell her, and she seemed to have all the time in the world to ask me about China and Chinese students. The delightful first visit encouraged me to send her occasional news about students, and she invited me once in a while to some of her meetings with student leaders, such as Joseph Lash of the National Student Federation. On one of my calls on Assistant Secretary Shaw, I thought of making an appointment to see Mrs. Roosevelt. She was very sympathetic. After explaining briefly why the State Department could not act quickly, she phoned Lauchlin Currie, a special assistant to the president, asking him to see me.

Currie behaved more like a professor than a high official. He had been an economist at Harvard and had been in China. During my first long interview with him he answered a buzz on his phone and said, "Yes, Mr. President," then excused himself and left through the rear door. His position was close indeed to the seat of power! In less than two weeks he worked out a plan by which Chinese students could be aided immediately.

Currie explained to me that some funds in the State Department were available through the newly created Bureau of Intercultural Relations if the project could be designated as providing scholarships. Although the Bureau and its funds were intended to cultivate friendly relations with Latin-American countries, Currie believed Chinese students could be provided scholarship-in-aid by presidential directive because of the special Chinese situation. He suggested that

I organize a committee of three to make the scholarship awards and that China Institute should defray all administrative expenses.

My committee consisted of Dr. Duggan, Roger Greene, and me. The State Department appointed a counterpart committee—later enlarged—composed of the Assistant Secretary, the chief of the Far Eastern Section, and me. My committee formulated the rules, made the announcements, went over more than three thousand applications, and on behalf of the American Government made grants of 1,666 scholarships for study and 474 grants for on-the-job training. The available fund of $500,000 proved to be inadequate. While a request for more funds was pending, Currie hinted that I should also appeal to the Chinese Government, and that I could do so simply by going directly to T.V. Soong, the Foreign Minister, in Washington.

Soong's fortunes had risen rapidly with the advent of the Nationalist regime. He was a Harvard graduate, brother of Madame Chiang Kai-Shek, the First Lady of China, and well known as an efficient, American-style administrator. He received me promptly at the appointed hour, eleven o'clock in the morning, and after a short interview asked me to submit a written memorandum by four o'clock the same day. My memo outlined the needs of Chinese students and appealed for aid similar to that extended by the American Government. Within a week, Soong notified me that the Chinese Government would take similar action, but that he wanted to see me about how the scholarships should be awarded. The composition of the committee should be planned in strict confidence. He requested that I go to his home on a particular Sunday morning and be prepared to spend most of the day with him.

On the Sunday, Soong and I talked all morning and he insisted on my having lunch with him. At one o'clock, at a large table in a spacious dining room, the two of us sat down to eat his favorite dish of generous slices of rare roast beef. The chief reason why our planning took so long was that President Chiang Kai-shek had doubts about my qualifications. The Minister of Education wanted to nominate the administrator of the funds. Soong told me that the minister, Chen

Li-fu, had informed the president that I was anti-Kuomintang and that, in any event, it was within his jurisdiction to administer such funds. Chen Li-fu was one of the famous "Two Chen" brothers whom Chiang regarded as his right and left hands and who operated at the topmost levels of the party. Chen had a number of agents in the United States and their reports evidently convinced him that I must not be trusted by the Government.

Soong gave me two major details from this dossier and asked me for clarification. One concerned a speech I had made at a Chinese-student conference in which I said that America's two-party system and the checks and balances built into its governmental structure were more congenial to our Chinese tradition of the Mandate of Heaven than the current one-party dictatorship of the Kuomintang without universal suffrage. My second offense was connected with the San Min Chu I Youth Corps. In 1938 the commandant of the corps, General Chiang Chih-chung, appointed me an adviser of the branch corps in the United States, urging me to use my influence to expand its membership among Chinese youth in America. I found some of the regulations of the corps unacceptable. For example, one article specified that a member should vow absolute loyalty to the commandant and his deputies personally. Another prescribed that a delinquent member should be deprived of his liberty after two warnings for violation of any regulations. I declined the appointment and explained my action to the officers of the corps in New York.

Those two "offenses" of mine had been so exaggerated and reported so often that I had been put on the KMT black list. Thus, Minister Chen's representations to Chiang Kai-shek, requesting that the funds be turned over to his ministry for administration by Dr. Z. Y. Kuo, one of the party faithful.

I admitted to Soong that I had done those two things. But my motive had not been political. Aside from my youthful involvement in the May Fourth Movement, I had never engaged in political activities or held political office. I was director of China Institute, a private American corporation, of which I was a full-time employee. Because of my work among Chinese students in the United States I had been awarded the honorific title of director of the Chinese Educational Mission in charge of Tsing Hua and other Chinese governmental scholarships and traineeships.

Furthermore, the Secretary of State had taken the unprecedented action of appointing me to the State Department's Advisory Committee on Aid to Chinese Students as the only member not an American citizen. "Dr. Soong," I asked, "don't you think the United States Government and American educators will wonder why Minister Chen wants to disqualify me?"

After considering the implications, Dr. Soong decided that it would not be good public relations for the Chinese Government to inject politics into the matter of student aid. But he said, "I have to satisfy Minister Chen and the party. The official procedure will be for me to ask him to appoint a committee to investigate you and render a report to the president before I can make funds available." I urged him to act quickly because of the urgent need, and also because American universities expected prompt action by the Chinese Government. "Permit me to make one suggestion," I added. "Please try to include on that committee someone in whose impartiality you have complete confidence." He accepted my suggestion and managed to appoint Dr. J. Heng Liu, head of the Peking Union Medical College, who was on leave in the United States to procure medical supplies.

In about three weeks, Dr. Soong phoned to say that the committee had cleared me, and that we could proceed with planning the administration of the aid funds. Knowing now that I was ignorant of the intricacies of politics, he was good enough to advise me to structure the administration of the funds in such a way as to fend off further party complications.

Accordingly, the Committee on Wartime Planning for Chinese Students in the United States was formed with five honorary chairmen, two honorary vice-chairmen, the usual array of officers, and twelve members—in sum, an imaginative mix and subtle balance of Chinese interests and influences at home and abroad. The honorary chairmen were Dr. Soong, his brother-in-law and political rival H. H. Kung, my friend and outspoken KMT critic Hu Shih, a party loyalist Wei Tao-ming, and the redoubtable Chen Li-fu. The vice-chairmen were China Institute's businessman-trustee, K. C. Li, and Li Meng (no relation), a prominent banker in Shanghai. Among the officers, Dr. Kuo, former director of China Institute, was chairman; T. P. Hou, Tientsin industrialist, was vice-chairman; Hsi Te-mou, banker, was treasurer, and Chang Chi-yun, a KMT leader, was secretary.

Committee members were Chang Kia-ngau, former cabinet member; Y. R. Chao of Harvard; S. R. Chow, an expert in international law; Kan Lee, special assistant to Soong; Liu Chieh, counselor of the Chinese embassy; the impartial Dr. J. Heng Liu; S. C. Mong, educator; Kin-wei Shaw, industrialist; T. F. Tsiang, diplomat; P. Tsou, agricultural specialist; S. C. Wang, scientist, and Consul General James Yu.

As can be seen, there were important men to lend weight to our endeavors, Kuomintang errand-runners to see that we did not go astray, bankers and businessmen to check our unworldly, academic impulsiveness, and just enough serious workers in our specialized field to get the job done. Face-saving is a necessity in human relations. It has been practiced throughout history by all nations, but in China it has perhaps been practiced longest and to the highest degree.

I was named executive director and a member of the executive committee.

Now both Governments extended aid to Chinese students and trainees. By the end of the war, some forty-seven hundred of them had been enabled to complete their courses of study and/or training. On a trip to the United States after the war, Chen Li-fu asked me for a private meeting in my office on a Sunday afternoon. At this meeting he reminded me that we had first met some twenty-five years before, when he was a student at the University of Pittsburgh. He expressed regret at the misunderstanding about my supposedly anti-Kuomintang actions. I appreciated his gesture.

Mrs. Roosevelt, Lauchlin Currie, and T.V. Soong each did a great deal to help Chinese students and to advance cultural relations

189

between China and the United States during those critical war years. I remember vividly one occasion in 1943 when Mrs. Roosevelt, in spite of her full schedule of travels and appointments, accepted my invitation to address Chinese students. The meeting was to be held at International House on Riverside Drive in New York. She asked me to meet her out front fifteen minutes before the hour to guide her to the auditorium. I expected to see some Secret Service men escorting the first lady. She arrived promptly, walking alone. After the meeting she asked me to escort her to the 125th Street subway station, where she boarded a downtown train, apparently by herself.

During the era of McCarthyism, Currie left the United States for Brazil, where he stayed for the rest of his life. I remember him as one who cared for economic reforms in China, and as a man of action in aiding Chinese students.

T. V. Soong's reputation suffered when *Thunder Out of China,* by Theodore H. White and Annalee Jacoby, led to a series of exposés of corruption in high places in the Nationalist Government. After the Communists drove the Nationalists from the mainland to Taiwan, Soong retired and lived in New York. I called on him several times at his Fifth Avenue apartment to persuade him to take an active part in the work of China Institute. His interests, however, seemed to be entirely in governmental and trade affairs. He wondered whether I could open a club for the purpose of bringing together important officials and businessmen at luncheons or cocktails, but he shunned public life and avoided meeting with students. He died in San Francisco in 1971.

By 1942 China Institute and its activities had become well known. We were recognized by the United States and Chinese Governments, and educational institutions in both countries were using us to administer scholarships, and exchange scholars, writers, and others. Cooperating with us were a number of local committees in both countries.

In the twelve years since I had taken charge, its work had grown by leaps and bounds. I had started the new corporation with two rooms, a staff consisting of a secretary and me, and a bank balance of less than $250. By 1943 we were administering scholarships amounting to over $2,500,000, conducting two pilot in-service teachers' projects on Chinese history and culture, and coordinating forty centers of information and hospitality throughout the country. But I had been a poor administrator, not aggressive enough to build up a staff or to expand office space to cope with the escalating volume of work. My inclination had been to enlist volunteers. Our staff had increased only to five, while our office had added only two more rooms.

Two of our trustees were successful administrators: Dan Douty, head of United States Testing, and Walter Mallory, of the Council on Foreign Relations. They kept urging me to plan for a more adequate staff and office space, but I preferred to devote my time to carrying out programs and to traveling and meeting more people, instead of raising funds to meet an increased overhead. Consequently, we were so crammed and crowded with visitors that some of them had to stand and wait outside in the corridors. Dan often remarked of me at trustees' meetings, "I have never seen anybody who could stretch a nickel so far."

In my frequent calls on Walter Mallory, who succeeded Paul Monroe as president of the trustees, I envied him his Council House which provided rooms for discussion, a library, and dinner meetings. How much more China Institute could do with a similar house, and how pressing was our need for classrooms.

The trustees approved my proposal for securing adequate headquarters for China Institute. We struggled for more than a year with no indication of success, mainly because I was inexperienced and did not have enough time to devote to fund raising. One day, walking back from seeing Walter Mallory to his office, I awakened to the fact that his Council House had been donated by a single patron. "Is there anyone who is rich enough and who would consider giving a house to China Institute?" I asked myself. The name of Henry R. Luce sprang to mind.

Henry R. Luce, known to his friends as Harry, was the son

of Dr. Henry Winters Luce, my friend who had done so much for Christian education in China and the promotion of better understanding of Chinese culture among churches in the United States. Dr. and Mrs. Luce had their start in Shantung province, where Harry was born, just before the Boxers' uprising. I had met Harry but did not get to know him until 1933 at the IPR Conference at Banff Springs, Canada, where we were members of our respective national delegations. He was a tall, athletic man and a fine tennis player. We played "mixed" doubles one afternoon, Harry pairing with a Chinese delegate, N. W. Liu, and I with an American delegate, James Mooney of General Motors. The American players were much more competitive and aggressive. Harry made a terrific overhead smash at the net and James called it out. Harry came over, examined the mark, and insisted that the shot had clipped the line. They called on Liu and me to judge. The line on the clay court was rather blurred and there were quite a few ball marks around where James Mooney was pointing. Liu and I were at a loss as to what to do. We finally suggested playing the point over. Later Harry scolded us, saying, "When are you people going to quit saving face and be honest for a change?"

By the autumn of 1943 I had gathered enough courage to tell Luce what I wanted to see him for. He invited me to lunch with him in Time's private dining room in the Time-Life Building, then in Rockefeller Center. There he told me that his father and sister had mentioned to him how cramped the Institute was for office space and expressed his willingness to help. After our talk he escorted me to the elevators, where the hall lights were much brighter. He looked at my face and asked me to go with him to his office. After a few minutes of careful scrutiny of my eyes, he said firmly, "You probably have what I got a few years back—jaundice." He urged me to get medical advice without delay at the Columbia-Presbyterian Medical Center. The findings confirmed his judgment: I had catarrhal jaundice. I was confined to Harkness Pavilion for twenty-five days.

Harry sent two dozen red roses and the message, "Get well soon so that we can look for a house together." Together we looked at twenty-seven houses for sale on the East Side, between 60th and 80th Streets. His first choice was the Arthur Curtiss James house at 68th and Park Avenue, his second the Frederick Leigh house at 65th between Park and Lexington Avenues. He was prepared to acquire either one and present it to us as a gift.

The trustees accepted the Leigh House. It was much smaller and the cost of maintenance would be less. But we soon had reason to regret that we had not taken Harry Luce's realistic assessement of the space we would require. In less than two years we wished we had taken the James house.

One of the trustees, William M. Chadbourne, proposed that the Institute, which was to be the owner of China House, should change its incorporation, to conform more closely to the nature of its purposes and program, and also to obtain tax-exemptions for the building. Accordingly, in 1944, China Institute dissolved as a membership corporation and reincorporated as an educational institution chartered under the University of the State of New York.

Hundreds of members and friends indicated their desire to see China House. In order to accommodate them, three events were scheduled: a celebration at Town Hall, open to all; a dedication ceremony at China House for members; and a public opening of China House with three days of exhibitions and lectures.

The celebration took place on the 2495th anniversary of the birth of Confucius (August 27, 1944). Town Hall was filled to capacity; many had to stand. The program symbolized the relevance of old and new, of Confucian and Christian. Marian Anderson sang two spirituals, "My Soul Is Anchored in the Lord" and "Sometimes I Feel Like a Motherless Child." She most graciously contributed her performance because she knew my extensive relations with black educators and colleges. The China Institute Chorus responded with Chinese folk songs, "The Song of the Hoe" and "Rhythm of the Sea."

Dr. H. H. Kung spoke on the Chinese wisdom of "culture,

not race, is meaningful in life" and "under Heaven all is one family."
Dr. Kung's presence was appropriate. He was not only vice-premier of
China and honorary president of China Institute in America, but a
seventy-fifth lineal descendant of the Sage. (In Chinese his name was
Kung Hsiang-hsi; his ancestor's was Kung Fu-tze.) He came from a
well-to-do banking family in Shansi. His father had business dealings
with English firms and was, as a result, among the first Christian
converts massacred by the Boxers. "H. H." carried on the family tradition—as banker and as Christian. He came to the United States for
his education, obtaining his B.A. from Oberlin in 1906, his M.A. from
Yale in 1907. While a student in the United States, he joined the
revolutionary movement of Sun Yat-sen. After returning home his
business prospered and he helped to establish Ming Hsien Academy,
a school for Christian education which became known as Oberlin-in-
Shansi. He married the eldest of the three Soong sisters, Ai-ling, a
Georgia Wesleyan College graduate, and joined Chiang Kai-shek's
Government, in which he held a number of high cabinet posts.

At Town Hall he was followed by Wendell Wilkie, the
Republican candidate for president, who spoke on his ideal of "One
World." Messages of congratulation were read from Eleanor Roosevelt,
Vice-President Henry A. Wallace, Pearl Buck, and John Dewey, among
others.

The dedication took place later the same day. Before a large
assembly of trustees and members, plus their families and friends,
China House was presented by Harry Luce on behalf of the Henry
Luce Foundation as a memorial to his father. Dr. Kung accepted it for
the Institute.

Chiang Kai-shek sent a scroll bearing the characters: "The
Way is one and the winds blow together."

In his presentation address, Henry Luce said in part: "As
we meet to dedicate China House, we remember that passage in the
Doctrine of the Mean where Confucius expresses his awareness of
invisible spirits: 'Like the rush of mighty waters, the presence of unseen
spirits is felt above and around us.'

"Of all those spirits, the first of whose presence we are most keenly aware is that of Master Kung, the ancestor of Dr. H. H. Kung. Another of whose invisible presence we are conscious today is China's great philosopher of democracy, Mencius. He, too, is ably represented by a direct descendant in Chih Meng, upon whom will rest much of the burden of guiding the destiny of China House."

The interior of the House was still in the process of being remodeled, but the entrance was already guarded by two Ming dynasty stone lions lent by C. F. Yau. The entrance door was painted Chinese vermilion. Facing the entrance, in the center of the wall, there was placed this plaque inscribed with beautiful golden Chinese characters and in English:

China House
Given in memory of
Henry Winters Luce

"The Brotherhood of Man
has its end, as its beginning,
in the Fatherhood of God."

December 1, 1944, was the date chosen for the formal opening to allow time for the completion of alterations to the building and for arranging the exhibitions. George Nelson, editor of *Architectural Forum,* designed the floor plan, which utilized all four floors of our red brick building, plus the basement. Aside from offices and classrooms, we had an art gallery, library, music room, board room, and an office for Tsing Hua University and the China Foundation.

Our technical adviser, Henry Murphy, Yenching's architect, decided to retain the beautiful exterior designed by Charles A. Platt and considered one of the fine specimens of American-Georgian architecture. Some additional Chinese touches were introduced by placing a "T'ang Horse and Groom" sculpture in the foyer alcove, replacing four panels of Italian oil painting with scrolls of stone rubbings and putting a fountain and Kuan Yin statuette in the garden.

As these public preparations were moving ahead, I was also involved in private preparation to marry Miss Huan Shou Kwoh, a recent Juilliard graduate and like myself a native of Shantung province. At one of the China Institute committee meetings, Mrs. C. V. Starr, who had learned of my personal plans, turned to me and said, "Why don't you have your wedding here in China House? It will be a wonderful way to bless a new house according to Chinese tradition." Mrs. Starr, like Harry Luce, had been born and brought up in Shantung of missionary parents and spoke Chinese with a Shantung accent. Her question was turned into a proposal warmly made and applauded by all present.

Miss Kwoh and I thought highly of the suggestion and we chose September 23 as the date. We were married both in a Chinese civil ceremony and an American Presbyterian sacrament. Hu Shih officiated at the much simplified and modernized Chinese ceremony. C. F. Yau represented the bride's family and Y. C. James Yen the groom's; Consul-General James T. C. Yu represented the Republic of China. Dr. Hu stated that Miss Kwoh and Mr. Meng had found mutual affection and purpose in life, and with the approval of their families pledged to marry in front of their assembled relatives and friends. The bride and groom then bowed to the four officials, to the assembled guests, and to each other. A red certificate was signed by the four official witnesses and by the groom and the bride, whose signature was Kwoh Huan Shou of Meng Family.

Through the introduction of Mrs. Francis C. Huyck, the minister of the First Presbyterian Church, the Reverend J. V. Moldenhower, saw to it that we had also a perfect American wedding, including the classical wedding march, exchange of marriage vows and two rings, and biblical blessings. The pronouncement "till death do us part" did not harmonize with our tradition and still sounds strange to our ears whenever we hear it today. Chinese cosmology teaches that souls or spirits continue their identities and relationships after death.

How simplified was this ceremony compared with the wedding of First Sister! On her wedding day the groom came in a red satin sedan chair, with an entourage of an orchestra, eight page boys in colorful costumes, and banners, and a second four-man sedan chair of embroidered green satin. The procession halted at our front gate. The groom descended from his chair, raised his ceremonial bow, and shot an arrow at the gate, which opened to admit the entourage. Accompanied by soft music, the groom was ushered to our family altar at the sides of which sat our parents. Following the rhythmic chanting of the ushers, he performed the three kneelings and nine kowtowings to the present and spiritual members of our family. The groom was guided to the boudoir of the bride and, with his ceremonial sword, he tapped on the door. The bride, heavily veiled in multicolored embroidered satin, emerged, supported by two bridesmaids, and was escorted to the green sedan chair.

The wedding procession now advanced to the groom's home, where his parents were waiting beside the family altar. The couple performed the same extreme obeisances to his ancestors. The bride and the maids, followed by the groom, then went to the bridal chamber, where a symbolic feast was ready. As soon as the bride crossed the threshold, the groom, with his sword, gently lifted the veil. More often than not, it was the first sight he had had of his bride. The couple then sat at the feast, attended by the maids, who assisted them each to eat half of a *chiao tze* (crescent-shaped prototype of ravioli) and to drink half of a cup of wine from the same cup.

The time soon came for China House's three-day formal opening. The feature event of the first day was an afternoon reception, at which the guests were briefed on the activities of China Institute. For the opening, more than six hundred invited guests came from Washington, Boston, and Philadelphia, as well as New York. In the receiving line, in addition to the officers and trustees of China Institute, were the Chinese Ambassador and Madame T. M. Wei, Mrs. Henry W. Luce, Henry R. Luce, Elisabeth Luce Moore, and Dr. Hu Shih.

On the second day, a number of documentary films about China were shown. They were used in the Institute's nationwide educational program and covered a wide and interesting range of subjects:

rural life, rice cultivation, extracting salt, education, painting and glass-blowing techniques, and making dry plasma at China's first blood bank, in Kunming. Among them was my own *Glimpses of Modern China*, two black-and-white reels shot in 1936 and 1937 showing some of the economic and educational advances China was making before war consumed the country's energies.

Such films owed their beginning to the initiative of Mary Brady, director of the Harmon Foundation, and their development to the brilliant achievements of Wango H. C. Weng. Miss Brady's persistent and inspired coaching made possible the training of all the Chinese makers of those films, and their production and distribution for use throughout the United States. Originals of these films were deposited in the National Archives in Washington.

Wango Weng is from a most remarkable family which produced not only two *chuang yuan*, or "Number One national scholars," but also a noted calligrapher. It owned one of the best private collections of Chinese paintings and literature. Like most idealistic students of his generation, Wango came to the United States. He studied electrical engineering at Purdue, and upon graduation sought my advice on his career. Two problems occupied him: the raging war in China and his natural inclination toward aesthetics. I suggested that he consider applying his engineering training to Chinese art, specifically the production of films on Chinese art. I was instrumental in introducing him to Miss Brady and filmmaking. The other happy result was his meeting another trainee, Virginia Dzung, at the Harmon Foundation. They married and became collaborators in filmmaking. Years later they produced a film on Buddhism in China and a series on *The History of Chinese Art*, perhaps China Institute's most important teaching tool. The series was the gift of C. T. Shen, who served with distinction both as trustee and vice chairman of the Institute. A successful industrialist, C. T. is also a scholar and teacher of Buddhism whose discourse has enriched and enlightened many American friends.

For the third day of China House's opening we presented an exhibition of Chinese art, and of memorabilia of the coming of Chinese students to the United States. It was Mr. C. F. Yau's idea to start a series of Chinese art exhibitions. The front room of the first floor was permanently converted into a gallery. For the inaugural we had a display of rare Chinese ceramics lent by different collectors.

The first three Chinese students in America were brought by the Reverend Samuel Robbins Brown in 1847. Brown (Yale 1832) had gone to Canton to preach the gospel in 1839, at the outbreak of the Opium War. British merchants in China controlled the profitable opium trade, and the so-called "war" was simply Britain's overwhelming military response when China sought to halt the traffic and protect its people from the ravages of addiction. The settlement imposed by Britain established the precedents for China's subjection to the western powers for a century to come.

For eight long years the Reverend Mr. Brown encountered hostility from the Chinese: They thought he was an Englishman and could not believe that a nation which forced the odious drug on helpless people to enrich its businessmen could also send missionaries to preach brotherhood. He concluded that the only way to convince the Chinese that America was not England was to enable some Chinese people to journey abroad and see for themselves. He was able to persuade three Chinese boys to enroll at his father's private school, Monson Academy, at Monson, Massachusetts, not far from Springfield.

One of the three, Yung Wing, went on to Yale, where he was a popular fellow and, as a graduate in 1854, the first Chinese to earn a four-year degree at an American university. His other achievement was a successful intermarriage with Lucie Kellogg, the daughter of a prominent Hartford family.

The second, Wong Foon, achieved distinction as the first Chinese physician and surgeon trained in western medicine. The third, Wong Shing, chiefly because of frail health, became a translator and interpreter.

Yung Wing entered the service of the Viceroy Tseng Kuo-fan in 1863, and returned to the United States the following year to buy machinery to equip Kiang Nan, one of China's few productive arsenals, near Shanghai. He also pleaded with officialdom to give more Chinese youths an American education, but in vain. Finally, through a ruse, he managed to get Government funds to provide scholarships for thirty boys a year to study in the United States. Since the officials had turned a deaf ear—for some seventeen years!—to his plea for modern American education, he played on China's desperate need for modern weapons. Instead of training young students as such, he urged, why not train them how to make guns? Europe was reluctant to supply China with up-to-date weapons, but the United States had no reason to keep her weak and unarmed. In 1872 he was appointed director of the Chinese Educational Mission with headquarters at Hartford, and the first thirty boys arrived for their western education. Of course, it had nothing to do with gun-making.

The ruse was exposed when the Government sent a special envoy to check how well the young gunsmiths were learning their trade. The envoy knew hardly anything about America. He was a typical imperial bureaucrat, extremely jealous of his rank and prerogatives. He held an audience and noted that two of the students did not kneel and that one of the pair had short hair. When they were examined by the envoy about these delinquencies, they explained, "Recently, the governor of Connecticut invited us students to his home to tea. He insisted that we must not kneel to greet him. He even asked us not to stand up when he passed around the cookies." The cutting off of the queue—the sign of subjection to the throne— could not be explained so easily. The boy was severely reprimanded and ordered to wear a false queue until he grew a natural one.

Yung Wing explained more or less successfully the slow process of learning gun-making; it took years to learn the language, basic science, mechanics, and so forth. But the envoy was not pleased. He recommended that the mission should be abolished and the students be sent home lest they become so Americanized that they would no longer be loyal subjects to the emperor. Thus, the project was terminated after benefiting a mere one hundred and twenty students.

The "boy" who did not kneel and who cut off his queue was Tsai Ting-kan. His Hartford high-school friends called him "the fighting Chinaman." Ultimately, he joined the republican revolutionary forces and attained the rank of admiral. When I called on him in Peking in 1936 he remarked, "More than anything else, the scolding of the envoy drove me to be a rebel."

The other was Li Yen-fou, who later adopted journalism as his life work. His Americanization had a bad start, he told me later in Canton, where he was editor of the *Free Press*. His group of students was being escorted eastward in 1873 by a number of American friends from San Francisco when their train was held up by Jesse James' gang. Shots were fired and the passengers were ordered out. The American lady who took care of Li urged him to pray for divine protection. Li escaped unscathed, but his American escort was wounded by a bullet. "Lady," Li wondered aloud to her, "my God protected me but yours did not." They all survived, however, and Li managed to complete his college education. In retrospect, he felt that the aspect of American society which had meant most to him, and which he found most admirable, was freedom of the press.

Yung, the two Wongs, and the students of the original mission played pioneering roles in China's effort to modernize after the Opium War and particularly in the ill-fated attempt to become an American-style republic. There were then very few men in all of China who could read or speak foreign languages, let alone handle the western world's many gadgets and appliances. Although "Yung Wing's boys" were recalled in 1881, abruptly and more or less in disgrace, all of them were immediately in demand and placed in suitable positions.

Yung himself was sent to Peru in 1874 to investigate the treatment of Chinese laborers there. At the same time he was appointed, concurrently, associate Chinese minister to Peru, the United States, and Spain. He returned to China in 1881, after the collapse of his program, and launched into one enterprising scheme after another: a plan for the suppression of the opium trade with India, the establishment of a national banking system, the construction of a seven-hundred-and-fifty-mile railroad from Tientsin to Chen-chiang. He aided the reform movement, and he died in 1912 at the age of eighty-four. Two sons also were graduates of Yale.

When, as fortune would have it, I was appointed in 1933 to a post similar to Yung Wing's, my curiosity about him and the mission was aroused. I was able to find in Hartford quite a few of Yung's Kellogg relatives and met people who knew some of the students during their years in school. The Carringtons gave me a number of snapshots and school photos, the Bartletts showed me letters they had received from their Chinese "boys," and I heard many of the local legends about those "pigtailed kids" and their fights with anyone who tried to pull their queues or made fun of their "Chink" talk.

The careers of one hundred and twenty students are interesting. Except for five who went into business and twenty-five who failed to return, died early, or dropped from sight, all were in Government service, including three teachers of English, two newspaper editors, and two physicians. The largest number, nineteen, went into the navy, mostly in technical service branches such as engineering and communications. Only two became combat officers. Eighteen went into the diplomatic service, seventeen into railroading, sixteen into telegraphs, ten into mining, and three into the customs service. Almost all of the ninety-five were successful. Most of them retired well-to-do or wealthy.

Their social adjustment was something else again. They had come to the United States in their adolescence and spent impressionable years living with American families and going to school with American students. They were highly Americanized. Many of them preferred American clothes and American apple pie all their lives. When it came to having fun, they were most "at home" with their Yale or Amherst schoolmates singing American alma-mater songs and recalling American college days, yarns, and anecdotes. It is not too much of an exaggeration to say that those early American-educated Chinese students felt more or less like guests in their homeland and at home in America.

Another significant development was that virtually all of the ninety-five sent their children to the United States to study. Many of them had American godparents and maintained close to their alma maters. Some New England schools, like Phillips Academy, Amherst, Brown, Harvard, and Yale, have had four generations of Chinese graduates from the same families. Thus, although it was not until the United States Congress in 1908 first allotted Boxer Indemnity funds for scholarships that another major influx began, the steady trickle of Chinese students coming to the United States never stopped.

Many movingly human stories can be found in the personal letters of Chinese students to their American friends. My best find was the collection of letters from "the Chinese boys" to Mr. and Mrs. H. D. Fearing of Amherst, Massachusetts, after their return to China in 1881—a period of seventeen years during which they had to cope with their old-fashioned families, equally old-fashioned etiquette, and the obstinate imperial officialdom.

After China became a republic in 1911, the collective psyche of Chinese students in the United States changed in step with the drastic changes occurring in their homeland. The students felt, and were encouraged to feel, that they were much-needed potential leaders of their newly established Republic. The initial tendency was to search for American solutions to Chinese problems. Previously, most Chinese students had been satisfied with undergraduate studies. Now many wanted to obtain M.A.'s or Ph.D.'s. Their stays lengthened from an average of four or five to seven years. Some stayed as long as fifteen.

I have newspaper clippings about Miss Kang Tung-bac, daughter of Kung Yu-wei, a famous reformer who advocated constitutional monarchy and who was the leader of the ill-fated Reform of 1898. She could not matriculate at Wellesley or any other college, but was permitted to audit courses in political science at Harvard and to get some tutoring. She was too eager and impatient to fulfill academic requirements and study for degrees. She seems to have absorbed enough of the American inclination to political action to go to New

York, where she organized the Chinese Women's Freedom Association. She even staged a parade and a press conference, at which she unwound the bandages of her bound feet to symbolize her liberation from her own traditional bondage.

Another Chinese girl who made front-page headlines was Chin Ya-mei (Yamei Kin). Dr. and Mrs. McCarter of the American Presbyterian Mission had adopted Yamei, an orphan. She was the first Chinese woman to earn an American M.D. (Women's Medical College, Philadelphia, 1885). She interned at New York Infirmary. Because she was tiny (about five feet tall), looked like a teen-ager, and was Chinese, the hospital authorities offered to excuse her from ambulance service. She refused, insisting on bearing her share of the load. New York newspapers had great fun publicizing Yamei Kin's ambulance-riding and treating of accident victims, a frail but fearless Chinese girl in a white uniform. Among her many firsts, Dr. Kin founded the Peiyang Woman's Hospital in Tientsin, and did early (1917) research for the United States Department of Agriculture on the use of soybeans which helped to convince American farmers to grow the crop on a large scale.

I visited Dr. Kin in her home in Peking in 1937, and she reminisced fondly on her sixteen student years in the United States. After living and working in her homeland for more than half a century, she still talked and gestured like an American. Except for her ineradicable Chinese face, there was nothing Chinese about her. She wore an American dress, and the furniture and pictures on the walls of her living room were also American.

Immediately after its opening, China House hummed like a beehive with activity. Visitors, students, VIP's came by the hundreds each day during office hours, and in the evenings the public rooms were used by alumni associations and professional societies, for forums, weddings, and classes. In the first six months alone nearly two thousand Chinese and American visitors signed the guest register, which did not include those who attended special meetings, social parties, and classes. During the same six-month period, one hundred and two evening events took place, including a weekly "Friday Open House" and a celebration of John Dewey's eighty-fifth birthday.

To manage China House, China Institute had a staff of seven executives and thirteen clerical assistants. The executives were a treasurer, personnel manager, and the heads of our four principal departments: Students (scholarships, counseling, and other student services), Education (classes and public lectures), Publications, and Associates (supporters of the Institute, formerly "Members"). Plus me as director.

The volume of work was far too much for this small staff. Fortunately, volunteers had been and remained the backbone of China Institute. Three of our trustees—Mrs. W. Murray Crane, Walter H. Mallory, and Mrs. F. Louis Slade—extended to us the hospitality of their homes at all times. Mrs. Maurice T. Moore—Elisabeth Luce Moore, daughter of Henry W. and sister of Henry R.—was de-facto high adviser to the director and coordinator of public relations of the Institute. Our on-the-job trainee programs owed much to the guidance of Thomas J. Watson, Jr., of IBM and to Reginald E. Gilmor of Sperry Rand. The Americans among our advisers gave generously of their time and resources.

Private institutions devoted to the public good, plus the fund-raising necessary for their support, are an integral part of American culture. I relied on experienced trustees, especially Walter Mallory, Edward Carter, and Beth Moore. Mallory knew how to communicate his own conviction of the importance of the study of foreign relations, and he had been very successful in obtaining substantial financial support from Americans who were concerned with such problems. Carter did well for the Institute of Pacific Relations by focusing on the same motivation. But for China Institute there were no prospects of raising funds in war-torn China, and there were only a few wealthy Chinese in the United States who could be persuaded to see the worth of our work when they were faced with many other urgent appeals for contributions from China itself and from Chinatowns in the United States.

With Beth Moore's guidance, we therefore undertook the arduous task of raising funds from prominent New Yorkers interested in China, and from foundations, notably the China Foundation, the C. T. Loo, Josephine B. Crane, George Frederick Jewett, Starr, Vincent Astor, and Henry Luce foundations.

Trustees such as K. C. Li, Governor Charles Edison, Ambassador Edwin Stanton, Roswell Gilpatric, Pierre Goodrich of Indianapolis, Philo Parker, James Pickering, Alexander Calhoun, C. T. Shen, Gordon Tweedy, Alberta Gim, Thomas J. Watson, Louise Crane, Morley Cho, Mrs. James Augustus Thomas, Pang Won Hsu, C. C. Wong, William E. Little, and S. J. Yue were enormously helpful in developing important programs and finding the necessary support. They were joined by a host of enthusiastic friends, including Paul Douglas, Walter Judd, Mrs. Tsuyee Pei, Mansfield Freeman, Earl Morse, C. Y. Tung, and Mr. and Mrs. C. Y. Chen.

Dr. Ho Ching Yang was among our most distinguished board chairmen. A highly successful investment banker in New York, he had long been a doctor in China and had worked unstintingly to save soldiers and civilians wounded in the long war against Japan. He had served China Institute as chairman for only a few months when the exhausting war years took their toll, and he died. His widow, Von Sung Yang, took his place on the board and has continued her generous support in his memory. The China Institute Women's Association was organized, not only to support China House but to develop lively programs to be enjoyed by Chinese and Americans together. For many years we maintained hospitality committees in major cities across the country. Served by leading citizens of each community, they perpetuated the tradition of a warm welcome to, and friendly concern for, Chinese students and scholars.

Early in 1942, soon after the United States and China became allies, I was invited to help plan a nationwide campaign to encourage a feeling of comradeship between Americans and the Chinese people. The idea was the brainchild of Brigadier General Frederick Osborn, the busi-

China Institute, trustees and staff,
1959. Front, from left: Virginia Runton,
Emiline Nollen, Mrs. Charles W. Perdue, Mrs.
Edwin F. Stanton, Elisabeth Luce Moore,
Mrs. Chih Meng, Mrs. Alexander D. Calhoun.
Rear: K. Y. Ai, Mr. Calhoun, C. P.
Cheng, Henry R. Luce, Charles Edison,
Philo W. Parker, Walter H. Mallory, Mr.
Stanton, F. T. Cheng, C. F. Yau, author.
Bottom: Entrance to China House.

nessman-banker who became director of the Army's division of information and education, and Dr. Harry Stack Sullivan, the noted psychiatrist who headed the William Alanson White Foundation and the Washington (DC) School of Psychiatry. They told me that this need could be met instantly by a campaign in this country with the help of Chinese students. China Institute knew who the qualified and talented students were and was in a position to mobilize them.

After several consultations, we agreed that Chinese students throughout the country should be asked to participate in public meetings, and the Institute, together with local Chinese clubs, would compile lists of speakers, musicians, and others who were qualified and ready to help. It was agreed also that Chinese students who volunteered for, or who were drafted into, the American armed forces should be awarded American citizenship, just as were non-Asiatic aliens. This took quite a little doing because of American immigration regulations, which discriminated against naturalizing Asiatics. Our public program, however, was an immediate success. Hundreds of Chinese students helped to correct the general impression existing in many parts of the country that all "Chinamen" were laundrymen or chop-suey cooks.

From Pearl Harbor to VJ Day, Americans and Chinese were comrades-in-arms, and they joined in all kinds of activities pertaining to their common war. Chinese speakers were welcome and applauded in all kinds of public meetings, and so were street demonstrations by Chinese people. Newspapers and magazines increased their news and background coverage of China. I was deeply impressed that coordinated efforts could accomplish so much and so quickly. I expressed my admiration to General Osborn and Dr. Sullivan for their expertise and success, but also requested them, in no uncertain terms and more than once, to develop an equally effective psychological campaign for promoting peace and avoiding war in future.

There were many other events which brought China into greater public awareness in the United States.

The president of the University of Rochester, Alan Valentine, took the initiative of organizing a China Week for Rochester in

April, 1942. Chinese lecturers spoke to classes at the university and to women's and other clubs in the city. The climax was a mass meeting at the Eastman Theater, featuring an address by Hu Shih, now ambassador to Washington, and music by the Eastman-Rochester Symphony Orchestra.

Dr. Howard Hanson, the conductor, wanted to introduce the Chinese national anthem and some Chinese folk songs and war songs. Hu recommended me. Accompanied by the orchestra, I sang the Chinese national anthem, "San Min Chu I," two war songs, "Chi Lai" (Arise) and "The Great Wall," and a love song, "Can I Help But Think of Her?" before an overflow audience of some four thousand people.

This unexpected and unusual success bolstered my courage and led me to the realization that singing could give people a unity of purpose and feeling. I made up my mind to promote the singing of Chinese songs. Fortunately, there were in New York some fifteen Chinese students majoring in music, including two voice majors, J. K. Li and Florence Wong. Mr. Li, a tenor, had had considerable experience in conducting in China. Miss Wong was an accomplished performer with a beautiful soprano voice. On my staff at China Institute was J. Y. Yen (Yen Jen-ying), a lover of music who assumed the role of manager. The four of us organized the Chinese Chorus, or more formally, the National Reconstruction Choral Society. In two years we recruited and trained some forty members. We contributed our services to mass meetings and parades. We gave concerts in Carnegie Hall and the Brooklyn Academy of Music, and several radio stations broadcast our performances on their nationwide networks.

To celebrate China's independence day in 1944—October 10, "Double Ten"—the Columbia Broadcasting System requested me to repeat what I had done for Rochester. During rehearsals and the performance, an American watched over me all the time. I asked him whether he was assigned by CBS to be my bodyguard. "No," he replied, "I am your stand-in according to the requirements of the Musicians' Union." He was paid $60 an hour for all the time I spent with the orchestra. The broadcast was heard all over the United States and rebroadcast to China.

A rather sour note, however, came from Chungking saying that I had used a wrong word in singing the national anthem. "San Min Chu I"—The Three Principles of the People—was adopted when the Principles were the professed aim of the Kuomintang, and when the KMT advocated one-party government pending the establishment of a constitutional government. Hence, the first two lines were:

"San Min Chu I,
"Our party's aim."

I thought the Three Principles also were the aim of the whole nation. The Chinese people were fighting the war, not just the members of a single political party. Therefore, in the second line I substituted the word "nation" for "party." The Chinese Government Information Office in New York notified me of my error and demanded that I stop using this substitution. I discussed the matter with the head of that office, but firmly insisted that, since "San Min Chu I" was the national anthem, "nation" rather than "party" was the appropriate word.

A number of academic specialists on China volunteered their services. Professor John K. Fairbank of Harvard and his wife, Wilma Cannon, became associated with the State Department in Washington and worked with our committees on educational exchange. They maintained close contacts with Chinese scholars, and because of their extensive knowledge of China were able to give well-considered interpretations regarding situations and trends in China. They were mainly responsible for inaugurating the exchange of scholars and intellectuals between the two countries. Professor Howard Wilson of the Harvard School of Education helped the American Council on Education publish a series of pamphlets to widen and deepen the understanding of China among teachers, students, and others who wanted to know more of China's history and culture but could not do their own research.

210   American gourmets had an opportunity to become ac-

Activities at China House: Secretary
of State George C.Marshall (below) addresses an
audience in library. At speaker's table are
General Albert C. Wedemeyer; Wang
Shih-chieh, Chinese foreign minister,
and Henry R. Luce (1947). Bottom: Author
teaches a class on Chinese history and
culture (1965).

quainted with classical Chinese cuisine through three refugees stranded in New York. Mrs. H. H. Li, a middle-school principal in Canton, fled the Japanese invasion and opened a small restaurant in New York to support her large family. Her initiative won recógnition and her business prospered. Her spectacular success with both Chinese and Americans spurred others to follow and started a city-wide and then nation-wide movement for authentic Chinese cooking and a demand for Chinese cooking classes and cookbooks. Dorothy Chuan Lee, from Peking, a graduate in home economics from Cornell, could not return home. Florence Lin, a woman guerrilla fighter against the Japanese, managed to escape to New York. They proved themselves to be skilled in Chinese culinary arts, and helped the Institute to organize Chinese cooking classes.

Peking Opera also gained popularity, due to the efforts of J. Y. Yen, my colleague in the formation of the China Chorus. He was the grandson of Yen Fan-sun, a founder of Nankai School and a reporter for *Ta Kung Pao* of Tientsin. He was a gregarious fellow who seemed to enjoy company twenty-four hours a day. He endeared himself to all who knew him by his devotion to his friends and his public spirit. He was broad and heavily built, with an unusually large head and thick neck; his Nankai contemporaries called him "sea monster" (hippopotamus). He came to New York University in 1941 for further study. When he was unable to go back home because of the war, I employed him as my assistant for student activities. He was a fine amateur "warrior-baritone," a term describing the heavy voice required for one of the basic roles in Peking Opera. Hao Yeh-yuan, his Nankai schoolmate, also studying at NYU, was a professional Peking Opera singer, having been brought up by his famous father, Hao Shou-chen, a notable "painted-face" warrior. Yen and Hao gathered around them a number of talented amateurs and opera buffs who became the Peking Opera Club. They practiced regularly at China Institute. Soon they were able to give full-fledged performances that were worthy successors to Mei Lan-fang's pioneering tour. The club became so popular and its membership grew so large that it split into the Ya Chi and the Yeh

Yu Clubs, both of which still give regular performances in and around New York.

Western folk songs have spread through China for over a hundred years. At first they were Christian hymns sung in mission churches by Chinese converts. When modern schools were established at the turn of the century, more western music was introduced and many American-oriented schools adapted Chinese words to western melodies for their school songs. Nankai blended its Chinese lyric beautifully with the old German tune of "O Tannenbaum," thanks to Bob Gailey, who also taught us cheers for athletic meets and the American custom of organizing alumni associations. In the past sixty years Chinese alumni associations have multiplied as American "school spirit" infused our students. Nankai and Tsing Hua association meetings always are graced by school colors of purple and white and cheered by the lusty singing of our respective school songs.

For their part, Chinese folk songs began attracting notice in the United States around the 1920's, when American educators first thought of intellectual interchanges. Yenching University and the YWCA took the lead in publishing albums of Chinese songs translated into English and transcribed in modern notation. During World War II, two famous American singers, Paul Robeson and Margaret Speaks, learned and sang Chinese songs for vast audiences. I coached both of them on their Chinese diction. Miss Speaks's favorite was "Ssu Chi Hsiang Ssu" (Four Seasons Mutual Longing), a traditional love song. "Chi Lai" was popularized by Robeson. He introduced me to some of his favorite spirituals and urged me especially to learn "Old Man River" and consider the lot of his fellow blacks.

The International Ladies Garment Workers Union appointed Rose Pesotta, one of its vice-presidents, to organize Chinese women workers in New York. She saw me leading a Chinese women's parade down Fifth Avenue, past Twenty-third Street, near where she lived. She invited me to her home and asked me to help in her work. I had to admit that the Chinese women in my demonstration were not workers, but students and their relatives and friends. In our several meetings afterward, I did bring with me people who knew Chinatown, including Mr. and Mrs. Pan King Mok. They both had M.A.'s in education but could not get jobs in teaching. He was running a hand laundry and she was sewing in a sweat shop. We agreed that there was no quick way to organize women. The ILGWU must educate them in unionism first.

One result of those discussions was that Rose Pesotta got interested in knowing more about China. She invited me to talk to the members of her union at their recreational center, Unity House, in Pennsylvania, a spacious and beautiful campus with a lake, tennis courts, and indoor and outdoor theaters. At her suggestion, I gave Chinese song recitals and lectures, and brought my wife, Huan Shou, as my accompanist. I visited the Center for four summers, during which I got to know David Dubinsky and gained an insight into his union. Both he, as president, and Rose Pesotta had professional outreach and a sincere feeling for workers of all nations.

VJ Day and final victory in the Pacific marked the climax of China's collaboration with the United States in war and in planning for postwar reconstruction. Emotions had been built up around the success of our united war efforts and it seemed that even greater successes could be expected from the two countries' cooperation in time of peace.

The Chinese Students Activities Council of Greater New York took the initiative in organizing celebrations. The Council got enthusiastic support from the Chinese community in staging mass meetings, parades, and in particular our victory banquet, which was held in December, 1945, in the grand ballroom of the Hotel Roosevelt in New York City. The assembly of Chinese and Americans included more than five hundred graduates and faculty members of all Chinese universities, joined by a hundred distinguished guests representing American educational institutions, businesses, and industries. Chinese and American songs were sung by a male quartet. The concluding number was a *pi-pa* solo entitled "The Battle of Shanghai," rendered

214

by Shou-kuan Tam of Shanghai Conservatory and Yale.

As toastmaster I singled out for introduction from the honored guests Mrs. Wendell Willkie, widow of the late presidential candidate and "One World" advocate; Dr. Wu Yi-fang, president of Ginling College at Nanking; Walter Mallory, representing the Council on Foreign Relations; and Dr. Li Shu-hua, former minister of education and recent delegate to the UNESCO conference.

Our speakers included Dr. J. Leighton Stuart and Lin Yutang, who described vividly how American-educated Chinese professors had borne up during the war in spite of near starvation and repeated Japanese bombings.

Hu Shih was the main speaker. He summarized the essence of Chinese-American relations over the past forty years and affirmed that "The thousands of Chinese students educated in American schools and trained in American industries constitute the best salesmen of American products, material, intellectual, and spiritual."

As Hu predicted at the victory dinner, China Institute became a hub of activities aimed at the reconstruction of war-torn China.

I personally took charge of organizing China Reconstruction forums, in which Chinese and American specialists and students were invited to present papers or projects for open discussion. The proceedings were published in eight volumes of the *National Reconstruction Journal* (1942 to 1947). Major interests were assigned to different university and industrial centers, according to the concentrations of Chinese students and their special studies and their on-the-job training. Forums were conducted at four University of California campuses, at Chicago, Columbia, Cornell, Harvard, Illinois, Iowa, Michigan, MIT, Minnesota, Missouri, New York, Pennsylvania, Pittsburgh, Purdue, Washington, Wisconsin, and Yale. Detroit was a center for automotive studies, Milwaukee for farm machinery, Akron for the rubber industry, and San Francisco for international trade.

On the cultural level, China Institute cooperated with the State Department and China Foundation on educational exchange programs for students, scholars, writers, and artists. In the spiritual sphere we helped to locate Christian Chinese students and initiate small gatherings which we called Chinese Christian fellowships. Our policy was to expand from such intimate student groups to include their relatives and friends. Any groups finding it desirable might go on to form a church. This policy was recommended in order to by-pass theological, ritualistic, or denominational differences until the group should grow large and strong enough to pursue its own preferences. The ensuing years have proved the wisdom of this policy. Most Chinese Christian student fellowships are nonsectarian and self-led and self-supported. Some groups have grown to become congregations or churches, and a few are affiliated with American churches.

There was one other sphere Hu Shih did not mention specifically in his speech at the victory banquet: the sphere of human rights and democracy. Through the war years many Chinese students and scholars and their American friends had felt distressed by the Kuomintang dictatorship in China, but refrained from voicing their protest publicly for fear of hampering the war effort. Victory released some of us from the restraints war had imposed. I began to hold forums on human rights at China House. Three of those open forums attracted wide attention because of the speakers I invited: Li Huang, head of the moderate Young China Party; Feng Yu-hsiang, the "Christian General," of the KMT, and Tung Pi-wu, a founder of the Chinese Communist Party, who was in the United States briefly during the creation of the United Nations. The last of these forums, featuring a discussion of the CCP, caused complications for me. To my surprise, because I knew how busy he was, running Time, Life, and Fortune, Harry Luce attended all three forums from beginning to end and participated in the question-and-answer periods. Not long afterward, he told me that a report of the forum had reached Nanking, and that a high official had written to inquire whether Tung had been invited with his—Luce's—approval. Harry was quick to assure me that he really enjoyed that particular discussion. He had answered the Nanking letter by saying that, as director of China Institute, I had the authority to organize such open discussions, and that he, though chairman of the Board of Trustees, did not require prior approval. Of course, he knew my stand on one-party dictatorship, and from his own correspondent, Theodore White, had just learned of an American-educated middle-school principal who had been jailed and another American-educated professor who had been assassinated simply because they publicly advocated the legalization of other political parties. Nonetheless, like most Americans, he preferred to believe KMT assurances that its one-party tutelage would be temporary.

In appreciation for American aid to Chinese students during the war, the Chinese Ministry of Education offered a program of scholarships for Americans who had served in China during the war. The scholarships provided means to study Chinese culture in America, as well as in China, for periods of one to three years. China Institute was given responsibility for administering the program. With Hu Shih, now president of Peking National University, Professor Y. R. Chao of Harvard, Professor L. Carrington Goodrich of Columbia, and Roger Greene of the China Foundation, I served on the selection committee.

Our choices were ten young men, formerly of the army, navy, or Marine Corps, who now wished to study the Chinese, Japanese, or Russian languages and various aspects of Far Eastern history or contemporary political and cultural affairs. The awards were made at a special convocation in September, 1946, held in the library of China House. Ambassador V. K. Wellington Koo came from Washington to present the awards in behalf of the Chinese Government. John Foster Dulles, General Courtney Hodges and Admiral Thomas C. Kinkaid, military heroes of World War II, and Generals P. T. Mao and T. J. Kung of China were among the guests of honor. General Douglas MacArthur cabled a message of congratulations from Tokyo.

During the war we had assisted the founding and development of a sister China Institute of New Jersey. We called it our sister institute because it was founded by women and continuously administered by

217

women for fifteen years. Its story began when Dr. and Mrs. Phillips Greene returned from China in 1942 to Upper Montclair, New Jersey, after years of missionary work. They had been student volunteers—he from Harvard Medical School, and she from Wellesley College—and he had been teaching at Yale-in-China's Hsiang Ya Medical School. To their surprise, they found that American college people, faculties as well as students, were not much better informed about China than the Americans they had known nineteen years earlier.

Dr. Edward Hume, Hsiang Ya's president, had also returned and was head of the Postgraduate Medical School of New York when I succeeded in getting him to be secretary of the Board of Trustees of China Institute. He introduced me to the Greenes. Dr. Greene had taken up the practice of surgery, but Ruth Greene wanted to do something about promoting better understanding of China among colleges in northern New Jersey, and asked me for advice and help. Dr. Hume and I shared with her the experiences of our Institute and suggested that she attempt first to educate public school teachers through summer workshops at Montclair State Teachers College.

Mrs. Greene thought well of our suggestions and persuaded a few friends to help. Soon they were able to convince Dr. Harry A. Sprague, the president of the College, to organize the China Institute of New Jersey. Their first China workshop was held in the summer of 1943, with Dr. Sprague generously providing the facilities of the College, while I assembled a number of Chinese scholars as faculty. In the first five summers our instructors and lecturers included: W. T. Chan, professor of philosophy, Dartmouth College; K. C. Chen, former professor of psychology, Nanking University; Fung Yu-lan, professor of philosophy, National Tsing Hua University; Hu Shih; William Hung, professor of history, Harvard; Orient Lee, professor of history, National Central University; P. C. Lee, former dean of the Chinese National Conservatory of Music; Moushing Lin, director, Human Rights Sections, United Nations; Wu-chi Liu, visiting professor of literature, Yale; Y. P. Mei, former president of Yenching; Ai-lien Tai, Chinese dancer; Ya-chen Wang, former professor of fine art, Shanghai Art Institute;

and Na-sun Wu, specialist in Chinese art.

There were intensive two-week workshops, which offered classes each day from nine until four p.m. Evenings were devoted to lectures, concerts, dances, and films which were open to the public. The College granted three points toward a master's degree to those who passed a final examination and submitted a satisfactory written project.

All the registrants were elementary and secondary school teachers. Special efforts were made to help teachers who wished to introduce Chinese subjects in their classes. As a result of her study of Chinese art, Mrs. Doris Fox created a particularly original and noteworthy project at the Memorial Junior High and Grammar School in Passaic. Mrs. Fox arranged for a ten-week course to be devoted to Chinese-style art. Because the heritage and environment of China was so different from America, pupils and teachers made no attempt to imitate the manner or the skilled technique of the Chinese artist. These the children developed themselves. But everything they did was based upon the study of things Chinese. The end result was a knowledge of the Chinese way of life, and an appreciation of the fine arts of China, as well as an unusual understanding of some basic art principles.

The work created by the children, some of whom took the ten-week course over and over again in advanced forms because of their intense liking for it, was gathered into an exhibit. Along the third floor of the school, a double row of Chinese block designs, pictures, and posters representing Chinese life lined both sides of the hall. The children had listened to old Chinese fairy tales, ancient folk tales about the Chinese conception of the creation of the earth, stories of the celebration of New Year—just such stories as I had grown up with. Inspired by these, they painted their own imaginative pictures. The art room displayed wonderful Chinese figurines, modeled in clay, painted and fired in the school's kiln. Masks of demons and Buddhas were made from clay and papier-mâché. Pictures of Chinese dragons, portraits of famous Chinese, portraits of ordinary families, and scenes depicting family life were done in pastels, crayons, and water colors.

219

One wall was entirely devoted to the children's own impressions of Chinese classical art. Black-and-white pen drawings of graceful trees and plants broke up space in a truly Chinese manner. A feature was a shoulder-high screen painted in varying shades of blue and yellow, with scenes of trees, water, sky, and yellow birds.

Through the four hundred and fifty alumni of these workshops and their friends, interest in studying China spread to other parts of New Jersey and to school districts in Delaware and Pennsylvania, and many teachers came to China House for further information and teaching aids. Professor Floy Hurlbut of Ball State College of Muncie, Indiana, visited a workshop and was convinced that her college should inaugurate a similar summer session. As a result, Dr. John R. Emens, Ball State's president, invited me in 1950 to organize China Institute of the Midwest, which in turn stimulated a number of colleges in Indiana to introduce their own courses or workshops on China.

With the momentum and experience of New Jersey and Indiana, I was able to initiate between 1948 and 1961 similar projects for public school teachers at the University of Washington in Seattle, Mills College in Stockton, California, Cortland State Teachers' College, Cortland, New York, Central College at New Britain, Connecticut, and State College at San Francisco, California.

Alvin Johnson opened up for me the field of adult—or "continuing"—education. The New School for Social Research, which he had helped to establish, was intended to provide opportunities for adults to broaden their knowledge on new subjects and explore new fields of experience. Many suburban communities had similar adult schools. New York University, too, conducted adult-education classes in a number of places throughout Greater New York. By 1954 I had learned enough about these programs to offer my services to those in charge at NYU and various local school systems. In time, I succeeded in introducing classes on China in two dozen adult schools in Long Island, Westchester, New Jersey, and Connecticut.

The sizes of my classes varied from ten to ninety-seven, according to the subjects, the more popular ones being Chinese folklore and literature, and contemporary China. Practically all my students were college graduates; they included retired couples, and active club and church leaders. Most of them attended classes regularly and took the lectures seriously.

Many who attended kept in touch by writing or visiting me, and by inviting me to speak to their clubs, synagogues, and churches, and often by volunteering help to China Institute. Mrs. Ione Eckersen of Englewood, New Jersey, a graduate of my first class, offered an elective course on China at Dwight Morrow High School for eighteen years, until her retirement. Mrs. H. Kingsley Blake of Scarsdale introduced two courses at her Women's Club and organized the American Friends of China in Westchester, which raised funds for scholarships for needy Chinese students.

When I met Loo Ching-tsai in Paris in 1928, he was already well known in France as a wealthy Chinese art dealer and a generous giver to Franco-Chinese philanthropies, for which the French Government made him a *Chevalier de la Légion d'honneur*. His firm, C. T. Loo et Cie, had branches in London and New York. Except for short business trips, however, he had never really stayed in the United States until he departed France during the Nazi occupation and came to live in New York City.

Mr. Loo and C. F. Yau were old friends; Yau soon got him to help mount the art exhibitions at China House. Mr. Loo contributed a number of showcases, lent art objects from his New York branch office, and helped to secure loan collections from his wealthy friends and clients.

One wintry evening in 1949, my wife cooked a typical Peking "home-informal-dinner" for the Loos and the Yaus which they especially enjoyed because, except for Mrs. Loo, who was French, they were from Chekiang in South China. After dinner we sat around the glowing fireplace, talking. Conversation rambled to old times, our respective overseas sojourns, and the current war situation. Loo was induced to talk most because he was the senior and because we all

221

wanted to know more about his early life. In 1900, as an idealistic youth of twenty he had gone to France to prepare himself to reform his country. He had difficulty getting admitted to a French college. Lonely and discouraged, he joined a group of young Chinese republican revolutionaries, followers of Sun Yat-sen who had found refuge in France. They were recruiting new members from among Chinese students and raising funds to supply arms to Sun's forces in Shanghai and Canton. They did well financially by introducing and marketing soybeans and soy-bean foods. Their sale of Chinese art objects, too, prospered. Loo educated himself and became a specialist in Chinese antiques. With relish he related to us his discoveries of valuable Chinese art objects on farms outside of Lyon, many of which he purchased at small fractions of their market value. They had been brought home by French troops who had looted Peking in the punitive expeditions of 1860 and 1900.

In turn, Loo asked us about the Luce family, and how the Luce Foundation figured in the gift of China House. He commented on the comparative merits of the Chinese and American way of philanthropy. "In this modern age," he said, "the American way is perhaps better. Personal giving was all right in a simple society. Now giving should be entrusted to impersonal and expert management." In the ensuing months, Loo and I held several meetings with friends and attorneys who advised him how he could contribute beneficially to the needs of philanthropy. The result was that in May, 1950, the C. T. Loo Chinese Educational Fund was incorporated. Mr. Loo was to serve as president, my old friend Professor Goodrich as treasurer, Ferdinand W. Coudert as secretary and counsel. I became executive director.

The officers decided to make grants-in-aid to Chinese graduate students in the United States who were majoring in science and engineering, and to entrust China Institute with selection of the grantees. The Committee on Awards was composed of eminent scholars, such as Dr. Claude E. Forkner of Cornell Medical School, and Professors Franklin Ho (economics) and Chien-shiung Wu (physics) of Columbia. The accomplishments of the first ten groups of grantees

222

were testimony to the collective wisdom of the committee.

By 1966 scholarships and other grants for graduate students had become so abundant that the Loo scholarships were no longer needed. On the other hand, the fast-increasing number of Chinese students and intellectuals, and the confused Cold War situation, seemed to call for a more organized exchange of information and opinion among Chinese expatriates, and between Chinese leaders and their American counterparts. The Loo Fund directors obtained the cooperation of China Institute and provided funds to hold annual conferences for Chinese students and scholars, and on Chinese-American cultural relations.

Altogether, during the years 1933 to 1967, China Institute administered scholarship and fellowship funds deriving from no less than thirteen sources: Tsing Hua University, China Foundation, Chinese Geological Survey, Sino-British Boxer Indemnity, Frank M. Shu Fund, C. T. Loo Chinese Educational Fund, the Chinese Ministries of Agriculture, Education, and Railways, Yunnan Province, the United States Department of State, the Wartime Planning Committee for Chinese students stranded in the United States, and the program for training workers on the Burma Road.

As C. T. Loo was planning his Educational Fund, other Chinese associates and friends of China Institute were discussing how they might contribute to meeting China's postwar needs. Among the prime movers were shipping magnates C. Y. Chen and C. T. Shen, and filmmaker Wango H. C. Weng. They needed legal advice and American help in organizing. Edward Hume and I arranged meetings in 1948 and 1949 between them and Newbold Morris, then a prominent New York attorney, and Professor Magnus Gregersen of Columbia, a physiologist and articulate advocate of war relief for China. The result was the establishment of the China International Foundation, which contributed medical aid to China and provided funds for a much-needed survey of Chinese students and professionals in the United States. China Institute conducted the survey in 1950–1.

223

Peace had not come to China after victory in East Asia. With the defeat and withdrawal of Japan, Chiang Kai-shek's Nationalists and Mao Tse-tung's Communists rushed to fill the vacuum, and civil war resulted. Since the United States aided the Nationalists, the victorious Communists started a hate-America campaign and began a purge of all Chinese with an American education or American connections. In the new exodus, it was estimated that more than twelve thousand Chinese intellectuals managed to escape to the United States by the end of 1949.

United China Relief, formed during the war by concerned Christian churches and other relief organizations, turned its attention to the problems of stranded Chinese students and escapees. In 1948, its chairman was Charles Edison—son of Thomas A. Edison, the inventor—who had been Secretary of the Navy and also governor of New Jersey. He became so interested in helping Chinese students that he joined China Institute and worked hard as chairman of its Finance Committee. He frequently invited groups of Chinese students to his home in Menlo Park and personally conducted them through his father's historic laboratory.

The findings of our survey made it possible for both China Institute and United China Relief to focus efforts and funds where they were most needed. In addition to giving vocational information and guidance, China Institute encouraged the organization of academic and professional associations, the largest of which were the Chinese Medical Association and the Chinese Institute of Engineers.

Perhaps the most significant development in the succeeding years was the increased employment of Chinese teachers in American schools. During the academic year, 1959–60, China Institute learned that more than eleven hundred Chinese scholars had attained professional rank on the faculties of nearly three hundred American colleges and universities. Sixty-two were teaching specifically Chinese subjects, while the rest were teaching or conducting research in different fields of science and engineering. Twelve colleges and universities had twenty or more Chinese faculty members: California 79, Illinois 65, Yale 39, Michigan 36, Wisconsin 32, MIT 31, Harvard 30, Iowa 29, Maryland 28, Washington (Seattle) 23, Columbia 21, and Hawaii 20. We also received interesting reports about Chinese teachers in the public-school system, but it would have been beyond our resources to survey the public schools properly. Since 1960 the number of Chinese teachers and Chinese students in American schools has increased many fold.

By 1955 the continuing discussions on China's postwar reconstruction had been completed, but China Institute's trustees and associates wanted to capitalize on the momentum which had been built up. Accordingly, the Institute offered a series of public lectures, which were so well attended that we had to set up a sound system so that lectures could be broadcast to guests seated in other parts of the building. Among our lecturers—and their topics—were:

Dr. Hu Shih, "Three Founders of Chinese Thought."

Dr. Y. P. Mei, Princeton, "Buddhist China and Chinese Buddhism."

Dr. William Hung, Harvard, "Tu Fu, the Greatest Chinese Poet."

Dr. Hsin-Hai Chang, Long Island University, "Chinese Influences on Western Culture."

Dr. P. C. Chang, Nankai University, "Chinese Theater: Development and Technique."

Dr. Wu-chi Liu, Yale, "Great Novels of China."

Dr. Shao-chang Lee, Michigan State, "The Spirit of Chinese Culture as Reflected in Chinese Houses and Gardens."

Dr. Lien-shen Yang, Harvard, "Interpretations of Chinese History."

Dr. Wing-tsit Chan, Dartmouth, "China's Contribution in Philosophy."

Dr. Frank W. Price, Missionary Research Library, "China's Contribution in Religion."

Dr. L. Carrington Goodrich, Columbia, "China's Contribution in Science."

Dr. Nelson Wu, Yale, "China's Contribution in Art."

Dr. Lin Yutang, "Chinese Calligraphy as Abstract Art."

Chou Wen-chung, composer, "Chinese Music and Its Significance."

Ssu-cheng Liang, architect, "Chinese Architecture: Some of Its Historical, Philosophical, and Aesthetic Aspects."

Dr. Arthur W. Hummel, Library of Congress, "The Art of Social Relationships in China."

In order to focus public attention on Chinese-American cultural relations and to bring together representatives in this field from other parts of the country, China Institure decided also to hold an annual round-table conference. Seeking adequate facilities in a convenient location, we were fortunate to have the help of our associate, Dr. Adolf E. Zucker, professor of German literature, and chairman of the Faculty Committee on International Relations at the University of Maryland. Dr. Zucker also had taught me German at Tsing Hua, and we were devotees of the Peking Opera; in fact, he wrote a book about it: *The Chinese Theater.* When I began work at China Institute he was among the first to volunteer to help. He persuaded Maryland to join the Institute in staging annual conferences on Chinese-American cultural relations, a total of ten between 1955 and 1966. They were attended by a hundred to a hundred and fifty representatives at closed sessions and by hundreds of others at open meetings. Conference reports were widely distributed in the United States and China. At the tenth conference the Institute and the University appointed a Continuation Committee which recommended that a professional organization be formed to carry on some of the programs suggested by the conferences. The result was the American Association for Chinese Studies, which is composed of Chinese and American teachers active throughout the United States in a variety of fields, including Chinese language and literature.

Our prolonged isolation from mainland China after the People's Republic lowered its "Bamboo Curtain" in 1949 caused some of us at

China Institute to see visions and dream dreams. One was a project for a Chinese university-in-exile which received the enthusiastic approval of many Chinese and American associates of the Institute before the "normalization" of relations between the United States and China in 1978 removed its raison d'être.

Although the project itself was overtaken by events, its objectives and programs still are relevant. They included research on agricultural sciences and industrialization; training for public administration and management, and a staff for the compilation and translation of related documents. I hope that these needs will not be overlooked by existing American institutions interested in China.

I would like to believe that a second dream still is viable. This was a proposal to erect in New York an authentic Chinese building of pure classical architecture, which would be not only a thing of beauty, but a profitable enterprise. According to Liang Ssu-cheng, director of the Institute of Chinese Architecture in Peking and visiting lecturer at Yale, there was not a single building truly representative of classical Chinese architecture in the United States. Liang was a graduate of Tsing Hua, where his famous father, the great Confucian scholar Liang Chi-chao, was my professor of philosophy. His sister, Ssu-yi, was on my staff. In our frequent visits the dream of such a building emerged. We consulted K. C. Li and C. F. Yau. They believed that the building could be a commercial success, and went so far as to look for desirable locations and sound out probable tenants.

In the block next to China House there was an abandoned trolley-car barn. The entire site between East 65th and 66th Streets, and Lexington and Third Avenues, was for sale. All three of my colleagues worked hard at planning a building which would include not only office space, but a theater, bazaar, restaurant, and an outdoor rock garden. Liang promised to design the building and garden in Peking Palace style, while Messrs. Li and Yau were raising the required capital investment among their friends. Liang, however, died while making the drawings; the block was sold and an apartment house went up on the site.

227

K. C. Li and I later attempted to revive the project by rebuilding the two blocks of Chinatown bounded by Mott, the Bowery, Mulberry, and Bayard Streets. We got the endorsement of the eminent Robert Moses in his capacity as consultant to the New York City Planning Commission, and of Herman Stichman, commissioner of public works. We also obtained the moral support of much of the Chinese community and the Chinese consul general. The project had to be abandoned, however, because of opposition from the landlords in the area.

In the past, Chinese art and art objects were an esoteric preserve of museums, specialists, and art collectors. However, a few educators found art to be very effective in conveying cultural traits and patterns when properly taught. In New York, for example, Miss Helen Parkhurst, principal of Dalton School, approached China Institute as early as 1931 concerning the use of Chinese art in her school. C. F. Yau was asked to assist in lending the school objects suitable for exhibition and teaching purposes. This experimental project led to classes in Chinese paper cutting and folding, kite making and flying, and so on, for the lower grades, with classes in painting and ceramics for high-school grades, and special exhibits and conducted tours of museums for teachers. Other private schools, such as Lincoln and Horace Mann, also found these undertakings fruitful.

When the Institute acquired China House, Mr. Yau proposed that the front room on the first floor be used as an art gallery for special exhibitions. He organized a committee to assist him and secured the cooperation of the Chinese Art Society and various art museums throughout the country. Following our highly regarded inaugural display of Chinese ceramics from the Han through the Sung dynasties, subsequent major exhibits were organized by a committee of distinguished art experts with Myron S. Falk, Jr., as the first chairman, followed by John Crawford and Gordon Washburn. Among the exhibitions were Lacquerwork, Three-Color Porcelain Figures of the K'ang Hsi Period, Animals and Birds in Ancient Chinese Bronzes,

Silver from the Han to the Ch'ing Dynasty, Imperial Textiles, Snuff Bottles of the 17th and 18th Centuries, Album Leaves from the Sung and Yuan Dynasties, Ming Porcelains, Silk Tapestry, Dragons in Chinese Art, and Tantric Buddhist Art. Guest curators from various museums installed the exhibitions and edited our handsomely illustrated catalogues. The shows were reviewed enthusiastically by newspapers and art journals. Between major exhibitions the gallery is used to show the work of contemporary Chinese artists and that of students in China Institute's own art classes.

One day early in 1957, K. C. Li summoned me to his office in the Woolworth Building to meet a distinguished gentleman who wanted to talk with me. The visitor was Li's old friend, Dr. F. T. Cheng, whom he had known since they were students together in London. Dr. Cheng wished to explore a proposal I had made to bring over from China a unique art exhibit.

Cheng's life had been a remarkable story of uninterrupted success in law and diplomacy, and his personality was a perfect blending of the best quallities of East and West. At seventy-three he had retired to the private practice of law after more than forty years of public service, including such posts as chief justice of the Supreme Court of China, member of the Permanent Court of International Justice at The Hague, and Chinese ambassador to the Court of St. James's. More than this, he was an authority on Chinese art. In 1935, when the British Government succeeded in borrowing a collection of Chinese art objects from the Peking Palace Museum, Dr. Cheng had been appointed high commissioner responsible for conveying the priceless cargo to London for Queen Victoria's Diamond Jubilee celebration. The objects had never before been shown, even in China, and their exhibition was such a great international success that it was extended an additional year.

In 1952 I had begun to think about an historical landmark in Chinese-American cultural relations: the approaching hundredth anniversary of Yung Wing's graduation from Yale. K. C. had shown me catalogues and newspaper clippings about the British exhibition, and we thought how wonderful it would be to bring it here to be shown to the American public. I thought Yale and China Institute might approach the Chinese Government, now reestablished on Taiwan, to borrow the same or a similar art collection to celebrate the Yung Wing centennial. I consulted Henry R. Luce and Han Lih-wu, Minister of Education and a director of the Palace Museum, and submitted a proposal in 1953 which was adopted by the trustees and approved by the minister, and agreed to by A. Whitney Griswold, then president of Yale.

We soon discovered that one year was not enough time to arrange for safe transportation of the objects. The Chinese Government wanted guarantees similar to those made by the British, including ocean transportation by American warships. After four years our negotiations still were snarled in bureaucratic red tape.

At our meeting, it was clear that Dr. Cheng knew all about our proposal. Since we could no longer use the Yung Wing centennial as our rationale, he suggested that a group of major American museums make a joint request of the two Governments to provide facilities to transport the collection safely.

With Henry Luce prodding both Governments, the proposal moved slowly through the machinery of Washington and Taiwan. It took another four years for them to agree on details, and for the appointed committees to select two hundred and thirty-one art treasures: 112 paintings, twelve displays of calligraphy, three embroidered silk tapestries, five bronzes, ten jade carvings, fifty-six ceramic pieces, sixteen pieces of enamel work and cloisonné, eight lacquer pieces, and nine carvings in bamboo, wood, and ivory. All the objects would be seen in the United States for the first time, some of them for the first time ever outside of China. The collection was brought over in 1961 in American naval ships and exhibited at the National Gallery of Art in Washington, the Metropolitan Museum of Art in New York, the Museum of Fine Arts in Boston, the Art Institute in Chicago, and the De Young Memorial Museum in San Francisco. In New York, China

Institute was given the privilege of sponsoring a private showing at the Metropolitan attended by more than twelve hundred associates and friends.

Dr. Cheng subsequently was elected a trustee of China Institute, a role he undertook conscientiously. He attended trustees' meetings regularly, often coming from London to do so, and he lectured frequently on the teachings of Confucius and Mencius. He was an excellent cook and enjoyed making exotic dishes for the elegant dinners he served the inner circle of his friends.

Incidentally, President Griswold did arrange a special convocation at Yale to celebrate the centennial of Yung Wing's graduation on June 13, 1954, with an academic procession and commemorative addresses by Hu Shih, Edward H. Hume, and me.

An air of unreality pervades my recollection of the Cold War and Bamboo Curtain years. I remember them as a period to get over with as soon as practicable. For Chinese in the United States there was plenty to occupy us. We tried to become good citizens and raise good children. Personally, I tried to have China Institute meet the rising demands of nonspecialists for opportunities to study China in schools, clubs, churches and synagogues, and to promote cultural relations with Taiwan. In our public lectures and forums, we had to avoid political issues because there was division both among the Chinese and their American friends, and, more often than not, the divided opinions were charged with emotion and personal involvement.

While celebrating the fortieth anniversary of the founding of China Institute in 1966, I came to the realization that I had been engaged in the search for Chinese-American understanding for more than sixty years—the span of time known in the West as a "cycle of Cathay." In my search I had traveled to hundreds of Chinese and American educational centers, and had talked to, taught, and met thousands of individuals. Meanwhile, the interest of many younger spirits had been kindled on both sides of the Pacific and they had taken up the cause. China Institute had acquired binational recognition and sup-

231

port, and a stable financial base. It was time for me to retire.

My trustees were most considerate. They allowed one year for me to plan my retirement and for them to find a successor. At the annual trustees' meeting in 1967 I gave my farewell address, summarizing my stewardship as director for the past thirty-seven years.

"The first thing which comes to mind," I remember saying, "is that China Institute means so much business and hard work—but it is more than all that. Personal friendship and dedication to a common interest brought about its birth, nourished its growth, and stood by it through thick and thin. In my *lao ma* ["old horse"] statement—a farewell address—I referred to this. As fellow-workers in a common cause, we have gone through periods of ups and downs. But our strivings together add deeper meaning and produce enduring values to the managing of our business operation and achievements.

"Today is the festival of *yuan hsiao* (the first full moon), or the Feast of Lanterns of the Year of Ting Wei. My heart is full of happiness and gratitude to all of you here, and to many others who are not here, for our many years of association and for your unfailing friendship and support."

Before I left office, the trustees gave me a testimonial dinner. Henry Luce III was the chief speaker, and I include here some of his remarks, not out of vanity, but because I always have been pleased to be included among the valiant company of missionaries, so many of whom helped to set my feet in the path I have followed.

"As most of you know," Henry said, "my grandfather was a missionary to China, and in one way or another, the quality of missionary was the one which stood highest in my father's constellation. As he saw it, it is the statesmen, journalists, theologians, and educators who carry the word and the truth in this world, and thus all of them are missionaries.

"So we are gathered here tonight to pay tribute to a missionary—a missionary from China to America. Paul Meng's mission to America began, believe it or not, some forty-eight years ago, and its purpose was to spread the word and the truth about his country and his people. It often seemed during that time that, if ever there was a labor of love among the heathen, it was the effort to explain China to Americans. For at certain critical times and in certain critical places, the American understanding of China was tragically faulty. But I think it can now be said that the labor has succeeded, and that there is indeed in America a more informed understanding, a more accurate appreciation, and a more practical awareness of China than exists in any other country of the world.

"The association of the Luce family with the Meng mission goes back farther than some of you may suppose. For it was my grandfather who conferred on Dr. Meng his anglicized name of Paul the name of the greatest missionary of them all. . . .

"Paul, it was twenty-three years ago that you and my father looked over this building and decided to make it China House. Ever since you have managed it with patience, imagination, wisdom, and enough of that missionary zeal to make it thrive and to make its presence felt from 65th Street to wherever there has been sympathetic concern for friendly understanding between Americans and Chinese."

From its headquarters in China House, China Institute in America continues to seek the way to mutual understanding for people of good will in both nations. Near the end of a life devoted to that goal and closely intertwined both with the Institute and the House, I take most satisfaction from the many strong friendships that have developed among those engaged in this effort. In China the most treasured friendship is *shih chiao*—"generations of mutuality." *Shih chiao,* I think, has been achieved by the many representatives and associates of China Institute, whether staff or volunteer, across America. To my successors: heartfelt good wishes. May your efforts be fruitful. May your light continue to shine.

Reflections

In my student years at Nankai and Tsing Hua, Chinese and western ways of life were subjects of hot debate in and out of the classroom. What seemed the obvious superiority of modern western culture influenced students to downgrade traditional religion and humanism, and to look up to science and technology. Hu Shih and his associates, such as V. T. Ting, the noted geologist, emerged as the most forceful and eloquent advocates of scientific living, which, in their view, included pragmatism and atheism. They went to the extreme of advocating abandonment of the institution of familyism, and total adoption of western culture.

Ironically, while this avant-garde was wholeheartedly seeing western science and technology as a panacea for China's ills, some western historians and scientists were arguing that study of Chinese history and philosophy might benefit western nations. (It was Bertrand Russell's conviction that "a civilized Chinese is the most civilized person in the world.") Nor was this western interest in the Chinese model new. In the eighteenth century China fascinated the West at all levels of society, from prime minister to storekeeper. The civil-service examination system adopted in England and later copied in the United States owed much to the inspiration English reformers found in China's civil structure.

Indeed, there has been no lack of recognition of the potential importance of Chinese culture to the world. Yet it would be hard to say that the West has genuinely learned much from Chinese culture or the Chinese way of life. Certainly the world, including America, still needs to learn more, if it can, about how to live "long and contentedly."

As the earlier portions of my story perhaps have made obvious, it seems to me that the world would benefit greatly if popular attitudes and ideals could move more toward those of the Chinese in such matters as the importance of the family, and in respect for things of the spirit and for the pacific way of life, as against the materialistic pursuit of wealth and power, which, to my mind, is ultimately inseparable from militarism and war. If it is important to master professions and technologies, it is more important, more urgent, for mankind to find a common meaning to life, and to commit itself to a common

234

course of action. Only thus can men avoid the dire consequences of repeating history and discover new ways to achieve a more civilized and happy world.

The traditional Chinese attitude toward all social structures, including national governments, is based on the philosophy of familyism. The relations between men and women lead naturally to family relations and then, by projection, to national and international relations. The relation of a ruler to the people ruled was equated with the relation of a parent to his children. Instead of checks and balances and adversary procedures, social, political, and legal philosophy all emphasize reasonableness, accommodation, and acceptance of reciprocal obligations for the common good. That individual rights, for example, or even the rights of particular ethnic groups or labor unions, could take precedence over the welfare of the nation as a whole would be unthinkable in Chinese society.

Chinese regard for the family is inseparably connected with the Chinese attitude toward sex. Here, too, it would be far better, in my mind, for the West to learn from China than for China to copy the West. Since the 1960's the trend in the United States has been toward extreme individualism. As an aspect of this, sexuality seems to have become more or less an end in itself. For many, the institution of the family has become incidental; similarly, family solidarity and continuity.

The Chinese word for sex is *hsing,* which also is the word for nature. The dual meanings in western terms of this one word illustrate the Chinese view of the central importance of sex in both the social and physical world. From time immemorial, all Chinese people have believed that the cosmos originated from the twin principles of Yin and Yang, female and male principles, which attract and also repel each other. In classical literature, Yin is always mentioned first because we believe it underlies water, moon, and motherliness, and all other creative and reproductive elements and virtues.

Yin and Yang manifest themselves in women and men most poetically and dramatically. Sex relations, when properly conducted, are beautiful and romantic, but when misdirected can be ugly and degrading. In Chinese, sexual intercourse is *hsing chiao* (nature mutual). At its most desirable, it is a factor of marriage, begetting offspring, and perpetuating the family. To Chinese, family life, birth, marriage, and death are the major events and concerns. We talk about, plan and prepare for them so we may experience them, celebrate them, and derive from them appropriate observances and the rightful meanings. For instance, conception or pregnancy is called *yo hsi* (acquiring joy). Begetting children is not accidental, not an afterthought or by-product. It is regarded as the most important and creative mission in life. It preserves the continuity, the "flowing fragrance," of the family, and by extension of society as a whole.

To Chinese, sexuality is thus too universal and too powerful for individuals to establish self-gratification as an ideal. In their current fascination with sex, Americans may be surprised to know that China in its distant past went through similar cycles in man-woman relations. The sixth century B.C., for example, was a period of permissiveness. Boys and girls met freely, marriage was taken lightly, divorce was easy. It was Confucius and his followers who established the dominance in Chinese culture of the moral values of familyism. By the Han dynasty (208 B.C.–A.D. 222), customs and etiquette governing man-woman relations were firmly established, and they have remained more or less constant, except for one two-hundred year disruption.

We learned our lesson from that one major disruption, when China was overrun and ruled by five tribes of barbarians from the North (386–589). During the period, pleasure resorts and a cosmetics industry flourished and sexual indulgence was rampant. Urban high society lived riotously all night and slept all day, and its women went around barebreasted and barebacked and bathed nude in public. The reaction to this period was puritanical.

Yet Chinese pornographic art flourished sub rosa during Sung dynasty (960-1279), when this Puritanism was at its most severe. Like other brushworks of that period, these Sung paintings and their later imitations are symbolic and suggestive rather than realistic. They can be characterized as graphic guidelines to the enjoyment of sex.

I have already mentioned the existence of certain plays and novels which young people were not supposed to read, such as the drama, *Romance of the Western Chamber,* and the novel, *Golden Lotus.* The latter was so graphic that it was banned even in England when it was first translated, and as late as World War II it was difficult to find an unabridged translation in bookstores and libraries in the United States. In 1937 the curator of the Peking Palace Museum showed me forty-seven scrolls of beautifully painted, multicolored pornography which had been discovered in the living quarters of the Purple Forbidden City.

Such pornographic literature and pictures were, by usage, permitted only to married people. The pictures bore the designation *Chún Kung* (Spring Palace, scenes). Spring, the Chinese learned long ago, is the time when nature generates interaction between Yin and Yang. Likewise, *chún yi* (spring idea), *chún ssu, chún chíng,* etc., are terms for the fancies of romantic young people. And so we have developed expressions and terms to denote relations between women and men and processes or forces of nature. Copulation is called *chiao ho,* (mutual union), or *yün yü* (cloud rain = orgasm), or *yü shueh chih huan* (fish-in-water joy). Romantic love is *feng liu* (breeze trended). Sexual aberrations, however, are treated as deviations from nature. Adultery is termed *yin* (pronounced with a rising inflection; not to be confused with the term for female principle), which literally means "too much water." For more than twenty-one centuries it has been the Chinese belief that, just as the greatest mission in life is to bring up good children, the greatest sin is adultery.

Chinese wisdom warns: "Balance the sex instinct with virtue" and "Restrain the indulgence in sex when blood and emotion are hot and strong." I should think American parents and teachers would find it desirable to do more than is done today to help young people to develop a healthy and balanced view toward sex and to resist the temptation of easy access to pills and promiscuity. Prudence and firmness are needed to guide young people away from drugs and harmful foods; greater wisdom and determination are required to educate young people in how to differentiate between the prurient and the romantic.

Cultural interchange, however, is and should be a two-way street. What, beyond technical knowledge, has China to learn from the West? In a sense, this was the question I encountered in 1936, when I was asked to make recommendations as to how the Chinese Ministry of Education should structure its program of scholarships to students for study in the United States. My answer was emphatic: the purpose of sending Chinese students to the United States should be twofold. The first was, indeed, to acquire up-to-date information and specialized methodology in science and technology. But a second and equally important purpose was to study the American way of life for guidance in making social progress and political reform in China.

My recommendation became entirely moot and remained so throughout the years of war, the aftermath of war, and the period of the Bamboo Curtain which isolated mainland China from the United States after 1949. With relations once again normalized, however, the policy of sending Chinese students to the United States deserves fresh scrutiny and a revival of open discussion. I hope that modern China will see its way to restoring a two-way people-to-people cultural exchange, the freer the better. There still are sizable groups of Chinese people, not all of them ideological Communists, who regard Americans as profit-motivated imperialists. There still are Americans, I am sorry to say, who think of the Chinese as heathens of a lesser breed. Most disturbing to me, quite a number of Chinese who have received highly specialized training in the large urban graduate schools of the United States understand little of traditional American values, and are prejudiced against them by what they see and hear of American lawlessness and civil strife.

Any program of cultural interchange which does not include as a principal goal mutual understanding at the popular level is entirely inadequate to the modern situation. During the past sixty years an impressive number of Chinese and Americans have been engaged in promoting such understanding to the best of their ability. They have, of course, not achieved their goal, and some of their efforts may have produced misunderstandings, in spite of good intentions. Yet my own search has convinced me that these efforts have been worthwhile, and that—quite apart from matters of technological progress—China has on balance clearly benefited.

Most American commentators, I believe, have been overly critical of the American missionary effort and of "do-gooders" who have attempted to change China. It is such do-gooders who have blazed the trail for bringing Chinese students to the United States ever since the days of Yung Wing and his fellows, who have introduced Chinese studies in American universities, and who, through their support of such schools as Tsing Hua and Nankai, Yenching and Nanking, created for generations of Chinese a window onto the western world. The Chinese still have much to learn from America which need not violate their traditional values. The tradition of individual freedom, so precious to Americans, would be a most important contribution to Chinese society if it could be reconciled, as I believe it can, with individual discipline, so that personal liberty is not permitted to be destructive of the welfare of the nation. China and the Chinese still have an excessive concern with personal status, one manifestation of which is the importance of "face." The imperial potentate who expected Chinese students whom he interviewed in the United States to kneel before him represented an attitude all too prevalent in Chinese officialdom. A greater willingness to deal with people on the basis of human equality and mutual respect would be salutary—and completely in accordance with the teachings of China's great philosophers. Finally, China and the Chinese remain too ethnocentric culturally. They are inward-looking rather than outward-looking. Over the next sixty years a more global outlook will be imperative, and a wide cultural opening to the United States can be the catalyst.

As I have grown older, I have come more and more to feel that there can be no higher priority for human effort than the cause of peace. During my last year at Tsing Hua I met Norman Thomas and became

239

Family: Huan Shou Kwoh and Chih Meng
with Elizabeth and Paul (rear), Virginia
and James (front). Left: Author
returns—with pleasure—to scenes of
youth at Silver Bay (1976).

interested in the pacifist movement he was fostering among American students. Since then, student antiwar sentiment has flared up strongly from time to time, most prominently perhaps in demonstrations against the Vietnam war. Yet it cannot be said that pacifism as an ideal has ever played a central role in American thought or national policy. Is it too much to hope that this might change, and that in this, as in the case of the noble principles of liberty and equality enshrined in the Declaration of Independence, the United States might again provide spiritual leadership to the world?

One psychological difficulty is surely that war continues to be honored in the belief systems of the West. The heroes of the past are very largely war heroes, and the history actually taught is largely a history of wars. Prominent among the virtues held up to young people for imitation are the classical military virtues.

For China the reverse is true. In *Spring and Autumn,* our oldest history classic, it is clearly stated that no war is righteous. In the *Four Books* Mencius teaches that benevolence and good government, not force or the use of armies, are the only way to win the allegiance of the people and secure peace among states. Throughout China there are hardly any war monuments, and statues of war heroes are few and far between. But shrines have been erected in practically all town and cities in honor of gentle and virtuous folk who have personified the ten virtues laid down in our classics and universally admired by all Chinese people:

温 Wen—Moderation and warmth

良 Liang—Goodness

恭 Kung—Respectability

儉 Chien—Frugality

讓 Jang—Modesty

仁 Jen—Benevolence

義 Yi—Righteousness

禮 Li—Politeness

智 Chih—Wisdom

信 Hsin—Sincerity

These ten qualities are extolled in folklore and folk tales as well as in festivals and on stage. Young children are trained and praised for acquiring them, rather than for physical prowess.

It most be confessed that China's philosophical dedication to pacifism has not spared the Chinese people the pains of war. Yet Americans have a proven genius for innovation and a capacity for leadership which, if dedicated to this greatest of all goals, fortified by a genuine belief that the path of peace is the only path open if man is to have a future, might achieve what neither philosophers nor religious leaders of the past had been able to accomplish.

Nations of the world cannot just coexist without firmly agreeing on which of their ideals and goals are basic, and without accepting the necessity of flexibility on all other differences. Surely the irreducible minimum goal must be the renunciation of war as a way of settling differences. It is almost a cliché then to say that disputes must be referred to the United Nations or some other appropriate body for reconciliation.

From the dawn of civilization, thinkers and religious leaders have formulated Utopias, and prayed under one name or another, for the Kingdom of Heaven on earth—what Chinese philosophers have called the Ta Tung, or Great Commonweal. Human progress in this, as in all else, must come through vision, and then faith, just such vision and faith as are the quintessence of every religious system, even, I suggest, that of communism. All religions converge on a belief in the brotherhood of man.

Such a faith cannot be inculcated in the peoples of the world by the demonstrative methods of experimental science. I believe, however, that they can be led toward it through humility and a convergence of collective experience.

In my lifelong search for Chinese-American understanding I have hoped, within the limits of my capacity, to bring our peoples to recognize their brotherhood, and thus to advance the cause of world peace. Western democracies have not impressed the Third World with their devotion to peace and brotherhood. On the contrary, in the eyes of the Third World, western democracies, including the United States, have continued to play geopolitical games and have even adopted Communist "dirty tricks" to fight communism. American Christian leaders have been too preoccupied with their theological and sectarian infighting to resume their global leadership. Generations have grown up in contradictory and confusing situations which have generated revolt, cynicism, and despair. The cumulative result is the overturning of established values and of law and order, with a reign of terror spreading from within the home to local and international communities.

Materialism, militarism, and racism have sown the seeds of division. Another cycle of chaos has set in, quite like what Mencius described twenty-three centuries ago: "Society is degenerating; the way of life has become obscure; depraved philosophies and violence are on the rise; ministers are assassinating their lords and sons are murdering their fathers."

I refuse to despair. It was American idealism and leadership which established the League of Nations after World War I, and transformed it into the United Nations after World War II. For all their defects, these represent the first institutional effort on the part of humanity as a whole to solve its problems. The Kellogg-Briand Pact, abortive though it was, gave voice—again under American leadership— to mankind's longing for peace.

The Government of the United States ultimately reflects its people. If, as I have dreamed, it falls to the United States to be the prime mover in outlawing war and ending all forms of world hegemony, it will be because the idealism I have found so abundant in the American people has been translated into the practices of our society.

Mankind needs to follow the Great Way to realize the Great Commonweal. *Li Chi*, the *Classic of Rites*, one of the *Five Classics*, defined the goal for Confucius twenty-five hundred years ago: "When the Great Way prevails, the world belongs to all mankind. People choose for their leaders the wise and the able, and world order is based on fidelity and harmony. They care for their own parents and children, and see to it that all old people enjoy their old age, all the able bodied are properly employed, and the young develop their talents. Provisions are made for widows and widowers and orphans, and homes are found for single men and women. Surplus wealth is not hoarded for personal gain, and manpower is not exploited for personal advantage. Consequently, theft and robbery do not arise, and gates need not be closed. This is Ta Tung, the Great Commonweal."

Trustees of China Institute, 1930–1967

Exchange Scholars and Artists, 1928–1967
Partial List, in Chronological Order

Tai Hsü   Abbott, Pu Tu Monastery, Amoy; founder, Chinese Buddhist Society

Mei Lan-fang   Actor (and his troupe)

J. J. L. Duyvendak   Professor of Chinese, Leiden University, Holland

Sidney D. Gamble   Sociologist and author

Berthold Laufer   Curator of Anthropology, Field Museum, Chicago

Chu Min-yi   Expert in Täi Chi Chúan

Y. R. Chao   Philologist, author, professor at Tsing Hua and Harvard

Paul Monroe   Educator

Carleton Washburne   Educator

Henry K. Murphy   Architect

Sophia Chen   Professor of History, Peking University

Kiung Kang-hu   Professor of Chinese and chairman of Chinese Department, McGill University, Canada

Herman C. E. Liu   President, Shanghai University

V. K. Ting   Secretary General, Academia Sinica

Y. H. Woo   Professor of Physics, Tsing Hua University

Yi-fang Wu   President, Ginling College

Hu Shih   Philosopher and diplomat

Sophia Han   Professor of Music, Peiping University

Tao Heng-Chih   Founder, Progressive Education Association of China

Francis Wei   President, Central China College

Leonard S. L. Hsu   Professor of Sociology, Yenching University

Chi Chao-ting   Lecturer, New School for Social Research

247

Chiu Kai-ming   Lecturer and librarian, Harvard-Yenching Institute

Li Fang-Kuei   Professor of Chinese Linguistics, Yale

Chang Po-Ling   President, Nankai University

Quo Tai-Chi   Chinese representative, Security Council of the United Nations

Pearl S. Buck   Nobel Prize winner for literature

W. E. Hocking   Professor of Philosophy, Harvard

George Kennedy   Professor of Chinese, Yale

William Hung   Professor of History, Yenching University

Wu-chi Liu   Author, professor of Chinese literature

Y. P. Mei   President, Yenching University

L. Carrington Goodrich   Professor of Chinese, Columbia

Tai Ai-lien   Folk dancer

Y. G. Chen   President, Nanking University

Lucy C. Wang   President, Hua Nan College

Y. K. Sze   Baritone

Liang Ssu-ching   Professor of Architecture, Tsing Hua

Fung Yu-lan   Professor of Philosophy, Peking University

Kao Chih-lan   Soprano

Ellie Mao   Soprano

S. Y. Shu (Lao Sheh)   Novelist

Chien Tuan-sheng   Professor of Government, Peking University

248   Franklin Ho   Professor of Economics, Nankai University

Wang Chi-chien   Landscape painter

Chang K'un-i   Painter and calligrapher

Timothy T. F. Lew   Dean, Yenching School of Religion

Walter C. Lowdermilk   Soil-conservation specialist, U.S. Department of Agriculture

Amar C. Bagwell   Engineer, International Telephone & Telegraph Co.

W. MacKenzie   Dean, School of Commerce, University of Maryland

George B. Cressey   Professor of Geography, Syracuse University

Lin Yutang   Author

Arthur W. Hummel   Curator of Orientalia, Library of Congress

Chang Kuan-chi   Archeologist

Cha Liang-chao   President, Tsing Hua Alumni Association

Horace H. F. Jayne   Vice-director, Metropolitan Museum of Art, New York

Ernest G. Osborne   Professor of Education, Teachers College, Columbia

William H. Kilpatric   Professor of Education, Teachers College, Columbia

Manley O. Hudson   Professor of International Law, Harvard

Kenneth S. Latourette   Professor of Missions, Yale Divinity School

Tung Tso-pin   Archeologist

C. L. Hsia   Professor of International Relations, Soochow University

Yang Lien-sheng   Professor of Chinese History, Harvard

H. H. Love   Professor of Plant Breeding, Cornell

Chamber Huang   Classical harmonica artist

Wang Ya-chun   Professor of Fine Art, Shanghai Art Institute

Index

Numbers in italic are picture pages

255